SUCCESSFUL GARDENING
A - Z of
PERENNIALS

Consultant editor: Lizzie Boyd

Typeset by SX Composing Limited in Century Schoolbook

PRINTED IN SPAIN

ISBN 0 276 42087 X

Opposite: The perennial joys of delphiniums, ox-eye daisies, spiky foxgloves and blue-flowered centaureas jostle in exuberant companionship.

Overleaf: Favourite border perennials include cheerful yellow coreopsis, blue and white campanulas, purple-leaved *Lobelia fulgens* and the woolly spikes of silvery *Stachys lanata*.

Pages 6-7: Blazing summer colours of bright red penstemons, cerise geraniums and orange-red spheres of *Lychnis chalcedonia* are tempered with pale blue delphiniums and pink goat's rue (*Galega officinalis*).

Reader's Digest

PUBLISHED BY THE READER'S DIGEST ASSOCIATION LIMITED
LONDON NEW YORK MONTREAL SYDNEY CAPE TOWN

Originally published in partwork form
by Eaglemoss Publications Limited

SUCCESSFUL GARDENING

A - Z of
PERENNIALS

CONTENTS

SPECIAL FEATURES

A-Z OF PERENNIALS

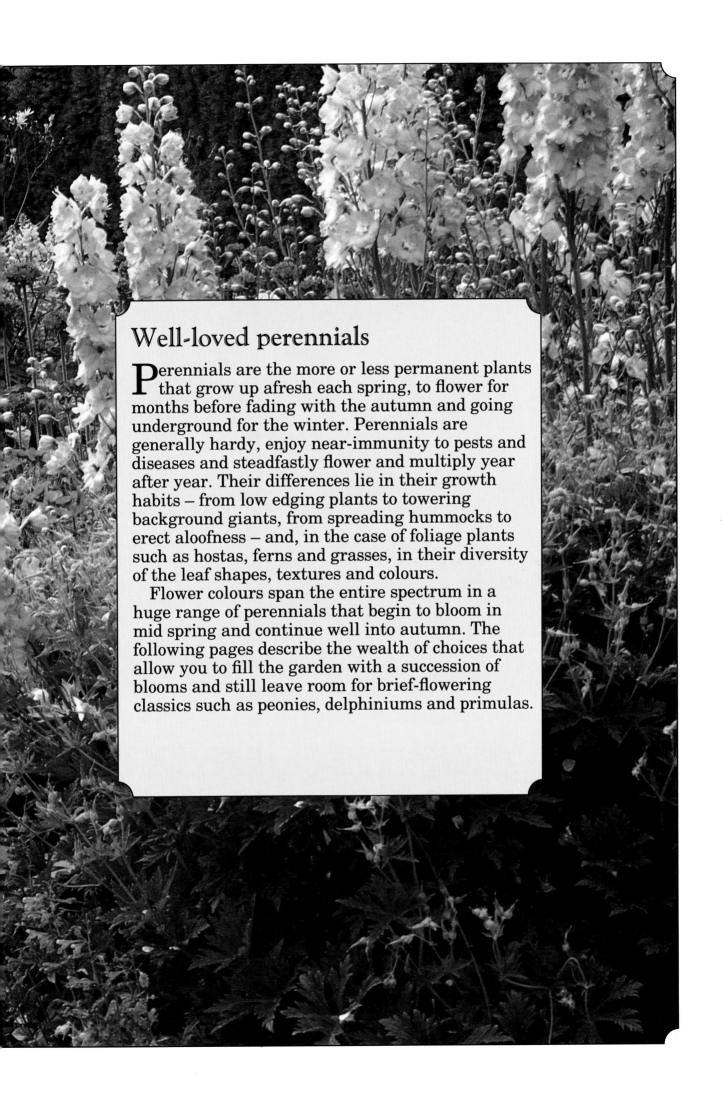

Well-loved perennials

Perennials are the more or less permanent plants that grow up afresh each spring, to flower for months before fading with the autumn and going underground for the winter. Perennials are generally hardy, enjoy near-immunity to pests and diseases and steadfastly flower and multiply year after year. Their differences lie in their growth habits – from low edging plants to towering background giants, from spreading hummocks to erect aloofness – and, in the case of foliage plants such as hostas, ferns and grasses, in their diversity of the leaf shapes, textures and colours.

Flower colours span the entire spectrum in a huge range of perennials that begin to bloom in mid spring and continue well into autumn. The following pages describe the wealth of choices that allow you to fill the garden with a succession of blooms and still leave room for brief-flowering classics such as peonies, delphiniums and primulas.

HERBACEOUS BORDERS

**Herbaceous perennials revel in company –
surrounded by their own peers or mixing happily with
transient annuals and long-lived shrubs.**

The traditional herbaceous border is one of the glories of the English garden. Wide rectangular beds were packed with perennial plants arranged in precise patterns according to colour and graduating in height towards a low front edging. Such borders peaked in early and mid summer and again in early autumn; in between they could look dull.

They have now largely disappeared from the average garden in favour of the mixed border, which involves less work. Here perennials join company with annuals and biennials, as well as deciduous and evergreen shrubs and sometimes small trees. So, by their very nature, mixed borders are informal and do not follow a clear pattern.

Planning a border

Study the proposed site carefully. A sunny or lightly shaded spot, reasonably protected from prevailing winds, with a fertile, well-drained but moisture-retentive soil is best. Few perennials are fussy about soil type, although pinks and scabious are happiest in alkaline conditions. Some shrubs have more exact requirements.

Take into account the backdrop to the border: established hedges and shrubberies are marvellous for dramatizing flower colours, but they also deplete the soil of moisture and nutrients. Walls and fences are obvious situations for growing a range of climbers.

Always plan a border in proportion to the size of the garden. Very wide borders are awkward to maintain, and narrow strips make a narrow garden look even more elongated. The traditional border is at least 3m (10ft) wide.

Draw up a plan to scale. Mark any relatively permanent plants such as trees and shrubs first.

Perennials in bold groups of three to seven plants should be plotted next; choose them for maximum summer impact. Intermingle them with spring and autumn plants and bulbs for secondary interest. Remember to include foliage plants as well as those which feature autumn colours, berries and fruit. Evergreens extend the interest to the winter months.

The choice of plants is always personal, but other important considerations are the plants' growth habit, density, height, colour and the time and duration of the flowering season.

▼ **Wild informality** Verbascums and heleniums jostle in sheets of golden-yellow around a clump of pale, dark-eyed delphiniums to create an exuberant semi-wild effect.

▲ **Colour coordination** The ordered formality of a purple-blue border scheme is strengthened dramatically by variety in flower and leaf form. Tall and graceful flower spikes of speedwell (*Veronica longifolia*) above narrow fresh green foliage relieve the severity of the dark-green spiny leaves that clothe the stiff stems of globe thistle (*Echinops*).

◄ **Foliage effects** In mixed borders of shrubs and herbaceous perennials, outstanding foliage plants have long-lasting impact. Centre stage in this group is held by *Hosta* 'Frances Williams' whose huge yellow-edged leaves contrast in shape and colour with the long and narrow pleated foliage of slender-stemmed false hellebore (*Veratrum nigrum*) towering above a low clump of golden grass.

▲ **Mixed borders** Set against a
background of deciduous trees and
flowering shrubs, hardy perennials in
full summer colour mingle happily with
bush roses and stately lilies. Low-
growing edging plants nestle close to a
lime-green froth of lady's mantle
(*Alchemilla mollis*). Tall slender spires of
verbascums add visual punctuation
marks.

► **Woodland setting** The light
shade of open woodland, with its leafy
soil, is the preferred habitat of such
moisture-lovers as green and
variegated hostas and arching
shuttlecocks of native ferns against moss
covered outcrops. Here, too, thrive such
perennial joys as purple-leaved
heucheras, majestic foxgloves and pink-
flowered physostegias.

▲ **Foxglove columns** Rising from
an immaculately striped lawn, perennial
foxgloves (*Digitalis* sp.), seen against a
hazy background of pale blue iris, hold
aloft their dense flower spires unaided
by sticks or canes. Their life-span is
comparatively short, but they are easily
perpetuated from seed to delight afresh
with their clear colours of pure white,
pink, rosy-carmines and peach. Dead-
heading prevents them from exhausting
themselves and often results in a
second, late-summer, burst of bloom.

► **Planned continuity** Old-time
favourites like russel lupins and *Iris
pallida* have their one glorious if brief
show of colour in early summer.
Thereafter, clever planning shifts the
interest to a foreground planting of the
silver-marbled *Pulmonaria saccharata*
and a backcloth of the poppy
(*Macleaya microcarpa*) whose
handsome foliage is topped in late
summer with clouds of buff-white
flowers.

▲ **Rose companions** The bare stems of standard-trained 'Ballerina' roses are concealed in this mixed border. The dense underplanting includes deep purple lavenders, pink alstroemerias and the silver-leaved, scarlet-headed flowers of perennial campion (*Lychnis flos-jovis*).

▼ **Dependable perennials** Long-lived and reliable, many perennials perform to perfection year after year. Among these are the popular red-hot pokers (*Kniphofia*) in stunning yellow and orange, the white-flowered *Chrysanthemum maximum* and the violet *Salvia* × *superba*.

▲ **Late-summer colour** Yellow and pink predominate in this herbaceous border. The clear yellow tasselled plumes of solidago vie for attention with tall, flat-headed achilleas and clear pink phlox seen against a tripod-trained vivid purple clematis.

◀ **Herbaceous splendour** High summer is epitomized in this border scene of pale blue delphinium spires, dark pink penstemon, pastel-coloured campanulas and exotic-looking, but tough, golden-orange day lilies (*Hemerocallis*). In the centre, a clump of goat's rue (*Galega officinalis*) adds brush strokes of pale pink.

Wall plant The accommodating euphorbias are superb foliage plants and thrive in the poorest of soils.

A-Z of Perennials

The descriptions of hardy perennials on the following pages are arranged in alphabetical order by the plants' botanical names, which are internationally used and recognized. Where they exist, common English names are also given, with cross-references to the botanical names of the plants. It is well worth getting to know plants by their botanical names, for only in that way is it possible to be certain of specifying a particular type. A species may contain one or more hybrids, varieties or cultivars that vary from the original type by, for instance, bearing flowers that are double, larger, a different colour or especially fragrant.

Most perennials are herbaceous plants which die back in autumn and send up new growth in spring; a few have evergreen foliage. The range of size, shape and colour is vast, and there are plants to suit every type of garden. Most adapt easily to any type of soil, but all perennials benefit from thoroughly dug, humus-rich and well-drained soil.

The flowering period of each plant may be brief or extend over several months. By using the plant descriptions as a guide it is possible to plan a display where some plants are in full bloom while others are still forming buds and yet others are putting on height and spread before preparing for the flowering season.

In general, most perennials need little maintenance, apart from keeping the border or bed weed-free, mulching in spring with organic matter and ensuring an adequate water supply. Most perennials should be lifted and divided every four or five years to prevent overcrowding.

Acanthus

bear's breeches

Acanthus spinosus

- ☐ Height 90cm-1.2m (3-4ft)
- ☐ Planting distance 90cm (3ft)
- ☐ Flowers in mid to late summer
- ☐ Any deep, well-drained soil
- ☐ Sunny or lightly shaded site
- ☐ Hardy, herbaceous

Grown as much for its immense glossy, dark green leaves as for its summer display of white and purple flowers, bear's breeches is a magnificent border plant. The flowers make a striking show on their upright 45cm (1½ft) long spikes and are suitable for fresh or dried flower arrangements.

Popular species
Acanthus mollis reaches a height of 90cm (3ft) and has mid to dark green leaves, broader and smoother than *Acanthus spinosus*. The white flowers have pinkish-purple bracts.
Acanthus spinosus reaches a height of up to 1.2m (4ft). The spiny leaves are deep-cut and hairy and the white and purple flowers have green bracts.

Cultivation
Plant between autumn and early spring in deep, well-drained soil in a sunny or lightly shaded site.
Propagation Sow seeds in early spring in boxes of seed compost in a cold frame. When the seedlings show two or three true leaves, prick them out, 15cm (6in) apart, into a nursery bed. Grow on for two years before planting out into their permanent positions.
　　Alternatively, take 7.5cm (3in) long cuttings of the thicker roots between mid and late winter.
Pests and diseases Trouble free.

Achillea

yarrow

Achillea millefolium 'Cerise Queen'

- ☐ Height 10cm-1.5m (4in-5ft)
- ☐ Planting distance 25cm-1.2m (10in-4ft)
- ☐ Flowers early to late summer
- ☐ Well-drained garden soil
- ☐ Sunny site
- ☐ Hardy, herbaceous and evergreen

Flat, wide heads or loose rounded clusters of little daisy flowers set against a delicate undercloth of ferny, aromatic leaves make yarrow one of the most popular and reliable of perennials. Tolerant of drought and demanding little attention, the larger species are good border plants and long lasting as cut flowers; and the shorter types are suitable for edging or as ground cover.

Popular species
Achillea clypeolata, with near silvery filigree and aromatic leaves, is evergreen and grows to a height of 45cm (18in), with a spread of 40cm (16in). During summer, it bears tightly packed heads, up to 12.5cm (5in) across, of tiny deep yellow flowers. For best performance it should be divided and replanted annually in spring. The outstanding variety "Moonshine", probably a hybrid between *Achillea clypeolata* and *A. taygetea*, is taller, at 60cm (2ft), with silver-grey foliage and flower heads that retain their clear yellow colour well.
Achillea filipendulina has a height and spread of 90cm-1.2m (3-4ft) and compact clusters of 15cm (6in) wide lemon-yellow flowers. The leaves are grey-green. Varieties include 'Coronation Gold' (flat, deep yellow flower heads) and 'Gold Plate' (deep yellow flowers on 1.5m (5ft)

Achillea × 'King Edward'

stems). All are good for drying).
Achillea × 'King Edward', syn. *A. lewisii*, is a dwarf hybrid, 10-15cm (4-6in) high and 20cm (8in) across that forms a neat hummock. The foliage is grey-green and the buff-yellow flower heads are up to 6cm (2½in) wide and produced from late spring to early autumn.
Achillea millefolium has deep green leaves and flat 10cm (4in) wide heads of tiny white to cerise flowers. It grows to 60-75cm (2-2½ft). Improved varieties include 'Cerise Queen' (intense cherry-red flowers) and 'Flower of Sulphur' (bright yellow flowers and more delicate foliage).
Achillea ptarmica, or sneezewort, spreads rapidly. It carries 5-10cm (2-4in) wide clusters of loose daisy-like white flowers and has narrow tapering, toothed mid-green leaves. It grows to 75cm (2½ft) high and has a spread of 38cm (15in). Popular varieties include 'The Pearl' with loose white button-shaped double flowers appearing in late summer, and 'Snowball', up to 40cm (16in) tall with pure white flowers.
Achillea taygetea has pale yellow flat flower heads set against silver-grey and evergreen foliage. They are long-lasting as cut flowers. It stands 45cm (1½ft) high and has a spread of 15cm (6in).
Achillea tomentosa, useful for ground cover, reaches up to 23cm

Achillea ptarmica 'The Pearl'

Achillea 'Galaxy hybrid'

(9in) high with a 30cm (1ft) spread. The downy grey-green leaves are long and narrow and the dense, bright yellow flower heads are 7.5cm (3in) wide.

Cultivation
Plant between autumn and early spring in any well-drained garden soil in a sunny site. Cut faded flower stems back to ground level in late autumn.

Propagation In early spring divide the roots into portions with four or five young shoots and re-plant. Alternatively, sow seeds in a cold frame in early spring. Prick off the seedlings when large enough to handle and transfer them to an outdoor nursery bed when well developed. Move the young plants to their flowering positions in mid autumn or the following spring.

Pests and diseases Trouble free.

Achillea filipendulina 'Gold Plate'

Aconitum
monkshood

Aconitum carmichaelii 'Kelmscott'

- □ Height 90-120cm (3-4ft)
- □ Planting distance 40-45cm (16-18in)
- □ Flowers in mid summer to early autumn
- □ Moist, deep soil
- □ Partial shade
- □ Hardy, herbaceous

Monkshood, though poisonous, is a stately border plant with large and glossy, deeply cut leaves and tall spikes of blue, violet, lavender, white or pale pink hooded flowers.

Popular species
Aconitum carmichaelii, syn. *A. fischeri*, grows 90cm (3ft) tall and bears violet blue flower spikes in late summer. Varieties include 'Arendsii' (120cm (4ft) amethyst-blue flowers) and 'Kelmscott' (lavender-violet flowers).
Aconitum napellus, 1m (3½ft) tall, has deep blue flowers and leaves divided into pointed segments. Varieties include: 'Album' (off-white blooms); 'Bressingham Spire' (violet-blue); and 'Carneum' (pale shell-pink).

Aconitum 'Ivorine'

Aconitum 'Ivorine' (yellow-white flowers), of hybrid origin, 90cm (3ft) tall, with large leaves.

Cultivation
Plant from autumn to early spring in moist, deep soil in partial shade.
Propagation Divide the roots from autumn to early spring.
Pests and diseases Trouble free.

Actaea
baneberry

Actaea spicata

- □ Height 45-90cm (1½-3ft)
- □ Planting distance 45-90cm (1½-3ft)
- □ Flowers in late spring
- □ Rich, moist soil
- □ Partial shade
- □ Ultra-hardy, herbaceous

Baneberries, thriving in mixed borders and by the waterside, have attractive leaves, flowers and berries. They quickly form wide clumps of handsome foliage, deeply divided and fern-like, sometimes with rounded lobes. All species bear small fluffy spikes of white-bluish flowers in late spring and early summer, but it is for the showy clusters of berries in the autumn that these perennials are chiefly grown. The common name of baneberry is truly descriptive – while all parts of the plants are poisonous if eaten, the berries are particularly so.

Popular species
Actaea pachypoda, syn. *A. alba*, grows to a height of 60-90cm (2-3ft) and has an average spread of 45cm (1½ft). The leaves are fern-like, the flowers white, and by late summer the plant bears prominent clusters of pea-sized white berries on thick, scarlet stalks.
Actaea rubra resembles *A. pachypoda* but grows more upright, spreading to 30cm (1ft). The late-summer berries are glossy red, on slender stalks. It is sometimes wrongly listed as *Actaea spicata rubra* or *nigra*.

ADIANTUM

Adiantum
maidenhair fern

Actaea rubra

Actaea spicata, known as herb Christopher, has a height and spread of 45cm (1½ft). The dark green, toothed leaves are attractive, and the white flower clusters more conspicuous than on any of the other species. So, too, are the large, glistening black berries – and the most poisonous.

Cultivation
Baneberries do best in rich, moisture-retentive soil and in partial shade although they will tolerate some sun if the ground can be kept moist. Plant them during frost-free weather from October to March.
Propagation Divide and replant congested clumps in autumn or early spring.
Pests and diseases Slugs and snails may attack emerging shoots in spring.

Adiantum pedatum

☐ Height 15-45cm (6in-1½ft)
☐ Planting distance 23-60cm (9in-2ft)
☐ Foliage plant
☐ Moist, rich soil
☐ Semi-shaded site
☐ Hardy, herbaceous or semi-evergreen

Maidenhair fern unfurls in spring to form a mass of delicate foliage. It is a good foil for flowering plants and looks attractive beneath trees.

Popular species
Adiantum pedatum has purple stems bearing gracefully drooping fronds which form a cloud of light green foliage, darkening slightly as it matures. It is 45cm (1½ft) tall and 60cm (2ft) across. It dies down after the first frost.
Adiantum venustum has coppery pink fronds in spring, later becoming light green, then gaining a blue-green tinge as it matures. Fully grown it is 15cm (6in) tall and 23cm (9in) across. It turns a warm brown after the first frost.

Cultivation
Plant in mid spring in semi shade in moist soil enriched with bone-meal and leaf mould. Plant the rhizomes of *Adiantum pedatum* no more than 2.5cm (1in) deep, *Adiantum venustum* 12mm (½in) deep. Top dress with bone-meal each spring.
Propagation Divide in early spring or early autumn. Pot out in a shady place and keep moist.
Pests and diseases Woodlice and root mealy bugs may infest the roots and check growth.

AFRICAN LILY – see *Agapanthus*

Adiantum venustum

19

Agapanthus

African lily

Agapanthus campanulatus

- ☐ Height 60-90cm (2-3ft)
- ☐ Planting distance 60cm (2ft)
- ☐ Flowers in late summer to early autumn
- ☐ Any fertile, well-drained soil
- ☐ Sunny and sheltered site
- ☐ Hardy or half-hardy, deciduous or evergreen

The large rounded and loose flower clusters of the African lily lend an exotic air to the late-summer garden. Borne on tall and sturdy stems above clumps of narrow, strap-shaped mid-green leaves, the flowers are excellent for cutting, and the seed heads for dried arrangements. The hybrid varieties are generally hardier than supposed and can be grown in the open garden in the milder south and west; in other areas they succeed best in a sunny and sheltered position, with winter protection over the fleshy roots. African lilies are also ideal for growing in tubs and other deep containers.

Popular species

Agapanthus campanulatus is 60-75cm (2-2½ft) tall, with deciduous leaves. It is moderately hardy and bears flattish clusters, 10cm (4in) or more wide, of pale blue trumpet flowers. The slightly taller variety 'Isis' is a richer blue.

Agapanthus 'Headbourne Hybrids' are more readily available than the species, and hardier. The flower stems, growing to 75cm (2½ft) high above mounds of deciduous foliage, are topped with perfect, wide spheres of pale blue to deepest violet-blue flowers. Other named hybrid varieties have intensely blue or pure white flowers,

Agapanthus 'Headbourne Hybrids'

such as 'Bressingham White'. *Agapanthus praecox*, syn. *A. umbellatus*, is an evergreen species and not reliably hardy. Under suitable conditions it grows about 60cm (2ft) tall and produces large heads of pale or bright blue flowers; white varieties also occur.

Cultivation

Plant in April, setting the fleshy crowns at least 5cm (2in) deep, in good and well-drained soil or compost. All species and varieties require full sun and preferably shelter from strong winds. Once established, the roots resent disturbance and should be left alone until overcrowding makes division necessary. No staking is needed but cut the stems down to the leaf mounds after flowering unless they are wanted for drying. In cold gardens, protect the plants with a deep winter mulch.

Propagation Divide and replant the roots in April or May or raise new plants from bought or home-saved seed sown in mid spring at a temperature of 13-15°C (55-59°F). Prick off the seedlings into boxes when large enough to handle. Transfer the young plants singly to pots of compost and grow on. They will take a couple of years to reach flowering size and should be overwintered in a frost-free greenhouse.

Pests and diseases Generally trouble free.

Alchemilla
lady's mantle

Alchemilla mollis

- □ Height 15-45cm (6-18in)
- □ Planting distance 23-38cm (9-15in)
- □ Flowers early to late summer
- □ Moist well-drained soil
- □ Sunny or partially shaded site
- □ Hardy, herbaceous

A frothy mass of tiny, delicate star-shaped flowers and pale silvery green, long-lasting foliage have made *Alchemilla* a favourite with gardeners and flower arrangers alike. The flowers range in colour from pale yellow to lime-green and the leaves are rounded or divided into narrow leaflets. *Alchemilla* is a versatile perennial – it harmonizes gently with many other plants and spreads rapidly by self-sown seed, making it useful both for ground cover in partial shade and at the front of a border, perhaps spilling over on to a path.

Popular species
Alchemilla alpina has pale green, silvery leaves divided into narrow leaflets and green flowers gathered in clusters. It reaches a height of 23cm (9in) and a spread of 23-30cm (9-12in).
Alchemilla erythropoda is smaller, with a height of 15cm (6in) and a spread of 25cm (10in). The leaves have a bluish tinge and the flowers are pale yellow, sometimes tinged red in late summer.
Alchemilla mollis, the most well-known species, has loose, cloudy sprays of yellow-green flowers in intricately branched heads. The leaves have rounded lobes with serrated edges, and are covered with a fine down which traps dew, making them glisten in early morning sunlight. It grows up to 45cm (1½ft) tall and 38cm (15in) across.

Cultivation
Plant from mid autumn to early spring in a sunny or partially shaded position in any moist but well-drained garden soil. Provide twiggy sticks for support and cut back stems to 2.5cm (1in) above the ground after flowering.

The plant self-seeds readily, so cut off flower heads before they go to seed to prevent it becoming invasive.
Propagation Sow in early spring in seed compost in a cold frame. Prick out the seedlings and harden off in a nursery bed. Plant out in permanent positions between mid autumn and early spring.

Alternatively, divide and replant immediately, between mid autumn and early spring.
Pests and diseases Generally trouble free.

ALKANET – see *Anchusa*
ALPINE ASTER – see *Aster*

Alchemilla erythropoda

Anaphalis
pearl everlasting

Anaphalis triplinervis 'Summer Snow'

☐ Height 30-60cm (1-2ft)
☐ Planting distance 30-45cm (1-1½ft)
☐ Flowers mid summer to early autumn
☐ Well-drained soil
☐ Sunny or shady site
☐ Hardy, herbaceous

Anaphalis, a showy border plant, has flat white flower heads with yellow eyes and tapering silver or grey leaves. It is popular in fresh or dried arrangements.

Popular species
Anaphalis margaritacea has loose, pearly white flowers in late summer and grey-green leaves. It grows up to 45cm (1½ft) high.
Anaphalis triplinervis grows 30cm (1ft) high. The underside of the silvery leaves is woolly and small, bunched heads of flowers appear in late summer. A popular variety is 'Summer Snow', grown for its crisp flower heads.
Anaphalis yedoensis has closely bunched flowers from mid summer to early autumn, when the grey-green leaves turn a straw colour. It grows up to 60cm (2ft) tall.

Cultivation
Plant from early autumn to mid spring in a sunny site in well-drained soil, or in dry shade.
Propagation Divide between early autumn and mid spring or take 5-7.5cm (2-3in) cuttings of basal shoots in mid to late spring and root in a cold frame.
Sow seeds in early to mid spring in a cold frame. Harden off in a nursery bed and plant out between mid autumn and early spring.
Pests and diseases Trouble free.

Anchusa
alkanet, bugloss

Anchusa azurea

☐ Height 90cm-1.5m (3-5ft)
☐ Planting distance 30-45cm (1-1½ft)
☐ Flowers early to late summer
☐ Any fertile garden soil
☐ Sunny site
☐ Hardy, herbaceous

Anchusa azurea, syn. *A. italica*, provides a vivid, long-lasting display of summer colour. Seen at its best when planted in groups, scores of tiny, saucer-shaped flowers, each with a white or yellow eye, and borne on narrowly branching upright spikes, rise in clouds of vivid blue above the coarse, mid green foliage. The flowers appear on the top third of the plant, drawing attention away from the leaves. These grow on bristly stems, looking coarse and rather unattractive after the flowers die away. Alkanet is short-lived, but self-seeds easily.

Popular varieties
A few popular varieties have been developed from *Anchusa azurea*. 'Little John' has brilliant blue flowers and reaches a height of 45cm (1½ft); 'Loddon Royalist' grows to a height of 90cm (3ft) and has deep blue flowers similar in colour to gentians; 'Morning Glory' grows up to 1.5m (5ft) tall and has deep blue flowers; 'Opal' has sky-blue flowers on stems up to 1.2m (4ft) tall.

Cultivation
Plant between mid autumn and early spring in any fertile and deep garden soil in a sunny site. Support the stems with twiggy sticks and remove the upper half of the stems after flowering to encourage a further display. Cut down old stems in mid autumn.
Propagation Increase by root cuttings taken in mid or late winter. Root them in boxes of seed compost in a cold frame and set out in a nursery bed in late spring when new shoots have appeared. Plant out in permanent positions from mid autumn.
Pests and diseases Generally trouble free.

Anemone

Japanese anemone

Anemone tomentosa

☐ Height 60cm-1.5m (2-5ft)
☐ Planting distance 60cm (2ft)
☐ Flowers late summer to mid autumn
☐ Fertile, well-drained, moisture-
   retentive soil
☐ Partially shaded site
☐ Hardy, herbaceous

Japanese anemone (A. × *hybrida*, syn. A. *japonica* or A. × *elegans*) provides fine colour late in the flowering season when many other plants are past their best. They are delightful under trees where the petals of the palest varieties can look almost translucent in the dappled shade. Nodding blooms, in white or shades of rose-pink with yellow stamens, open out flat when mature, and are held in loose, open clusters above dark green, lobed leaves. The foliage, dense at the bottom of the plant, becomes lighter and smaller-leaved further up, leaving the upper 30-60cm (1-2ft) almost bare of leaves. The plants are free-flowering after their first year.

Popular varieties

'Alba' has large white flowers and grows up to 90cm (3ft) high; 'Bressingham Glow' is a small variety, 45cm (1½ft) tall, with rose-red, semi-double flowers; 'Honorine Jobert' has white flowers and grows up to 1.2m (4ft) tall; 'Krimhilde' has blush-pink, semi-double blooms; 'Lady Gilmour' has pendent, almost double, pink flowers on branching stems; 'Lorelei' is a delicate rose-pink; 'Louise Uhink'

Anemone × hybrida 'Lorelei'

Anemone × hybrida 'Louise Uhink'

Anthemis

anthemis

Anthemis tinctoria

Anemone × hybrida 'Queen Charlotte'

has white single blooms; 'Margarete' has deep pink, almost double flowers; 'Queen Charlotte' has semi-double, pale pink flowers; 'September Charm' has clear pink flowers; 'Whirlwind' has semi-double, white flowers.

Anemone tomentosa is similar to *A. × hybrida*, but with vine-like leaves and single pale pink flowers: It grows to 75cm (2½ft) and is often invasive.

Cultivation
Plant from early autumn to early spring in any fertile, well-drained, but moisture-retentive soil, in dappled shade.

Propagation Divide and replant during suitable weather between early autumn and early spring.

Take root cuttings during winter and root in a cold frame. When three leaves have developed, line out the young plants in nursery rows and plant out in early autumn of the following year.

Pests and diseases Flea beetles may eat small holes in the leaves of seedlings. Caterpillars eat the leaves, flower buds and stems of older plants. Aphids may infest stems and leaves, making them sticky and sooty. Several virus diseases may affect anemones. Symptoms include stunted growth, yellowing or distorted leaves and flowers of poor size and colour.

☐ Height 15-75cm (6-30in)
☐ Planting distance 30-45cm (1-1½ft)
☐ Flowers early to late summer
☐ Any well-drained soil
☐ Sunny site
☐ Hardy, herbaceous

The fern-like leaves of anthemis provide a light and aromatic setting for its daisy-like flowers, which appear from early to late summer and can be white, yellow or orange. Non-flowering varieties of *Anthemis nobilis* are used for chamomile lawns, which are sweetly scented, but do not wear well.

Popular species
Anthemis cupaniana has grey, finely dissected leaves and white flowers. It forms a spreading cushion up to 30cm (1ft) high and 38cm (15in) across.

Anthemis nobilis (common chamomile), to a 23cm (9in) high, spreads to a 38cm (15in) wide mat of finely dissected, mid-green mossy and aromatic foliage with small white flowers. The non-flowering, but vigorous, variety 'Treneague' is suitable as a lawn substitute.

Anthemis sancti-johannis has bright orange flowers and lobed, grey-green and hairy leaves. It grows up to 45cm (1½ft) high and 38cm (15in) wide.

Anthemis tinctoria (ox-eye chamomile) has golden yellow flowers and deep green toothed leaves. It grows up to 75cm (2½ft) tall and 45cm (1½ft) across.

Cultivation
Plant decorative species between early autumn and early spring in a sunny position in any ordinary, well-drained soil. Cut down old flower stems in early autumn. To grow *A. nobilis* as a lawn, set young plants in well-drained soil in an open position, 15cm (6in) apart, in early to mid spring.

Propagation Increase *A. nobilis* from 7.5cm (3in) long cuttings of lateral shoots between late spring and late summer and root in a cold frame. Plant out in early autumn or early spring.

Take 5-7.5cm (2-3in) long cuttings of basal shoots of decorative anthemis in early to mid spring. Root in a cold frame and plant out in early to mid autumn. Alternatively, divide and replant.

Pests and diseases Trouble free.

Anthemis cupaniana

Aquilegia
columbine, granny's bonnet

Aquilegia vulgaris 'Nora Barlow'

Aquilegia vulgaris 'McKana Hybrids'

Aquilegia flabellata 'Nana'

□ Height 25-90cm (10-36in)
□ Planting distance 20-45cm (8-18in)
□ Flowers late spring to mid summer
□ Well drained, moist garden soil
□ Sunny or partially shaded site
□ Hardy, herbaceous

Columbine is a pretty, old-fashioned perennial with dainty, spurred, white, pink, yellow, blue or red flowers and delicate light grey to grey-green foliage. They are long-lived and reliable border plants, but tend to cross pollinate and produce variable colour forms.

Popular varieties
Aquilegia canadensis, which grows to 60cm (2ft) high and spreads to 30cm (1ft), has distinctive lemon-yellow flowers with bright red spurs in early summer.
Aquilegia flabellata grows up to 25cm (10in) tall and produces white to violet-blue flowers from late spring to mid summer. 'Nana Alba' is pure white and 'Nana' has lilac and cream flowers.
Aquilegia vulgaris is less popular than the numerous varieties developed from it. They include: 'Crimson Star', up to 45cm (1½ft) tall with crimson and white flowers; 'McKana Hybrids' and 'Mrs. Scott Elliott', both up to 90cm (3ft) tall, with cream, red, blue, yellow or pink flowers. 'Nora Barlow' has double flowers, without spurs, coloured plum-red, shading to pink and green.

Cultivation
Plant between early autumn and early spring in a moist but well-drained humus-rich soil in a sunny or partially shaded site.
Propagation Sow seeds in mid to late summer, or in early spring in a cold frame. Alternatively, divide and replant immediately from mid autumn to early spring.
Pests and diseases Leaf miners may burrow into the leaves and aphids infest the stems.

Artemisia

artemisia

Artemisia schmidtiana 'Nana'

- ☐ Height 7.5cm-1.5m (3in-5ft)
- ☐ Planting distance 23-90cm (9-36in)
- ☐ Flowers mid summer to mid autumn
- ☐ Any well-drained soil
- ☐ Sunny site
- ☐ Hardy, herbaceous perennials and deciduous or evergreen sub-shrubs

Once used as a herbal remedy for many ailments, *Artemisias* are grown for the billowing clouds of silver foliage which has a pleasant sharp aroma when crushed. They are lovely specimen plants and can also act as foils for darker-foliaged plants. Shorter types are suitable for informal edging. The plume-like flowers, insignificant in most species, appear from early to mid autumn.

Popular species

Artemisia abrotanum, southernwood, is a shrubby, deciduous plant up to 1.2m (4ft) tall, with downy grey leaves and clusters of yellow flowers in autumn.

Artemisia absinthium, wormwood, is a deciduous shrub, 90cm (3ft) high and wide, grown for its silver-grey, filigree foliage. 'Powis Castle' is an outstanding form.

Artemisia lactiflora, an herbaceous species, has mid green, parsley-like foliage forming a clump 1.5m (5ft) high and 45cm (1½ft) across. Fragrant, creamy white flower plumes appear in early to mid autumn and are suitable for cutting.

Artemisia lanata, syn. *A. nitida*, is a shrubby evergreen forming glistening, grey-green cushions 5cm (2in) high and 23cm (9in) across. Yellow flowers appear from mid summer to early autumn.

Artemisia ludoviciana, an herbaceous species up to 1.2m (4ft) high, has woolly, whitish green leaves and plumes of silver-white brown-topped flowers in early to mid autumn.

Artemisia schmidtiana 'Nana', a shrubby evergreen, forms a 7.5-13cm (3-5in) high dome of silver-grey leaves, with dull yellow flowers in woolly silver bracts in early autumn.

Artemisia splendens a deciduous sub-shrub has silvery dainty foliage; it grows to 30cm (1ft) high and 45cm (1½ft) across.

Artemisia stelleriana, a shrubby, grey-white-leaved evergreen, bears tiny yellow flowers in late summer. 'Mori's Form' is up to 15cm (6in) tall with deeply lobed silver-grey leaves.

Cultivation

Plant herbaceous species from mid autumn to early spring in light, well-drained soil in full sun. *A. lactiflora* needs a moisture-retentive soil. Plant shrubby species in any well-drained garden soil in

Artemisia ludoviciana

early to mid spring.

Propagation Divide and replant herbaceous species between mid autumn and early spring. With shrubby species, take 7.5-10cm (3-4in) semi-hardwood cuttings with a heel in late summer and root in a cold frame. Plunge outdoors in a sheltered bed and plant out the following spring.

Pests and diseases Root aphids may infest the leaves. Rust shows as pale brown spots that later turn into almost black pustules.

Artemisia stelleriana 'Mori's Form'

Arum

arum

Arum italicum 'Pictum'

- ☐ Height 45cm (1½ft)
- ☐ Planting distance 30cm (1ft)
- ☐ Flowers in spring
- ☐ Fertile, moisture-retentive soil
- ☐ Partial shade or sun
- ☐ Hardy, herbaceous

A close relative of the distinctive wild flower known popularly as lords and ladies, (*Arum maculatum*), the garden form *Arum italicum* 'Pictum' is becoming increasingly popular. Its lovely grey and green marbled foliage provides winter interest and its scarlet spikes of berries, though poisonous, bring welcome spots of brilliant colour. The variety 'Marmoratum' has less heavily marbled leaves.

The stemless, spear-shaped leaves appear in a clump in early autumn as the berries ripen. They survive the winter, dying off soon after the flowers – yellowish green spathes – appear in spring.

Cultivation
Plant the tubers 10cm (4in) deep in fertile, moisture-retentive soil in autumn. Light shade is preferable though sun is tolerated, provided the soil is moist.

Propagation Lift the tubers in early autumn and divide the offsets. Replant immediately.

Pests and diseases Trouble free.

Aruncus

goat's beard

Aruncus dioicus

- ☐ Height 60cm-1.2m (2-4ft)
- ☐ Planting distance 60cm (2ft)
- ☐ Flowers early summer
- ☐ Deep, moist, loamy soil
- ☐ Partial shade
- ☐ Hardy, herbaceous

Aruncus is grown for its silky plumes of creamy white flowers which rise over and contrast gracefully with the bold light to mid green compound leaves. Rough to the touch, the foliage is effective throughout the growing season. The seed heads, though poisonous, are also ornamental, but appear only on female plants.

A large, shrub-like plant, *Aruncus* is suitable either as a specimen or in association with other plants, perhaps in partial shade at the rear of a border. It looks particularly effective close to water.

Popular species
Aruncus dioicus, syn. *A. sylvester* or *A. vulgaris*, carries tall plumes of creamy white flowers over a 1.2m (4ft) clump of handsome mid green foliage. The variety 'Kneiffii' is smaller, only up to 60cm (2ft) tall, and has finely divided, ferny and dark green leaves.

Aruncus plumosus 'Glasnevin' reaches a height of 1.2m (4ft) and bears plumes of white flowers against light green foliage.

Cultivation
Plant from mid autumn to early spring in partial shade in deep, moist loamy soil. Cut the stems down in mid autumn.

Propagation Divide and replant in mid autumn, though roots and stems are tough and rather difficult to separate.

Pests and diseases Sawfly larvae may eat holes in the leaves, often reducing them to skeletons of veins.

Asarum

wild ginger

Asarum europaeum

- ☐ Height 12-20cm (5-8in)
- ☐ Planting distance 30cm (1ft)
- ☐ Flowers in spring
- ☐ Rich moist soil
- ☐ Shady site
- ☐ Hardy, herbaceous or evergreen

Wild ginger provides useful ground cover for moist, shady places, perhaps under trees in woodland. The leaves, which are heart-shaped, grow on long stalks. In spring, curious bell-like brownish to greenish-purple flowers appear under the foliage, which may be evergreen or herbaceous.

Popular species

Asarum canadense is an herbaceous species. It has downy leaves up to 18cm (7in) wide, which may irritate the skin.

Asarum caudatum is an evergreen species with leaves up to 15cm (6in) wide.

Asarum europaeum is an evergreen, clump-forming and wide-spreading plant with leathery, rounded 7.5cm (3in) wide leaves.

Cultivation

Plant in autumn in rich moist soil in a shady position.

Propagation Divide and replant in autumn or spring.

Pests and diseases Trouble free.

Asphodeline

Jacob's rod, king's spear, yellow asphodel

Asphodeline lutea

- ☐ Height 90cm-1.2m (3-4ft)
- ☐ Planting distance 30cm (1ft)
- ☐ Flowers in late spring
- ☐ Any well-drained soil
- ☐ Sunny site
- ☐ Hardy, herbaceous

Asphodeline lutea, still sold by some nurseries under its old name, *Asphodelus lutea*, is a stately border plant with a pleasant fragrance. In late spring stiff spikes, up to 1.2m (4ft) tall, are covered with clusters of bright yellow starry blooms with red stamens. The flowers, which last for several weeks, are later replaced by seed heads which look decorative in the garden or as part of an indoor cut flower arrangement.

The furrowed leaves, grass-like and waxy, are up to 30cm (1ft) long and growing in tufts at the base of the flower spikes.

Cultivation

Plant from mid autumn to early spring in ordinary, well-drained soil in a sunny position. Take care not to damage the rhizomatous roots.

Propagation Divide the roots in spring or in early autumn and replant immediately. Alternatively, sow seed in a cold frame in spring. Pot on and plant out in permanent positions in spring.

Pests and diseases Generally trouble free.

Asplenium
spleenwort

Asplenium trichomanes

☐ Height 25cm-1.2m (10in-4ft)
☐ Planting distance 25-60cm (10-24in)
☐ Foliage plant
☐ Shady site
☐ Rich soil
☐ Hardy evergreen ferns

Asplenium is an attractive fern providing all-year-round interest for shady places in borders or woodland, walls and rock gardens. The long, graceful fronds resemble broad glossy straps, frilled, tough ribbons or double curving rows of tiny discs.

Popular species
Asplenium adiantum-nigrum, black spleenwort, 23cm (9in) high and wide, takes its name from purple-black stalks clothed with finely cut, glossy green fronds.
Asplenium scolopendrium, hart's tongue fern, has tongue-like fronds and thrives in woodland or shady borders. It reaches a height of 60cm (2ft), with a spread of 30cm (1ft). Popular varieties include: 'Crispum' (crisped fronds

and wavy margins); 'Cristatum' (the fronds have tassels at the tips); 'Kaye's Variety' (deep cut edges); and 'Undulatum' (a dwarf variety with wavy fronds).
Asplenium trichomanes, maidenhair spleenwort, has a height and spread of only 25cm (10in). It can be planted in rock gardens or the crevices of walls and has black stalks with round green lobes.

Cultivation
Plant smaller species in vertical or sloping crevices among rocks or stones during damp weather from mid spring to early autumn. *A. trichomanes* needs lime. Plant other species in moist, well-drained garden soil in a shady site in mid spring.
Propagation Sow the dust-like spores in early spring or mid to late summer. Or lift, divide and replant in spring.
Pests and diseases Woodlice may eat the roots and slugs and scale insects attack the fronds.

Aster
aster

Aster amellus 'Mauve Beauty'

☐ Height 38cm-1.5m (15in-5ft)
☐ Planting distance 30-45cm (12-18in)
☐ Any fertile, well-drained garden soil
☐ Sunny open site
☐ Hardy, herbaceous

Asters earn their place in the border with a burst of varied late summer to autumn colour – white, blue, purple, pink, red or lilac – when earlier-flowering perennials are past their best. Each daisy-like bloom is a mass of starry petals around a yellow centre. Borne in clusters, each flower can measure up to 5cm (2in) across or as little as 8mm (⅓in). The foliage, which provides a strong foil to the colourful flowers, is grey-green, mid green or dark green, with rather hairy, narrow leaves.

Border species have an upright habit and are heavily branched towards the top, with many leaves and flowers and look outstanding in any autumn border. They include the popular Michaelmas daisies in a variety of clear, bright colours. They deteriorate quickly and for the best effect, Michaelmas daisies should be divided and replanted at least every two years. All asters are excellent for cut flower arrangements.

Popular species
Aster amellus, Italian aster, is up to 60cm (2ft) high and 38cm (15in) across with rough, grey-green leaves. The flowers, up to 6cm (2½in) wide, appear on woody stems in late summer and early

Aster novi-belgii 'Patricia Ballard'

autumn. The species has been superseded by such popular varieties as 'King George' (violet-blue); 'Mauve Beauty' (mauve); 'Nocturne' (lavender); 'Pink Zenith' (clear pink); 'Sonia' (rosy-pink); and 'Violet Queen' (violet, on compact plants 45cm (1½ft) tall).

Aster cordifolius is up to 1.2m (4ft) tall with sprays of silvery-blue flowers, each 2cm (¾in) across. The variety 'Ideal' is pale blue.

Aster ericoides, heath aster, is up to 90cm (3ft) tall with mid green leaves. It bears numerous tiny white or pink-edged flowers on slender, much-branched stems in early to mid autumn. Varieties include: 'Blue Star' (palest blue); 'Delight' (white); and 'Ringdove' (rosy-mauve).

Aster farreri, only 45cm (1½ft) tall, is an early-flowering species, producing its violet, gold-centred flowers by mid summer.

Aster × frikartii is a 75cm (2½ft) high hybrid with orange-centred blue flowers from late summer to mid autumn and rough, dark green leaves. Varieties include: 'Flora's Delight' (lilac-pink); 'Mönch (lilac-blue and free-flowering)); and 'Wonder of Stafa' (pale lavender).

Aster linosyris is up to 60cm (2ft) tall with dull green leaves and small, button-like, bright yellow flowers appearing in dense clusters from late summer to early autumn. 'Gold Dust' is a superior, brighter variety.

Aster novae-angliae, New England aster, is a 1.2m (4ft) tall species producing pink to mauve flowers in loose clusters on woody stems in early autumn. Many varieties are grown, including: 'Alma Potschke' (salmon-pink); 'Autumn Snow' (glistening white); 'Harrington's Pink' (clear pink); 'September Ruby' (ruby-red); and

'Treasure' (lilac).

Aster novi-belgii, Michaelmas daisy, is up to 1.2m (4ft) tall, with deep green leaves and clusters of flowers on branched stems in early to mid autumn. Tall varieties include: 'Ada Ballard' (lavender-blue); 'Chequers' (violet); 'Eventide' (semi-double, violet-blue); 'Freda Ballard' (semi-double, pink-carmine); 'Marie Ballard' (double, light blue); 'Patricia Ballard' (semi-double, pink); and 'White Ladies' (white). Dwarf varieties, up to 30cm (1ft) tall, include: 'Jenny' (double, violet-purple); 'Kristina' (pure white); 'Lady in Blue' (semi-double, blue); 'Little Pink Beauty' (semi-double, pink); 'Snowsprite' (white); and 'Victor' (lavender).

Aster thomsonii 'Nana' is up to 38cm (15in) tall with lavender-blue flowers in late summer to mid autumn, and grey-green leaves.

Aster tongolensis, syn. *A. subcae-*

Aster novi-belgii 'Chequers'

Aster amellus 'King George'

ruleus, is up to 45cm (1½ft) tall with hairy, dark green leaves and bright blue-mauve flowers in high summer. The variety 'Napsbury' has deep blue flowers.

Cultivation
Plant in any fertile well-drained garden soil in a sunny open position from mid autumn to early spring. The soil must not dry out in late summer and autumn when most plants are in flower. Most of the taller asters need to be supported with twiggy sticks.

Propagation Divide and replant the roots from mid autumn to early spring. To raise large numbers of plants, pull the clumps apart into single shoots in early to mid spring and plant 15cm (6in) apart each way. Divide *A. novi-belgii* like this annually.

Pests and diseases Powdery mildew appears as a white powder on the leaves. Aster wilt affects many species and varieties, particularly *A. novi-belgii*. The stems may turn brown and wither, and the shoots wilt and die. *A. novae-angliae* and its varieties seem to be immune.

Aster × frikartii 'Wonder of Stafa'

Astilbe
astilbe

Astilbe × arendsii 'Fanal'

☐ Height 45cm-1.2m (1½-4ft)
☐ Planting distance 30-60cm (1-2ft)
☐ Flowers early to late summer
☐ Rich, moist soil
☐ Sunny or partially shaded site
☐ Hardy, herbaceous

The fluffy, long-lasting flower spires of *Astilbe*, in white, cream or shades of pink, lilac and red, rise above lush, deeply cut foliage. Ideal for damp borders, it looks particularly effective by water.

Popular species
Astilbe × arendsii, 60-90cm (2-3ft) high, has dark green fern-like foliage and a wide range of flower colours. Varieties include: 'Deutschland' (white); 'Fanal' (deep red); 'Federsee' (rosy-red); 'Hyacinth' (rose-pink); 'Irrlicht' (pure white); and 'Red Sentinel' (brick-red).
Astilbe chinensis, up to 90cm (3ft) tall, has rose-pink to purplish flowers and coarse-toothed leaves. The dwarf variety 'Pumila', 45cm (1½ft) high, has mid green, ferny

Astilbe × arendsii 'Deutschland'

foliage and mauve-pink flowers.
Astilbe × crispa, 20cm (8in) all, has mid green, crinkly leaves and white, pink or pale red flowers.
Astilbe simplicifolia, up to 30cm (1ft) high, has arching white or pink flower plumes above deeply cut leaves. 'Sprite' has outstanding shell-pink flower sprays that last for weeks.

Cultivation
Plant from mid autumn to early spring in rich, permanently moist soil in sun or partial shade. Give twiggy support to tall varieties in windy sites.
Propagation Divide and replant every three years in early to mid spring.
Pests and diseases Trouble free.

Astilbe chinensis 'Pumila'

Astrantia
masterwort

Astrantia major

☐ Height 30-90cm (1-3ft)
☐ Planting distance 23-38cm (9-15in)
☐ Flowers early to late summer
☐ Any garden soil
☐ Partially shaded or sunny site
☐ Hardy, herbaceous

A favourite in gardens since the 16th century, *Astrantia* is a lovely and versatile border plant. Its starry flowers – white, pink or greenish pink – are surrounded by white, green and white or plum-coloured bracts and are held in small clusters above clumps of coarsely dissected leaves. It grows up to 60cm (2ft) tall and is suitable for fresh or dried cut-flower arrangements. The flowers are up to 6cm (1½in) across.

Popular species
Astrantia carniolica, up to 60cm (2ft) high, has mid-green finely divided leaves and white flowers in mid to late summer, tinged with pink and surrounded by white bracts. The variety 'Rubra' is 30cm (1ft) high with purple-red flowers and bracts in mid summer. *Astrantia major* is up to 90cm (3ft) tall with greenish-pink rose or white flowers and pink-purple-tinged bracts in early to mid summer. Varieties include 'Variegata' with the leaves irregularly edged in cream.
Astrantia maxima, up to 60cm (2ft) tall, has bright green leaves and shell-pink flowers with pink bracts in early to mid summer.

Cultivation
Plant from mid autumn to early spring in any ordinary garden soil. A partially shaded site is best, but a sunny site will do if the soil stays reasonably moist in summer. Plants may need supporting with twiggy sticks.
Propagation Divide and replant from mid autumn to early spring. Or sow seeds in early autumn in a cold frame. Prick out in spring and plant out in a nursery bed in early to mid summer. Plant out into permanent positions the following spring.
Pests and diseases Trouble free.

Astrantia major 'Variegata'

Athyrium
athyrium

Athyrium filix-femina

☐ Height 30-90cm (1-3ft)
☐ Planting distance 45-90cm (1½-3ft)
☐ Foliage plant
☐ Moist, rich soil
☐ Lightly shaded site
☐ Hardy, herbaceous

In the light shade of a border the delicate fronds of *Athyrium* resemble green lace. This fern is at its best in spring when the fresh young fronds unfurl in a cloud of dainty foliage on darker stems. The lady fern, *Athyrium filix-femina*, is up to 90cm (3ft) high and wide, with fresh green fronds. Many varieties have been developed from it, including; 'Veroniae' with crisped and roughly triangular fronds; and 'Victoriae' with finely cut, crested fronds forming a lattice-work effect.

Cultivation
Plant in mid spring or early autumn in light shade in a humus-rich soil. Keep moist at all times. Lift and replant when the rootstock pushes above ground..
Propagation Sow the dust-like spores at any time, or divide and replant in mid spring.
Pests and diseases Generally trouble free.

AVENS – see *Geum*
BABY'S BREATH – see *Gypsophila*
BALLOON FLOWER – see *Platycodon*
BANEBERRY – see *Actaea*

Baptisia
false indigo

Baptisia australis

☐ Height 60-90cm (2-3ft)
☐ Planting distance 45cm (1½ft)
☐ Flowers early summer
☐ Deep moist soil
☐ Sunny or lightly shaded site
☐ Hardy, herbaceous

As an informal border plant, baptisia is easily grown and accommodating, thriving in rough places. Only one species, *Baptisia australis*, is generally available. This is an erect, leafy perennial growing about 90cm (3ft) high, with blue-green trifoliate leaves. In early summer it produces slender indigo-blue spikes of sweet-pea-like flowers good for cutting.

Cultivation
Plant during suitable weather from mid autumn to early spring, in deep moist soil and in full sun. Once established, the roots resent disturbance.
Propagation Sow seeds in mid spring, outdoors or in a cold frame. Transfer seedlings to a nursery bed and grow on for two years.
Pests and diseases Trouble free.

BARRENWORT – see *Epimedium*
BEAR'S BREECHES – see
Acanthus
BEDSTRAW – see *Galium*
BELLFLOWER – see *Campanula*

Bergenia
bergenia

Bergenia stracheyi

☐ Height 30-38cm (12-15in)
☐ Planting distance 30-60cm (1-2ft)
☐ Flowers early to late spring
☐ Any garden soil
☐ Sunny or partially shaded site
☐ Hardy, evergreen

The leathery, slightly glossy leaves of *Bergenia* provide bold mid to dark green year-round ground cover, tinted red or purple in winter. In late winter and through spring, clusters of white or palest pink to deep purple-red bell-shaped flowers rise over the foliage on tall, straight stems.

Popular species
Bergenia cordifolia, up to 30cm (1ft) tall, has drooping heads of lilac-rose flowers on reddish stems from early spring until early summer. The glossy green crinkle-edged leaves are up to 25cm (10in) long. The creeping rootstock forms close ground cover and edgings. The variety 'Purpurea' has purplish leaves in winter and pink-purple flowers.
Bergenia crassifolia, up to 30cm (1ft) high, has leaves tinted red in winter; lavender-pink flowers appear early in the New Year.
Bergenia purpurascens syn. *B. delavayi*, up to 38cm (15in) high, has loose heads of purple-pink to pink flowers. The leaves are reddish in winter.
Bergenia stracheyi is up to 30cm (1ft) tall with white to pink flowers. Hybrids include: 'Abend-

Bergenia purpurascens

glut' or 'Evening Glow' (magenta-crimson, heart-shaped leaves maroon in winter); 'Ballawley' (deep carmine-pink); and 'Silberlicht' or 'Silver Light' (white above broad leaves that turn bronze-red in winter). 'Baby Doll', only 30cm (1ft) tall, bears dense clusters of pale pink flowers.

Cultivation
Plant well-rooted plants from mid autumn to early spring in almost any soil in sun or partial shade, setting the plants 30cm (1ft) apart. Bergenias thrive in quite damp soils next to water and also do well in dry soil although growth is

Bergenia stracheyi 'Silberlicht'

Bergenia purpurascens

slower than in moist conditions. Lift and divide only when overcrowded. Remove stems after flowering.
Propagation Divide and replant in autumn or early spring.
Pests and diseases Large brown blotches on leaves are symptoms of leaf spot fungus.

Blechnum
hard fern

Blechnum spicant

☐ Height 15-60cm (6-24in)
☐ Planting distance 30-45cm (1-1½ft)
☐ Foliage plant
☐ Moist, well-drained, lime-free soil
☐ Shady, sheltered position
☐ Hardy, evergreen

Hard ferns have tough, leathery, dark green fronds resembling rosettes of curving double combs. They are very hardy evergreen foliage plants but hate alkaline soils.

Popular species
Blechnum penna-marina, (dwarf hard fern) up to 15cm (6in) tall, but spreading from creeping rhizomes, is suitable for rock gardens. It has narrow fronds.
Blechnum spicant (common hard fern) is up to 60cm (2ft) tall with densely set narrow fronds.

Cultivation
Plant in spring, in moist, well-drained acid soil, sheltered from drying winds. Mulch annually in spring with forest bark.
Propagation Divide and replant in spring or early autumn.
Pests and diseases Trouble free.

Brunnera
Siberian Bugloss

Brunnera macrophylla

☐ Height 30-45cm (12-18in)
☐ Planting distance 45cm (1½ft)
☐ Flowers late spring to mid summer
☐ Lightly shaded site
☐ Any ordinary garden soil
☐ Hardy, herbaceous

Brunnera macrophylla, syn. *Anchusa myosotidiflora*, is a handsome border plant, with heart-shaped matt green leaves, setting off a cloud of blue forget-me-not-like flowers. Useful for ground cover, popular varieties include: 'Langtrees' (leaves spotted with silver); and 'Variegata' (white-splashed leaves).

Cultivation
Plant from mid autumn to early spring in any ordinary soil. Brunnera tolerates sun, if the soil does not dry out, but prefers light shade. Remove any stems on variegated forms that revert to green.
Propagation Divide and replant in mid to late autumn. Or take root cuttings in mid to late autumn and root in a cold frame. Plant out in a nursery bed in late spring to early summer. Plant out in the flowering site in autumn.
Pests and disease Trouble free.

BETONY – see *Stachys*
BISHOP'S HAT – see *Epimedium*
BLACK SNAKEROOT – see *Cimicifuga*
BLADDER CHERRY – see *Physalis*
BLANKET FLOWER – see *Gaillardia*
BLAZING STAR – see *Liatris*

BLEEDING HEART – see *Dicentra*
BLUE CUPIDONE – see *Catananche*
BLUE-EYED GRASS – see *Sisyrinchium*
BONESET – see *Eupatorium*
BOWLES' GOLDEN GRASS – see *Milium*

BUCKLER FERN – see *Dryopteris*
BUGBANE – see *Cimicifuga*
BUGLOSS – see *Anchusa*
BURNET – see *Sanguisorba*
BURNING BUSH – see *Dictamnus*
BUTTERCUP – see *Ranunculus*
CALAMINT – see *Calamintha*

Calamintha
calamint

Calamintha nepetoides

☐ Height 30cm (1ft)
☐ Planting distance 30cm (1ft)
☐ Flowers late summer to mid autumn
☐ Ordinary well-drained soil
☐ Sunny site
☐ Hardy, herbaceous

Calamintha nepetoides, syn. *C. nepeta nepeta*, is a long-flowering member of the mint family, with a pleasant minty aroma to the leaves, irresistible to bees. It forms a bushy mound up to 30cm (1ft) high and across, with deep green leaves about 2.5cm (2in) long. From late summer a profuse show of small pale lilac, tubular-shaped flowers appear in whorls along erect, leafy stems.

Cultivation
Plant in mid spring in gritty, well-drained soil in a sunny site.
Propagation Divide and replant in spring, or sow seeds in a cold frame. Prick out seedlings into a nursery row and move the plants to permanent sites the following spring.
Pests and diseases Mint rust may affect shoots.

Campanula
bellflower

Campanula trachelium

☐ Height 15cm-1.5m (6in-5ft)
☐ Planting distance 23-60cm (9-24in)
☐ Flowers late spring to mid autumn
☐ Well-drained soil
☐ Sunny or partially shaded site
☐ Hardy, herbaceous

The nodding blooms of bellflower (*Campanula*) were a familiar sight in Shakespeare's day and before. Many species have truly bell-shaped flowers – in others they are formed like cups or stars. The delicate flowers bloom singly on branching stems, or are held in loose or tight clusters, or in spikes. The flowers come in shades of blue, violet, lavender, pink and white and the foliage is grey-green to mid or dark green. Hundreds of bellflower species occur, including perennial, biennial and annual types. Those described here are perennials suitable for growing in bold groups in herbaceous and mixed borders; some are invasive and should be sited with care.

Popular species
Campanula alliariifolia, up to 60cm (2ft) high, has spikes of creamy-white flowers in early to mid summer. 'Ivory Bells' has slightly larger flowers.
Campanula barbata (bearded bellflower) is a short-lived species up to 45cm (1½ft) high. It forms rosettes of lance-shaped, hairy mid green leaves and single stems bearing one-sided panicles of nodding bell flowers in early summer. They range in colour from bluish

Campanula persicifolia

purple to white and are distinguished by the long wooly hairs that protrude from the bells.
C. × *burghaltii* is a hybrid bellflower and grows 45-60cm (1½-2ft) tall. Clump-forming, with erect, wiry stems set with tufts of mid green leaves, it bears drooping, blue-grey bell flowers, 7.5cm (3in) long, in early summer. The variety 'Ivory Bells' has creamy white bells on arching stems from early to late summer.
Campanula carpatica is an alpine species, 23-30cm (2-12in) tall, and too invasive for any but the largest of rock gardens. It is, however, admirably suited for front edging of borders and beds where the leaf clumps quickly form neat hummocks of mid green, gently toothed ovate leaves. In mid and late summer, the plants are densely covered with showy cup-shaped flowers, 2.5-5cm (1-2in) across, in shades of blue and purple. Numerous varieties are available, including 'Blue Moonlight' (light blue); 'Bressingham White' (white); 'Chewton Joy' (china blue and free-flowering into early autumn); and 'Hannah' (white, compact and only 15cm/6in tall).
Campanula glomerata (clustered bellflower) is up to 45cm (1½ft) high with dense clusters of erect, purple bell-shaped flowers on rigid, leafy stems from late spring to mid autumn. Good varieties include: 'Purple Pixie' (purple); and 'Superba' (violet).

Campanula portenschlagiana

Campanula lactiflora (milky bell-flower) is up to 1.5m (5ft) tall with sprays of bell-shaped light lavender-blue or milk-white flowers in early to mid summer. Varieties include 'Loddon Anna' (soft pink); 'Pouffe' (up to 25cm/10in high with profuse lavender-blue flowers); 'Prichard's Variety' (deep lavender-blue); and 'White Pouffe' (white, up to 25cm/10in high).

Campanula latifolia (giant bell-flower) has tubular, purple-blue flowers on erect stems in mid summer and grows to 1.5m (5ft). Varieties include 'Gloaming' (smoky-blue) and 'White Ladies' (white).

Campanula persicifolia, syn. *C. grandis* or *C. latiloba* (peach-leaved bellflower), has evergreen basal leaves and slender stems up to 90cm (3ft) high with clustered saucer-shaped white, blue or purple-blue flowers from early to late summer. Varieties include: 'Alba' (white); 'Percy Piper' (deep blue); 'Pride of Exmouth' (semi-double, powder-blue); and 'Telham Beauty' (large, light blue).

Campanula portenschlagiana, syn. *C. muralis*, is an invasive plant up to 15cm (6in) high best grown in crevices in walls or paths. Deep purple, bell-shaped flowers are borne from mid summer to late autumn.

Campanula poscharskyana is a rampant species up to 30cm (1ft) tall and 90cm (3ft) across. Sprays of lavender-blue starry flowers appear in succession from mid summer to late autumn.

Campanula pyramidalis, chimney bellflower, is a very hardy, but short-lived perennial species best grown as a biennial as flowering deteriorates in the second year. The 1.2m (4ft) tall stems are clothed with rich green, heart-shaped leaves beneath the broad spikes of blue or white bells in high summer.

Campanula trachelium syn. *C. urticifolia* (nettle-leaved bell-flower), has nettle-like leaves and purple-blue flowers in late summer. It is up to 60cm (2ft) high. 'Bernice' has double, powder-blue flowers.

Cultivation

Plant from early autumn to mid spring in well-drained, fertile garden soil in a sunny or partially shaded site sheltered from winds. Tall varieties need staking.

Propagation Sow seeds in mid autumn or early to mid spring in a cold frame. Line out taller species in nursery rows and plant out in mid autumn. Grow on smaller species in pots until ready for planting out.

Divide and replant named varieties in mid autumn or early to mid spring. Or, take 2.5-5cm (1-2in) cuttings of non-flowering basal shoots in mid to late spring and root in a cold frame. Pot up and treat as seedlings.

Pests and diseases Slugs and snails may damage leaves and shoots.

CAMPION – see *Lychnis*

Carex stricta 'Bowles' Golden'

Carex
sedge

☐ Height 30cm-1.2m (1-4ft)
☐ Planting distance 30-90cm (1-3ft)
☐ Foliage plant
☐ Moist soil
☐ Sun or light shade
☐ Hardy, herbaceous

Sedges are evergreen grasses with green to yellow, sometimes variegated, arching foliage. Smaller species can be used to edge beds and borders, while larger species are good specimen clumps at margins of pools. Insignificant flowers appear on spikes with leafy bracts.

Popular species
Carex morrowii (Japanese sedge) is up to 30cm (1ft) tall. Varieties include: 'Evergold' (leaves striped golden-yellow); and 'Variegata' (leaves striped white).
Carex pendula (great drooping sedge), up to 1.2m (4ft) tall, has broad, yellow-green leaves and attractive pendent seed heads in autumn.
Carex stricta 'Bowles' Golden', syn. *C. elata* 'Aurea', is up to 60cm (2ft) tall. Its golden-yellow leaves become green in late summer.

Cultivation
Plant in autumn or spring in any well-drained, but moisture-retentive soil. *C. pendula* prefers constantly moist soil.
Propagation Divide and replant in spring. Or sow in early spring in a cold frame. Harden off in a nursery bed, plant out in autumn.
Pests and diseases Trouble free.

CARNATION – *Dianthus*

Catananche caerulea

Catananche
cupid's dart

☐ Height 45-75cm (1½-2½ft)
☐ Planting distance 38-45cm (15-28in)
☐ Flowers mid to late summer
☐ Light, well-drained soil
☐ Sunny site
☐ Hardy, herbaceous

The soft blue flowers of *Catananche caerulea* (cupid's dart, also called blue cupidone) are carried high over its narrow-leaved, sparse foliage. Shaped like double daisies on wiry stems, with deep blue centres and papery calyces, the flowers are suitable for both fresh and dried flower arrangements. The plant is up to 75cm (2½ft) high and looks decorative in borders. Varieties include: 'Major' (larger flowers in a richer shade of blue); and 'Perry's White'.

Cultivation
Plant from early autumn to mid spring in a sunny position in light, well-drained soil. The stems may need support in exposed positions.
Propagation Sow seeds during mid to late spring in a cold frame. Prick off into boxes, then into a nursery bed; move to permanent positions in autumn.
Increase named varieties by root cuttings taken in early spring and rooted in a cold frame.
Pests and diseases Generally trouble free.

CATMINT – see *Nepeta*
CELANDINE POPPY – see *Stylophorum*

Campanula lactiflora

Campanula latifolia

Campanula persicifolia 'Alba'

Centaurea

knapweed

Centaurea dealbata 'Steenbergii'

Centaurea macrocephala

☐ Height 45cm-1.5m (18-60in)
☐ Planting distance 30-60cm (12-24in)
☐ Flowers late spring to early autumn
☐ Any fertile, well-drained soil
☐ Sunny site
☐ Hardy, herbaceous

With its handsome thistle-like flower heads in shades of blue, lilac, rosy to deep pink or bright yellow, *Centaurea* is a striking border plant. Deeply cut leaves form a low-growing clump and may be deep green, silvery, or grey-green backed with silver.

Popular species

Centaurea dealbata (perennial cornflower), up to 60cm (2ft) high, has grey-green, silver-backed leaves. Its rose-pink flowers bloom in early to mid summer and again in early autumn. Varieties include: 'John Coutts' (pale yellow-centred); and 'Steenbergii' (white-centred).

Centaurea hypoleuca, 45cm (1½ft) high, is a vigorous but compact border plant, with greyish-green, deeply cut leaves. Pink cornflower-like blooms open from late spring to late summer.

Centaurea macrocephala, up to 1.5m (5ft) tall, has very large yellow, thistle-like flowers in early to mid summer. 'John Glover' has bright yellow flowers.

Centaurea montana, up to 60cm (2ft) tall, has deep green, hairy leaves. From late spring to early summer it produces a profusion of thinly petalled blue flowers.

Centaurea pulchra 'Major', 90cm (3ft) tall bears large pink flowers.

Cultivation

Plant from mid autumn to early spring in any fertile, well-drained soil in a sunny position.

Propagation Divide and replant every third or fourth year from mid autumn to early spring. Or sow seeds in mid spring in a cold frame. Prick off into boxes and grow on in a nursery bed. Pot seedlings of *C. dealbata* and *C. hypoleuca* singly and plunge outdoors. Move the plants to flowering sites in mid autumn; overwinter pot-grown species in a cold frame; plant out in permanent positions the following mid spring.

Pests and diseases Powdery mildew shows as a white coating on leaves, stems and flowers.

Centaurea montana

Centranthus

red valerian

Centranthus ruber and C. r. 'Albus'

☐ Height 45-90cm (1½-3ft)
☐ Planting distance 30cm (1ft)
☐ Flowers early to late summer
☐ Well-drained soil
☐ Sunny position
☐ Hardy, herbaceous

The distinctive reddish-pink flower heads of *Centranthus ruber* can be seen in southern England on chalk cliffs and old walls, where its powerful woody roots can split open brickwork. This strong, upright plant thrives in limestone or chalky soil, producing a long-lasting display of small star-shaped flowers held in upright clusters. The broad fleshy leaves are grey-green and up to 10cm (4in) long and can smell unpleasant when bruised. *Centranthus ruber* reaches a height of 90cm (3ft) and spreads across an area 30cm (1ft) wide.

Varieties include: 'Albus' (white flowers); and 'Coccineus' (red).

Cultivation

Plant in early to mid spring in a sunny position in well-drained, even poor soil. Chalk or limestone soils are particularly suitable. Cut down dead growth in autumn.
Propagation Sow seeds between mid spring and early summer, either where the plants are to flower or in a seed bed. If the seeds are sown in the flowering site, thin to the required distance; if in a seed bed, transplant while the plants are quite small.
Pests and diseases Generally trouble free.

CHAMOMILE – see *Anthemis*

Chelone

turtle-head

Chelone obliqua

☐ Height 60-90cm (2-3ft)
☐ Planting distance 30-60cm (1-2ft)
☐ Flowers mid summer to early autumn
☐ Deep well-drained soil
☐ Sunny or partially shaded site
☐ Hardy, herbaceous

The pink or deep rose flowers of *Chelone* are gathered in spikes, shaped rather like colourful turtles' heads. These accommodating, upright perennials are valuable additions to autumn borders.

Popular species

Chelone lyonii, up to 90cm (3ft) tall, has clusters of pink flowers. *Chelone obliqua*, up to 60cm (2ft) high, has deep rose flower spikes above dark green foliage.

Cultivation

Plant from early autumn to early spring in a sunny or partially shaded position in any deep and well-drained soil.
Propagation Sow seeds either under glass in early spring at 15°C (59°F) or in a cold frame in mid spring. Prick out into a nursery bed and plant out in permanent positions 1½-2 years after sowing.
Pests and diseases Generally trouble free.

CHEQUER MALLOW – see *Sidalcea*
CHINESE LANTERN – see *Physalis*
CHRISTMAS ROSE – see *Helleborus*

Chrysogonum

chrysogonum

Chrysogonum virginianum

☐ Height 30cm (1ft)
☐ Planting distance 20cm (8in)
☐ Flowers late spring to mid autumn
☐ Partially shaded or sunny site
☐ Hardy, evergreen

The starry golden flowers of *Chrysogonum virginianum* stand out vividly against its dense, bright green, toothed foliage throughout the long flowering season from late spring to mid autumn. Suitable for brightening up the front of a border, it roots where it touches the soil and spreads to an attractive carpet.

Cultivation

Plant in ordinary well-drained soil in a partially shaded position or in sun. Plant container specimens in early spring.
Propagation Divide and replant in early spring.

Alternatively, sow seeds in late spring or early summer, but expect variation in leaf size and flower colour.
Pests and diseases Generally trouble free.

Chrysanthemum

chrysanthemum

Semi-pompon chrysanthemum 'Charleston'

Spoon-petalled chrysanthemum 'Pennine Ace'

Pompon chrysanthemum 'Purple Fairy'

☐ Height 20cm-1.5m (8in-5ft)
☐ Planting distance 30-60cm (1-2ft)
☐ Flowers late summer to autumn
☐ Well-drained soil
☐ Sunny position
☐ Hardy and half-hardy, herbaceous

Chrysanthemums owe their popularity to their enormous diversity. The flowers come in shades of red, yellow, white, purple, pink, mauve or bronze. They range from the simplest, daisy-like form, to the more elaborate types developed by horticulturists – rayed petals with pin-cushion-like centres, petals curving up, petals curving down or petals massed tightly together to create an apparently solid ball of colour. In some types the flowers are small and gathered in loose clusters on branding stems; in others each stem bears one huge single bloom.

The simplest type of chrysanthemum produces daisy-like flowers, usually white with a yellow centre, but also in shades of pink or purple. They include annual, bedding and rock garden types as well as the border chrysanthemums described here.

The huge selection known as florists' chrysanthemums offers a much wider variety of colour and flower form, lasting well into autumn. In mild areas, particularly in sheltered gardens in the south, late-flowering varieties may still be in bloom at the beginning of winter. In cold gardens and in the north, late-flowering florists' chrysanthemums are best grown in pots that can be stood outside during the summer; by the end of September they should be moved into a greenhouse.

Florists' chrysanthemums are

Anemone-flowered chrysanthemum 'Pennine Twinkle'

Single chrysanthemum 'Purple Rockery'

hybrids of complex parentage and are suitable for growing in beds, borders or in pots. Left alone, they produce sprays of flowers up to 6cm (2½in) across. Disbudded, however, they produce magnificent, long-stemmed single blooms, each measuring 12cm (5in) across or more. They are not reliably hardy. In mild areas, they may survive the average winter, but second-year plants produce less impressive floral displays. They are best raised annually from basal cuttings taken from roots, lifted from the garden in late autumn and overwintered in a frost-free greenhouse or cold frame. Perennial border chrysanthemums are fully hardy and can be left in their permanent flowering positions.

Popular species

Chrysanthemum haradjanii, syn. *Tanacetum haradjanii* or *T. densum* 'Amani', is up to 25cm (10in) high, grown for its silvery, fernlike foliage. It has small, yellow, button flowers but these are best removed. The plant is suitable for bedding schemes and as accents at the front of borders.
Chrysanthemum leucanthemum, syn. *Leucanthemum vulgare* (ox-eye daisy or moon daisy) is an ultra-hardy border perennial. It reaches a height of 60cm (2ft) and has a profuse show of white daisy-like flowers in early summer.
Chrysanthemum maximum (the Shasta daisy) is up to 90cm (3ft) tall with white daisy flowers in mid to late summer. The leaves are dark green and toothed. Varieties include: 'Aglaia' (semi-double, white); 'Esther Read' (double white); 'Horace Read' (double creamy); 'H. Seibert' (white, frilled petals); 'Snowcap' (50cm/20in high, white); and 'Wirral Supreme' (double, white).
Chrysanthemum parthenium, syn. *Matricaria eximia*, commonly known as feverfew, is a hardy but short-lived perennial species usually grown as an annual. From 20-45cm (8-18in) high, it has light green, aromatic leaves and a profuse show of yellow or white, anemone-type flowers. Popular varieties include: 'Golden Ball' (golden-yellow, 25cm/10in high); and 'Snow Dwarf' (ivory-white, 30cm/1ft high).
Chrysanthemum rubellum has fragrant pink, yellow-eyed daisy flowers in late summer to early

autumn. It grows up to 75cm (2½ft). Varieties include: 'Apricot' (clear apricot, yellow centres); 'Clara Curtis' (clear pink); 'Mary Stoker' (soft yellow); and 'Royal Command' (semi-double, purple-red).
Chrysanthemum serotinum, syn. *C. uliginosum* (Hungarian or giant daisy) is up to 1.8m (6ft) high, bearing white flowers with a greenish-yellow centre in late autumn. It is suitable for growing at the back of borders.

Florists' types

Florists' chrysanthemums have deep green, pungent leaves divided into rounded lobes and can be grown in borders, beds, pots or greenhouses. There are two main sorts of florists' chrysanthemum – the large/medium type and the spray type.
LARGE/MEDIUM TYPES are disbudded, which encourages the development of one very large bloom per stem, sometimes reaching a width of 18cm (7in). The plants themselves are 1.2-1.5m (4-5ft) high. They are classified according to type of bloom.
Incurved Close, firm petals, curving in on each other to form a perfect globe. Varieties include: 'Creamist' (pale yellow); 'Daren Bailey' (white); 'John Lowe' (cream); 'Peter Rowe' (yellow); 'Susan Riley' (pink); and 'Woolman's Celebration' (white).
Reflexed Petals fall outwards and downwards, overlapping like feathers on a bird. Varieties include: 'Bronze, Eve Gray' (bronze);

Korean chrysanthemum 'Mabel'

Chrysanthemum rubellum 'Clara Curtis'

Chrysanthemum 'Pennine Jig'

Chrysanthemum haradjanii

Chrysanthemum maximum

'Eve Gray' (pink); 'Gambit' (purple); 'Jill Collins' (yellow); 'Joanne Hall' (white); 'John Riley' (red); 'Midnight' (purple); and 'Salmon Venice' (salmon-pink).

Intermediate Petals incurve loosely or are incurved towards the top and reflexed below. Varieties include: 'Bill Wade' (white); 'Creamery' (cream); 'Ginger Nut' (light bronze); 'Hazy Days' (buff-yellow); and 'Primrose Chessingham' (pale yellow).

Anemone A pincushion-like centre ringed with petals. Varieties include: 'Catina' (bronze); 'Premiere' (yellow); 'Thora' (white).

SPRAY TYPES, up to 1.2m (4ft) high, produce sprays of smaller flowers, each up to 6cm (2½in) across, with the following types of flower heads.

Double The centre of the flower is hidden by petals. Popular varieties include: 'Heide' (white); 'Lemon Margaret' (pale yellow); 'Lucida' (yellow); 'Margaret' (pink); and 'Pennine Zither' (bronze).

Single Five or less rows of petals around a central disc. Popular varieties include: 'Pennine Dancer' (pink); 'Pennine Signal' (red); 'Pennine Tango' (bronze); and 'Purple Rockery' (deep pink).

Anemone Varieties include: 'Pennine Gambol' (pink); 'Pennine Globe' (gold); 'Pennine Jig' (golden-yellow), 'Pennine Poppet' (white); Pennine Robin' (red); and 'Pennine Twinkle' (yellow).

Others Petals are shaped like spoons or quills, giving a spidery appearance. Varieties include:

'Pennine Ace' (pink, tipped white with spoon-shaped petals); and 'Pennine Alfie' (bronze-red with spoon/spider-shaped petals).

Pompon Clusters of small tightly packed heads on plants up to 30cm (1ft) high. Varieties include: 'Brighteye' (yellow and red); 'Bronze Fairie' (bronze); 'Cameo' (white); 'Charleston' (semi-pompon, orange-yellow); 'Purple Fairy (cerise-pink); and 'Solley' (lemon-yellow).

Korean Plants with single or double flowers up to 5cm (2in) across. Hardier than other florists' chrysanthemums, they can be left in permanent beds in most areas. Varieties include: 'Copper Nob' (double, bronze-red); 'Fairy' (single, rose-pink); 'Janice Bailey' (double, pink); 'Lemon Tench' (lemon-yellow); and 'Mabel' (red).

Cultivation

For florists' chrysanthemums, take out shallow planting holes in moist, well-drained humus-rich soil in late spring. Stake tall varieties and tie in the plants as they grow. When a plant is 15-20cm (6-8in) tall, pinch out the growing tip to stop further upward growth and hasten the development of lateral flowering shoots. Except on spray types, allow only six flowering stems to develop on each plant.

To obtain large blooms, remove all buds and side-shoots except the centre (crown) bud on each stem. This type of disbudding should start from mid summer onwards or when the side-shoots are about 18mm (¾in) long. Cut all stems down after flowering and lift the crowns before the first hard frost and overwinter in a greenhouse or cold frame.

Plant border chrysanthemums from early autumn to mid spring in a sunny position in well-drained fertile soil, preferably limed. Varieties of *C. rubellum* may produce such large flower clusters that the plants need support. Cut back all perennials to ground level after flowering.

Propagation To propagate florists' chrysanthemums, start the overwintered crowns (stools) into growth in late winter. Take 5-6cm (2-2½in) basal cuttings in early spring and root in a propagator or glass-covered box. Transfer rooted

Incurved chrysanthemum 'Daren Bailey'

Reflexed chrysanthemum 'Salmon Venice'

cuttings singly to 7.5cm (3in) pots of potting compost and keep them cool. Pot on as necessary when roots fill the pots and plant out in the flowering positions when all danger of frost is past.

Propagate border chrysanthemums by 5-75cm (2-3in) long basal cuttings in mid spring and root in a cold frame. Plant out when well rooted. Alternatively, lift and divide established clumps in spring.

Pests and diseases

Chrysanthemum leaf miner tunnels into leaf tissues, producing narrow mines which disfigure and weaken the plants.

Leaf spot appears on the leaves as circular black or brown spots up to 2.5cm (1in) in diameter.

Powdery mildew forms a white mealy covering on leaves, stems and flower buds.

Rust shows as red-brown powdery pustules, the size of a pinhead, on the undersides of leaves. The disease spreads rapidly.

Slugs and snails may feed on the leaves, stems and flowers.

Intermediate chrysanthemum 'Ginger Nut'

Cimicifuga
bugbane

Cimicifuga racemosa 'Atropurpurea'

☐ Height 60cm-1.8m (2-6ft)
☐ Planting distance 45-90cm (1½-3ft)
☐ Flowers mid summer to early autumn
☐ Moist, rich soil
☐ Lightly shaded site
☐ Hardy, herbaceous

Bugbane (*Cimicifuga*) is a graceful backdrop for any border. Its sometimes drooping, sometimes gently upright, feathery spikes of rather fluffy white or cream flowers are set against mid green, ferny leaves divided into many leaflets. The flowers are suitable for cutting.

Popular species
Cimicifuga americana has creamy white, fluffy, wand-like flower spikes up to 60cm (2ft) tall above 1.2m (4ft) high leaf clumps.
Cimicifuga japonica has drooping stems of feathery snow-white flowers and shiny lobed leaves. It grows up 1.2m (4ft) tall.
Cimicifuga racemosa (black snakeroot) has graceful spikes of feathery white flowers on 1.5m (5ft) tall plants in mid to late summer. The variety 'Atropurpurea'

has purplish leaves and purple stems with white flower spikes.
Cimicifuga simplex, up to 1.2m (4ft) high, has spikes of white flowers in early autumn. Varieties include 'Elstead Variety' (lilac buds, white flowers) and 'White Pearl' (pearly white flowers).

Cultivation
Plant during suitable weather from mid autumn to early spring. *Cimicifuga* will grow in dry soil but thrives in a lightly shaded position in rich, moist soil. Stems need support only in exposed positions. Once planted it should not be disturbed except to divide the roots for propagation.
Propagation Divide and replant the roots from mid autumn to early spring. Or sow seeds in a cold frame in autumn. Germination can be slow.
Pests and diseases Trouble free.

CINQUEFOIL – see *Potentilla*
CLARY – see *Salvia*

Clematis
clematis

Clematis integrifolia 'Hendersonii'

☐ Height 60cm-1.2m (2-4ft)
☐ Planting distance 30-45cm (1-1½ft)
☐ Flowers early to late summer
☐ Ordinary, preferably alkaline garden soil
☐ Sunny or partially shaded site
☐ Hardy, herbaceous

The ever-popular clematis group, usually thought of as climbers, includes several perennials which can fill the border with an outstanding floral display, later replaced with fluffy seed heads. The flowers are in shades of blue and purple, white or sometimes pink and are often fairly small. They may be starry, narrowly bell-shaped, or flat with distinctive stamens. Often they bear no resemblance to the typical flower of climbing clematis.

Popular species
Clematis × durandii is a very hardy sprawling plant that will climb up to 1.8m (6ft) tall if given support. In late summer it produces nodding dark violet flowers up to 10cm (4in) wide, with cream stamens.
Clematis heracleifolia has loose spikes of strongly scented, rather small, narrowly bell-shaped, purple-blue flowers in late summer. The leaves are dark green and the plant is sub-shrubby, sprawling across an area of up to 1.2m (4ft), with a height of 1m (3½ft) if supported. Varieties include: 'Crépuscule' (azure-blue with a light scent); *davidiana*

Clematis heracleifolia davidiana 'Wyevale'

(large, violet-blue with a light scent); and 'Wyevale' (flax-blue and fragrant flowers).

Clematis integrifolia has veined, mid green leaves and small, nodding indigo-blue flowers from early summer to early autumn. Only 60cm (2ft) tall, it will sprawl across an area 1.5m (5ft) wide unless supported. Varieties include: 'Hendersonii' (larger deep blue) and 'Rosea' (pink).

Clematis recta produces a mass of small, scented, starry white flowers in early to mid summer. They are followed by silky seed heads. This species, which is poisonous, has dark green leaves. It grows up to 1.2m (4ft) high. Varieties include 'Edward Prichard' (scented white flowers suffused with blue) and 'Purpurea' (leaves copper-purple when young).

Cultivation
Plant in a sunny border from mid autumn to late spring. Herbaceous clematis do well in any ordinary garden soil but thrive in alkaline soils. *C. recta* and its varieties need support – they look attractive climbing up low-growing shrubs. *C. integrifolia* needs twiggy sticks for support.

Mulch annually in spring, using compost, forest bark or well-rotted manure. Cut back the stems of *C. heracleifolia* and *C. recta* to about 15cm (6in) above ground level in mid autumn or early spring.

Propagation Take 7.5cm (3in) basal cuttings in mid to late spring and root in a cold frame. Pot up singly and plunge into an outdoor nursery bed. Plant out into permanent positions from mid autumn onwards.

Pests and diseases Young shoots may be eaten by slugs. Aphids may infest growing points. Earwigs may eat ragged holes in petals and leaves.

COLUMBINE – see *Aquilegia*
COMFREY – see *Symphytum*
CONEFLOWER – see *Echinaceae* and *Rudbeckia*
CORAL FLOWER – see *Heuchera*

Coreopsis
coreopsis

Coreopsis grandiflora 'Sunburst'

☐ Height 30-60cm (1-2ft)
☐ Planting distance 30-45cm (1-1½ft)
☐ Fertile, well-drained soil
☐ Open sunny site
☐ Hardy, herbaceous

Perennial *Coreopsis* species and varieties include some of the brightest plants for growing at the front of a border. The daisy-like flowers shine out cheerfully against the mid to bright green, deeply cut foliage and look just as attractive arranged in a vase. The plants withstand pollution and are generally long-lived, trouble-free border subjects.

Popular species
Coreopsis auriculata has 5cm (2in) wide flowers, blotched maroon in the variety 'Superba'. It grows about 45cm (1½ft) tall, but the variety 'Nana' reaches a height of only 15cm (6in) and is suited to the front of a border.

Coreopsis grandiflora (tickseed) is a robust but sometimes short-lived species up to 45cm (1½ft) high with narrow, deeply toothed mid green leaves. The bright yellow flowers, up to 6cm (2½in) across, are borne on long stems from early to late summer; they are good for cutting. Varieties include: 'Goldfink', also known as 'Goldfinch' (15-20cm/6-8in in height, bright yellow, longer lived); 'Mayfield Giant' (90cm/3ft, orange-yellow); and 'Sunburst' (75cm/2½ft, rich yellow, double).

Coreopsis verticillata is a long-lived species up to 60cm (2ft) high. It is upright and bushy with finely

Cortaderia

pampas grass

Cortaderia selloana 'Pumila'

- [ ] Height 1.5-3m (5-10ft)
- [ ] Planting distance 1.5-1.8m (5-6ft)
- [ ] Flowers late summer to autumn
- [ ] Any well-drained, fertile soil
- [ ] Reasonably sheltered sunny site
- [ ] Hardy, evergreen

One of the most popular and effective ornamental grasses, *Cortaderia selloana* provides year-round interest. In late summer it produces upright 60-75cm (2-2½ft) creamy plumes on stout stalks over a clump of slender, arching and rough-edged leaves. The plant makes an impressive focal point.

Popular varieties
'Gold Band' is up to 1.5m (5ft) tall with leaves narrowly striped in gold and green.
'Pumila', more compact than the species with a maximum height of 1.5m (5ft), is suitable for small gardens.
'Rendatleri' has purplish-silver plumes and grows up to 2.4m (8ft) high.
'Roi des Roses' has large pink-white plumes.
'Sunningdale Silver' grows up to 3m (10ft) high and has large, loose, white plumes.

Cultivation
Plant in mid spring in any well-drained fertile soil in a reasonably sheltered sunny site, either on a lawn or among shrubs. Wear gloves when removing dead leaves in spring as the edges are sharp.
Propagation Divide and replant in mid spring.
Pests and diseases Generally trouble free.

Coreopsis verticillata

divided, bright green, ferny leaves. The profuse show of clear yellow, 2.5cm (1in) wide flowers last from early summer to early autumn. Varieties include 'Grandiflora' syn. 'Golden Shower' (star-shaped rich yellow flowers); and 'Zagreb' (bright golden flowers on compact plants up to 30cm (1ft) tall.

Cultivation
Plant from mid autumn to early spring in any fertile and very well-drained garden soil in an open, sunny site. *C. grandiflora* should be staked with pea sticks at an early stage. The variety 'Sunburst' is very short-lived unless cut back after flowering.

Propagation Divide from mid autumn to early spring, making sure that each portion has a number of shoots. Replant immediately in permanent positions.

Alternatively, sow seeds in open ground in mid spring; prick out into a nursery bed and grow on. Transfer to the flowering site from mid autumn onwards.
Pests and diseases Froghoppers exude 'cuckoo-spit' in leaf axils, and suck sap from the stems. Slugs may eat leaves and flowers.

CORNFLOWER – see *Centaurea*
CORNFLOWER ASTER – see *Stokesia*

Corydalis

corydalis

Corydalis lutea

☐ Height 25-30cm (10-12in)
☐ Planting distance 30cm (12in)
☐ Flowers from late spring to mid autumn
☐ Well-drained, fertile garden soil
☐ Sunny or shady site
☐ Hardy, herbaceous

Corydalis is a soft, entrancing little plant with pale, delicate foliage decorated with a profuse and long-lasting show of quaint tubular spurred flowers. Some species seed themselves freely and are often seen growing in old walls and brickwork.

Popular species
Corydalis cheilanthifolia grows about 25cm (10in) high and is of neat tufted habit. It is the least invasive of the species and suitable for ground cover, for edging and for container growing. The attractive ferny foliage is tinted bronze-purple and handsomely shows off the dense spikes of bright yellow flowers that appear from late spring to autumn.
Corydalis lutea (common yellow corydalis) grows up to 30cm (1ft) tall. It has fern-like light green leaves and yellow flowers on arching stems from mid spring until late autumn. It is often seen on old walls and can be invasive.
Corydalis wilsonii has blue-green leaves and spikes of bright canary-yellow flowers. It grows up to 25cm (10in) tall.

Cultivation
Plant in early spring in any good, well-drained garden soil, in sun or light shade. *C. lutea* will grow in deep shade, and a rich soil encourages even more self-sown seedlings. For best results, grow the species in ordinary, even poor soil and pull up unwanted seedlings as soon as they appear.
Propagation Sow seeds in a cold frame in late winter to early spring or in early to mid autumn. Prick out when the first true leaf appears, as the root is very brittle on older seedlings. Pot up individually and overwinter in a cold frame. Plant out in early to mid spring. *C. lutea* can also be sown directly in the permanent site.
Pests and diseases Generally trouble free.

Cotyledon

lamb's tail

Cotyledon oppositifolium

☐ Height 15cm (6in)
☐ Planting distance 60cm (2ft)
☐ Flowers late spring to early summer
☐ Free-draining soil
☐ Shady or lightly sunny site
☐ Hardy, evergreen

Lamb's tail (*Cotyledon oppositifolium*, syn. *Cotyledon simplicifolia* or *Chiastophyllum oppositifolium*) is grown partly for the texture and colour of its interesting leaves and partly for its elegant flower racemes. It is a rosette-forming, succulent plant which forms a creeping, self-rooting mat. The light to mid green, fleshy leaves are oval and lightly toothed. In late spring to early summer, stems of yellow flowers arch over the foliage, to add to the colour and textural interest.
    Lamb's tail can be grown in clusters in walls and crevices.

Cultivation
Plant in any free-draining soil with added grit, in a cool shady site, surrounded with stone chippings.
Propagation Take 5-7.5cm (2-3in) softwood cuttings during early summer. Let the cut surfaces heal for 1-2 days before rooting in compost.
Pests and diseases Mealy bugs may cause conspicuous tufts of white wax on young growths.

COWSLIP – see *Primula*

Crambe

flowering seakale, giant seakale

Crambe cordifolia

- ☐ Height 1.8m (6ft)
- ☐ Planting distance 60-90cm (2-3ft)
- ☐ Flowers early to mid summer
- ☐ Fertile, well-drained soil
- ☐ Sun or partial shade
- ☐ Hardy, herbaceous

Crambe cordifolia is a magnificent plant for larger gardens. It has enormous, dark green, heart-shaped leaves, irregularly lobed and toothed, and measuring up to 90cm (3ft) long. In summer the great mound of foliage supports a charming cloud of tiny white, cross-shaped flowers held in widely branching sprays about 90cm (3ft) across.

In large borders *Crambe cordifolia* is useful for concealing a spring-flowering shrub that looks dull in summer. It also makes an imposing specimen plant.

Cultivation

Plant in autumn or spring in fertile, well-drained soil in a sunny or partially shaded site protected from strong winds. Mulch the root area annually in late spring. Cut back to ground level in autumn.
Propagation Sow seeds in a cold frame in spring. Prick the seedlings singly into pots and plant out in a nursery bed when well-rooted. Grow on for a year before transferring the young plants to their permanent sites; they should flower in their third year. Alternatively, take root cuttings in spring.
Pests and diseases Slugs and snails eat young leaves.

CRANE'S-BILL – see *Geranium*
CREEPING JENNY – see
Lysimachia

Crepis

hawkweed

Crepis aurea

- ☐ Height 10-23cm (4-9in)
- ☐ Planting distance 23-30cm (9-12in)
- ☐ Flowers mid summer to early autumn
- ☐ Any well-drained soil
- ☐ Sunny site
- ☐ Hardy, herbaceous

The pink or coppery-orange dandelion-like flowers of hawkweed (*Crepis*) look pretty in a rock garden, but they are just as welcome as edging to the front of an herbaceous border. The plant is very hardy and will grow in the poorest soil, provided it is in a sunny position.

Popular species

Crepis aurea, up to 15cm (6in) high, has light green, dandelion-like leaves and produces coppery-orange flowers from mid summer to early autumn.
Crepis incana, up to 23cm (9in) high, has hairy grey-green leaves and soft pink flowers from mid to late summer. It is clump-forming and ideal for edging.

Cultivation

Plant in any well-drained soil in a sunny position from late summer to early autumn.
Propagation Sow seeds in mid spring in a cold frame. Prick off in

Crepis incana

boxes, or singly; transplant to permanent positions in late summer or early autumn. Alternatively, divide and replant in mid spring.
Pests and diseases Generally trouble free.

CUPID'S DART – see *Catananche*

Cynoglossum

hound's tongue

Cynoglossum nervosum

☐ Height 45-60cm (1½-2ft)
☐ Planting distance 30cm (1ft)
☐ Flowers early to mid summer
☐ Rich, well-drained soil
☐ Sunny or lightly shaded site
☐ Hardy, herbaceous

Cynoglossum nervosum forms a dome up to 60cm (2ft) high of softly textured, mid green leaves which are hairy and narrowly tongue-shaped. In early to mid summer many intensely blue flowers, which look rather like forget-me-nots, rise over the foliage on branching stems. The plant is easy and accommodating.

Cultivation
Plant between mid autumn and early spring in a sunny or lightly shaded position in moderately rich, well-drained soil. Support *C. nervosum* with twiggy sticks and cut the stems down to ground level in autumn.
Propagation Sow seeds in early to mid spring in a cold frame. Prick out into a nursery bed and grow on; plant out in autumn. Or divide and replant between mid autumn and early spring.
Pests and diseases Generally trouble free.

Dactylorrhiza

orchis

Dactylorrhiza elata

☐ Height 45-60cm (1½-2ft)
☐ Planting distance 30cm (1ft)
☐ Flowers early to mid summer
☐ Humus-rich, moist soil
☐ Sunny or partially shaded site
☐ Moderately hardy, herbaceous

With a little care and suitable conditions, *Dactylorrhiza*, a member of the Orchid family, will produce its lovely flowers in a border. These beautiful, upright plants have lance-shaped leaves, sometimes speckled with brown and forming a sheath around the stem. The lobed flowers are in shades of purple, magenta or red.

Popular species
Dactylorrhiza elata, up to 60cm (2ft) tall, has dull green leaves and dense clusters of deep lilac-purple, slightly speckled flowers.
Dactylorrhiza fuchsii, syn. *D. maculata*, up to 50cm (20in) high, has leaves faintly mottled with red-dish-brown and dense spikes of spotted lilac-pink flowers.
Dactylorrhiza maderensis is up to 45cm (1½ft) high with shiny green leaves and red-purple flowers.
Dactylorrhiza purpurea (lady orchid), 45cm (1½ft) high, has broad leaves and dense clusters of scented purple-pink flowers.

Cultivation
Plant in autumn or spring in humus-rich soil in sun or semi-shade. Keep constantly moist.
Propagation Divide and replant the rhizomes in spring.
Pests and diseases Trouble free.

DAISY, PAINTED – see *Pyrethrum*
DAY LILY – see *Hemerocallis*
DAMASK VIOLET – see *Hesperis*
DEAD NETTLE – see *Lamium*

Delphinium
delphinium

Delphinium × belladonna 'Lamartine'

Delphinium elatum 'Clack's Choice'

- ☐ Height 60cm-2.4m (2-8ft)
- ☐ Planting distance 30-60cm (1-2ft)
- ☐ Flowers early to mid summer
- ☐ Deep, rich soil
- ☐ Sunny preferably sheltered site
- ☐ Hardy, herbaceous

Delphinium is an outstanding garden plant. Grown at the back of a border, the dense flower spikes of some varieties rise like stately Roman columns; others have a graceful branching appearance.

Spurred flowers cluster around upright stems, above the mid to dark green, deeply divided foliage. Famous for their dazzling range of blues, the flowers can also be pink, mauve, yellow, red or white, often with a contrasting central eye, or 'bee'. Delphiniums are short-lived and need care, but their appearance is worth it.

Popular species and varieties
Delphinium × belladonna, 1.1-1.4m (3½-4½ft) high, bears mainly white to dark blue flowers on slender, branching stems from early summer. Varieties, usually listed as Belladonna delphiniums, include: 'Lamartine' (deep blue); 'Moerheimii' (white) and 'Pink Sensation' (clear pink).

Delphinium elatum, 1-2.4m (3-8ft) tall, has sturdy stems terminating in dense spikes of flattish flowers, sometimes with a black or white central bee. Popular varieties, over 1.4m (4½ft) high, include: 'Butterball' (cream, yellow eye); 'Clack's Choice' (mid blue, black eye); 'Clifford Lass' (rosy-pink); 'Cream Cracker' (cream-white, yellow eye); 'Fanfare' (pale mauve, white eye); 'Fenella' (brilliant blue, black eye); 'Galahad' (white); and 'Strawberry Fair' (dusky-pink, white eye). Dwarf varieties, up to 1.4m (4½ft) tall, include: 'Blue Jade' (sky-blue, brown eye); 'Blue Nile' (brilliant blue, white eye); 'Mighty Atom' (deep lavender). Superior new completely perennial strains include the Pacific Hybrids and New Century Hybrids, 1.2-1.5m (4-5ft) tall, with majestic flower spikes in shades of white, pink, blue and purple.

Delphinium grandiflorum, up to 60cm (2ft) tall, has violet-blue flowers on branching stems in mid summer.

Delphinium nudicaule, up to 60cm (2ft) tall, has orange-red cup-shaped flowers in airy spikes.

Cultivation
Plant from early autumn to early spring in rich, deep soil in a sunny preferably sheltered position. Stake taller plants in mid spring.

Propagation For Elatum and Belladonna groups, take 7.5-10cm (304in) basal cuttings in mid spring and root in a cold frame. Grow on in nursery rows and plant out in early autumn. Or divide and replant in early to mid spring.

All perennial species can be raised from seeds sown in the permanent bed in summer or early autumn. The seeds, which are short-lived should be obtained from a reliable source to ensure true breeding to type.

Pests and diseases Snails and slugs may eat shoots. Crown rot may kill off top growth. Powdery mildew shows as a white coating.

Delphinium elatum 'Cream Cracker'

Delphinium elatum 'Blue Jade'

Delphinium elatum 'Fenella'

Delphinium elatum 'Clifford Lass'

Dianthus

pinks and carnations

Dianthus × arvernensis

'Daphne' (Modern pink)

- ☐ Height: carnations 30-90cm (1-3ft); pinks 7.5-45cm (3-18in)
- ☐ Planting distance 15-45cm (6-18in)
- ☐ Flowers late spring to mid autumn
- ☐ Well-drained, neutral or alkaline soil
- ☐ Sunny site
- ☐ Carnations – moderately hardy, evergreen
- ☐ Pinks – very hardy, evergreen

Few garden flowers are more delightful than pinks or more elegant than carnations. Usually scented and in numerous shades and colour combinations, these plants are true classics whose beauty has fascinated gardeners and flower arrangers since Roman slaves wove their blooms into garlands for festivals.

Pinks are generally smaller than carnations and should always be scented. The blooms, carried on erect and dainty stems, are either single, consisting of five slightly overlapping petals, or double. There are four colour classifications: self – all one colour; bicolour – the base of each petal has a patch of dark, contrasting colour; laced – the contrasting patch is extended in a band near the edge of each petal; and fancy – speckles or stripes of contrasting colour. Pinks are very versatile and can be grown in rock gardens, at the edge of a border, as fill-in plants, on walls, in beds, containers and in window boxes. Some types flower twice, once in summer and again in autumn.

Border carnations are up to 90cm (3ft) tall. Their large, heavy flowers, not always scented, may measure over 7.5cm (3in) across and are borne on stout stems which need to be staked. There are four main colour classifications: self – all one colour; fancy – a single colour background (white, yellow or apricot) with stripes or flecks in a contrasting colour; picotee – white or yellow ground colour with a contrasting colour around the margin of every petal; and clove – any colour or colour combination with a distinctive clove scent. Florists' or perpetual carnations – the ones you see in buttonholes at weddings – cannot be grown outdoors.

Popular pinks

MODERN PINKS (*Dianthus × allwoodii*), are the very successful result of crossing a perpetual-flowering carnation with an old-fashioned pink. Fast-growing, these border pinks flower profusely in early to mid summer and again in early to mid autumn. They grow up to 38cm (15in) high and have grassy, grey-green leaves. Popular varieties include: 'Cherry Ripe' (bright cherry-pink); 'Constance Finnis' (white with maroon-red lacing); 'Daphne' (palest pink, crimson eye); 'Diane' (salmon-red); 'Doris' (palest salmon-pink); 'Freckles' (silver-pink laced red); and 'London Poppet' (palest pink laced with ruby-red).
MINIATURE PINKS, of complex parentage, up to 15cm (6in) tall and suitable for rock gardens, raised beds and containers, include: 'Annabel' (pink); 'Fanal' (intense red); 'Little Jock' (pink with a darker eye); 'Oakington' (deep rose, double); and 'Wisp' (white, purple eye).
Dianthus alpinus, a rock pink, is up to 10cm (4in) high. It forms mid to deep green mats of foliage and from late spring to late summer produces pale pink to purple flowers with paler eyes surrounded by a ring of purple spots.
Dianthus arenarius, up to 30cm (1ft) high, forms a dense green or grey-green mat of leaves. The flowers are white with fringed petals and a green eye and appear from early to late summer.

'Constance Finnis' (Modern pink)

Dianthus × *arvernensis*, Auvergne pink, forms a hummock of leaves up to 15cm (6in) high and across and is suitable for rock gardens. The flowers, which appear on branched stems in late spring to mid summer, are rosy-pink with toothed edges. The variety 'Albus' is white.

Dianthus deltoides, maiden pink, up to 23cm (9in) high, looks pretty in crevices in paving. It has narrow, deep to mid green leaves, sometimes flushed with purple. The flowers, appearing from early summer until autumn, range in colour from red to pink and white. Popular varieties include: 'Albus' (white); 'Brilliant' (bright rose-pink); 'Flashing Light' (crimson); 'Samos' (brilliant carmine-red with dark purple leaves); and 'Wisley Variety' (carmine-red with dark green foliage).

Dianthus gratianopolitanus, syn. *D. caesius*, Cheddar pink, is 10-30cm (4-12in) high and creeps to form a grey-green mat up to 30cm (1ft) across. It is excellent for a rock garden. The fringed flowers are pink.

Dianthus neglectus, 10-23cm (4-9in) high, forms a dense grey-green tuft of foliage and produces pale pink to crimson flowers, buff-coloured on the underside, from mid to late summer.

OLD-FASHIONED PINKS are developed in part from *Dianthus plumarius*. They are slow-growing, to 38cm (15in), with grey-green leaves. The flowers appear in mid summer. Popular varieties include: 'Dad's Favourite' (white with purple-maroon lacing);

Dianthus deltoides 'Flashing Light'

'Inchmery' (pale pink); 'London Glow' (crimson with white lacing); and 'Mrs. Sinkins' (white, double). *Dianthus superbus*, 23-45cm (9-18in) tall, has mid green leaves and white or pale to deep lilac flowers from mid summer.

Popular carnations

Dianthus caryophyllus has grey-green, broadly grass-like foliage and clusters of often clove-scented, dull purple flowers on stems up to 60cm (2ft) high in mid summer. It is the main parent of the many border carnations whose smooth-petalled flowers measure up to 5cm (2in), or more if the plants are disbudded.

Popular border carnations include: 'Catherine Glover' (yellow flecked scarlet); 'Consul' (apricot); 'Eva Humphries' (white ground picotee with dark wine-red edging); 'Fiery Cross' (scarlet); 'Fingo Clove' (deep crimson, scented); 'Harmony' (grey-purple flecked cerise); 'Lavender Clove' (lavender, scented); 'Merlin Clove' (white, marked crimson, scented); 'Orange Maid' (apricot marked bronze); 'Robin Thain' (white marked crimson, scented; 'Salmon Clove' (salmon-coral, scented);

'Santa Claus' (yellow edged purple); 'Scarlet Fragrance' (scarlet-red, scented); 'Warrior' (white marked blood-red, scented); and 'Zebra' (yellow marked crimson).

Cultivation

Plant pinks and border carnations in spring or autumn, in shallow holes, in ordinary well-drained soil, alkaline to neutral, and in full sun. Stake carnations and tall pinks with bamboo canes. Do not mulch, or water except in excessively dry spells. Do not feed carnations which are short-lived and best perpetuated from layering every two years; old pinks can benefit from a spring feed of base fertilizer.

In mid spring, pinch out the tips of young pinks if they do not naturally produce several side-shoots. Carnations do not need stopping in the same way, but pinch out buds on all flowering stems to leave only the top or crown buds.

Propagation Increase pinks from cuttings of side-shoots during summer and root in a cold frame. Pot on singly. Layer carnations – and pinks – in mid to late summer and sever the layers after 6-8

Dicentra
Bleeding heart

'Fingo Clove' (Border carnation)

weeks. Plant immediately in flowering positions.

True species can be raised from seed in late spring or early summer; seedlings are often variable.
Pests and diseases Aphids may infest stems, leaves and flower stalks, fouling plants with honeydew and checking growth. Root aphids may infest the growing system. Powdery mildew may appear as a fine white powder.

Dicentra spectabilis 'Alba'

☐ Height 30-75cm (1-2½ft)
☐ Planting distance 30-45cm (1-1½ft)
☐ Flowers late spring to early autumn
☐ Moist, humus-enriched soil
☐ Partially-shaded site sheltered from wind and frost
☐ Hardy, herbaceous

The distinctive red, deep pink or white blooms of *Dicentra* look like dangling hearts, each with a pendent drop formed by protruding inner petals. They hang from stems arching over a mound of deeply cut grey-green, blue-green or bright green foliage. These graceful plants range in height from 30cm-75cm (12-30in) and flower in late spring and early summer, occasionally later.

Dicentra is an extremely picturesque specimen plant and looks delightful in borders. However, *Dicentra spectabilis*, the most commonly grown species, tends to die back and disappear below ground after flowering, so looks best if grown in association with other plants which will fill in the gap.

Popular species
Dicentra eximia (fringed bleeding heart) forms a clump up to 45cm

(1½ft) tall and 30cm (1ft) across. It has grey-green foliage and bright rose-pink flowers on drooping stems from late spring to early autumn. Popular varieties include: 'Alba' (white flowers) 'Luxuriant' (bright green foliage and brick-red flowers on 30cm/1ft compact plants); 'Spring Morning' (up to 50cm/20in tall, soft pink flowers); and 'Stuart Boothman' (grey-green leaves and flesh-pink blooms.

Dicentra formosa (western bleeding heart), up to 45cm (1½ft) high and across, has bright green leaves on long stalks and pink flowers from late spring to early summer. Popular hybrids between this and other species include: 'Adrian Bloom' (pink-red); 'Bountiful' (deep pink with blue-green leaves); 'Pearl Drops' (white faintly tinged pink, blue-green ferny foliage); and 'Sweetheart' (white).

Dicentra spectabilis (common bleeding heart), up to 75cm (2½ft) high and 45cm (1½ft) across, has grey-green leaves. The rose-red flowers, plumper than in the other species, have glistening white

'Mrs Sinkins' (Old-fashioned pink)

Dictamnus
burning bush, dittany

Dicentra spectabilis

protruding inner petals. The flowers appear in late spring and early summer. The variety 'Alba' has pure white flowers.

Cultivation
Plant between mid autumn and early spring in any well-drained garden soil enriched with organic matter in a partially-shaded site sheltered from spring frosts and strong winds. Keep well watered, especially in periods of drought. Once well-established, leave the plants alone as the brittle roots resent disturbance.

Propagation Divide and replant from mid autumn to early spring if overcrowding makes this necessary. At the same time take 7.5-10cm (3-4in) root cuttings. Root in a cold frame, grow on in a nursery bed and plant out in their permanent positions in mid autumn. The plants, like divisions, may take a year or two to become established.

Alternatively, germinate seeds indoors in early spring at a temperature of 15°C (59°F). Harden off the seedlings in a cold frame and plant out in their permanent positions in the following early spring.

Pests and diseases Generally trouble free.

Dictamnus albus

☐ Height 60cm-1m (2-3ft)
☐ Planting distance 45-60cm (1½-2ft)
☐ Flowers early to mid summer
☐ Well-drained, preferably alkaline soil
☐ Sunny site
☐ Hardy, herbaceous

Dictamnus albus, syn. *D. fraxinella*, is a large, showy plant forming a bush of lush, dark green toothed leaves which smell of lemons when crushed. Dense spikes of white or pink flowers, laced with a darker pink, are borne from early to mid summer and later replaced by seed pods. All parts of this poisonous plant, particularly the seed heads and flowers, give off an inflammable vapour. On a hot, still summer evening, a lighted match held near a flower will cause a slight pop as the volatile oils ignite, hence the common name, burning bush. Varieties include: 'Alba' (white); 'Purpura' (pink, red striped); and 'Rubra' (rose-purple).

Cultivation
Plant between mid autumn and early spring in a sunny position. The soil should be well-drained and preferably alkaline. If the soil is acidic, add lime at 50-125g per sq m (2-5oz per sq yd). Do not disturb the plants, particularly the large ones, once they are established. Cut back the stems to their base in mid to late autumn.

Propagation Sow freshly gathered seeds thinly in a seed bed outdoors in late summer or early autumn. Transplant the seedlings to their flowering positions two years later from mid autumn onwards. Plants may take three to four years to flower.

Pests and diseases Generally trouble free.

Digitalis
perennial foxglove

Digitalis × mertonensis

Digitalis grandiflora

☐ Height 30-90cm (1-3ft)
☐ Planting distance 30cm (1ft)
☐ Flowers late spring to early autumn
☐ Any moist garden soil
☐ Partial shade
☐ Hardy, evergreen

The upright stems of perennial foxglove carry columns of lovely bell-shaped yellow or pink flowers. Beneath them are the mid to dark green oval leaves which become larger towards ground level.

Perennial foxgloves are attractive plants for lightly shaded borders and are especially suited to woodland and wild-garden cultivation where they often become naturalized.

Foxgloves should be propagated frequently as many seed-raised plants tend to produce shorter and sparser flower spikes after the second or third year.

Popular species
Digitalis grandiflora syn *D. ambigua*, 60-90cm (2-3ft) high, is a long-lived and reliable species. It has soft, hairy leaves and, in mid to late summer, slightly arching stems of soft yellow, 5cm (2in) long flowers that are much frequented by bees.

Digitalis lutea, 30-90cm (1-3ft) high, has yellow 18mm (¾in) long flowers on tapering spikes from late spring to mid summer. The glossy lance-shaped leaves are finely serrated.

Digitalis × mertonensis is a hybrid between *D. grandiflora* and the common foxglove, the biennial *D. purpurea*. It grows 60-90cm (2-3ft) high. From mid summer to early autumn it produces densely packed tapering spikes of 5cm (2in) long flowers the colour of crushed strawberries. Frequent replacement of this short-lived plant is recommended.

Cultivation
Plant from mid autumn to mid spring in partial shade in any good moist garden soil. Remove the faded spikes after flowering to encourage the formation of side-shoots that will produce later, and shorter spikes. In mid autumn cut plants down to ground level.

Perennial foxgloves, particularly *D. × mertonensis*, are short-lived and biennial in habit.

Propagation Scatter seeds outside in late spring or early summer, gently raking them in. A thin covering of damp seed compost improves germination. Transplant the seedlings to a nursery bed. Space them 15cm (6in) apart and move to the flowering positions in early autumn.

Pests and diseases Plants grown in over-wet soil may develop crown rot and root rot in winter. Affected plants show discoloured leaves, die-back of stems and finally collapse. There is no effective chemical control; new plants should be grown in a different site and soil conditions improved.

DITTANY – see *Dictamnus*

Doronicum

leopard's bane

Doronicum pardalianches

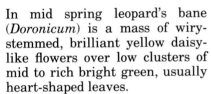

- ☐ Height 20-90cm (8-36in)
- ☐ Planting distance 23-45cm (9-18in)
- ☐ Flowers mid spring to mid summer
- ☐ Deep, moist soil
- ☐ Sun or partial shade
- ☐ Hardy, herbaceous

In mid spring leopard's bane (*Doronicum*) is a mass of wiry-stemmed, brilliant yellow daisy-like flowers over low clusters of mid to rich bright green, usually heart-shaped leaves.

It dies down quite early in th season, so is best grown in associa tion with plants which will fill the gap it leaves. The flowers are good for cutting.

Popular species

Doronicum columnae, syn. *D. cordatum* or *D. cordifolium*, is up to 30cm (1ft) high with bright green kidney-shaped leaves and single, golden-yellow flowers in mid to late spring. Popular varieties include: 'Magnificum' (golden-yellow, 5-7.5cm/2-3in wide); 'Miss Mason' (bright yellow, up to 6cm/2½in across, clump-forming); and 'Spring Beauty' (38cm/15in high, double, deep yellow flowers).
Doronicum pardalianches (great leopard's bane) is a robust species up to 90cm (3ft) tall with tufts of broad, pale green basal leaves. The bright yellow flowers, up to 7.5cm (3in) wide, appear from late spring to mid summer. The variety 'Gold Bunch' is 75cm (2½ft) high.
Doronicum plantagineum, up to 60cm (2ft) tall, produces golden-

Doronicum columnae 'Spring Beauty'

Doronicum columnae 'Miss Mason'

yellow flowers from mid spring to early summer. The bright green leaves are heart-shaped and slightly hairy. Varieties include 'Excelsum', syn. 'Harpur Crewe', with several golden-yellow flowers per stem.

Cultivation

Plant from mid autumn to early spring in sun or partial shade in deep, moist soil. Plants in exposed positions may need supporting.
Propagation Divide and replant the roots from mid autumn to early spring.
Pests and diseases Powdery mildew may show as a white powdery coating on the leaves. Slugs and snails may devour young plants.

Dryopteris
buckler fern

Dryopteris filix-mas

☐ Height 45cm-1.2m (1½-4ft)
☐ Planting distance 60cm-1.2m (2-4ft)
☐ Foliage plant
☐ Rich, moist soil
☐ Shady site
☐ Hardy deciduous or semi-evergreen
   ferns

Dryopteris is an attractive group of ferns many of which grow wild in the British Isles. The delicate, pale fronds lighten shady corners of the garden, where they thrive in moist soil. In mild areas, the fronds remain evergreen, elsewhere they take on attractive russet colours after frost before withering and dying down.

Popular species
Dryopteris cristata, crested buckler fern, grows up to 60cm (2ft) high and as much across, with arching and spreading fronds, pale or yellow green in colour and leathery in texture. It thrives in boggy wet ground.
Dryopteris dilatata, syn. *D. austriaca*, is commonly known as broad buckler fern. Up to 1.2m

(4ft) tall and 60cm (2ft) across, it has deciduous, elegant, arching fronds with a broad triangular shape. It grows particularly well by water and is often used as background foliage for exhibition dahlias. The variety 'Grandiceps' has very large crests on the fronds.
Dryopteris erythrosora (Japanese buckler fern or Japanese shield fern) is a striking plant up to 90cm (3ft) high. The broad triangular fronds are pink and coppery when young, maturing to pale green, and the spore capsules are red. Hardy only in sheltered gardens, it is evergreen if kept under glass.
Dryopteris filix-mas (male fern), up to 1.2m (4ft) high, is a robust, semi-evergreen species, with light green fronds on brownish stems. It tolerates dry, poor soils, sunny positions as well as deep shade, and is useful for ground cover, looking particularly attractive in wild gardens. Popular varieties include: 'Crispa' (up to 45cm/1½ft high with crisped fronds); 'Cristata' (up to 40cm/16in, crisped and

crested); 'Grandiceps' (up to 60cm/2ft tall with very large crests); and 'Linearis' (upright with finely cut fronds).
Dryopteris marginalis is up to 45cm (1½ft) tall with evergreen shiny, bluish-green, leathery fronds growing from a rather woody crown.
Dryopteris pseudo-mas, syn. *D. borreri*, known as golden-sealed male fern, up to 1.2m (4ft) tall, is semi-evergreen. The large, arching fronds are golden-green when young, darkening to rich green with scaly golden stems. It tolerates dry soil. The variety *D. pseudo-mas cristata* 'The King' has large crests on fronds up to 90cm (3ft).

Cultivation
Plant in early to mid spring in shade in humus-rich, acid to neutral soil, moist and even boggy for varieties of the crested buckler fern, and in light or deep shade. Cut top growth of faded fronds back to ground level in autumn.

Echinacea
cone flower

Dryopteris filix-mas

Propagation Divide and replant the crowns in mid spring.

Alternatively, sow the dust-like spores thinly in compost, and germinate under glass in a greenhouse. Keep moist. Prick off and pot the seedlings up singly when large enough to handle. Plant out in autumn or spring.

Pests and diseases Rust may show as scattered or loosely grouped brown spore pustules on the undersurface of the fronds.

Echinacea purpurea 'Robert Bloom'

☐ Height 60cm-1.2m (2-4ft)
☐ Planting distance 45cm (1½ft)
☐ Flowers mid summer to early autumn
☐ Any fertile, well-drained soil
☐ Sunny site
☐ Hardy, herbaceous

The long-lasting flowers of *Echinacea purpurea* (purple cone flower) have drooping daisy-like petals in a deep shade of dusky pink, surrounding prominent cone-shaped centres. These splendid flowers are set against rough, mid green, lance-shaped leaves, with slightly toothed edges. They look magnificent in any sunny border and are excellent for cutting.

Popular varieties
'Bressingham Hybrids', up to 90cm (3ft) tall, provide a mixture of pink-purple shades.
'Bright Star', up to 90cm (3ft) tall, has rosy-red flowers.
'Crimson Star' is 60cm (2ft) tall with crimson flowers.
'Robert Bloom' is up to 90cm (3ft) tall with intense cerise-purple flowers.

'The King', up to 1.2m (4ft) tall, has coral-maroon flowers.
'White Lustre', up to 90cm (3ft) tall, has white flowers.

Cultivation
Plant from mid autumn to early spring in a sunny position in any fertile, well-drained soil.
Propagation Divide and replant from mid autumn to early spring.

Take root cuttings in late winter and root in a cold frame. Plant out in a nursery bed when young leaves appear and then into flowering positions from mid autumn onwards.

Alternatively, sow seeds in early spring under glass at a temperature of 13°C (55°F). Prick out into boxes and harden off before setting outdoors in a nursery bed in early to late summer. Plant out from mid autumn onwards; or sow in a sunny bed in mid autumn, prick out into a nursery bed and finally plant out in autumn.
Pests and diseases Generally trouble free.

Echinops
globe thistle

Echinops humilis 'Taplow Blue'

- ☐ Height 90cm-1.5m (3-5ft)
- ☐ Planting distance 60cm (2ft)
- ☐ Flowers mid summer to early autumn
- ☐ Any ordinary well-drained soil
- ☐ Sunny position
- ☐ Hardy, herbaceous

Globe thistle is a striking plant whose dense, perfectly globular and prickly, deep mauve to blue-green flower heads, set off by jagged metallic, thistle-like leaves, provide long lasting architectural interest for borders.

A useful plant, globe thistle tolerates poor soil and drought, and the flower heads may be cut and dried for winter decoration.

Popular species
Echinops banaticus, up to 1.2m (4ft) high, has slender, spiny, dark green leaves which are downy on the underside. Globular heads of grey-blue flowers, about 2.5cm (1in) across, are borne on branching stems in mid to late summer.
Echinops humilis, up to 1.5m (5ft) high, has dark green, almost spineless, wavy-edged leaves, cobwebby above and hairy beneath. Blue flowers appear from late summer to early autumn. The best variety is 'Taplow Blue' up to 1.2m (4ft) high, with soft blue flowers and grey-green leaves.
Echinops ritro reaches a maximum height of 1.2m (4ft) and is more compact than *E. humilis*. Its deep grey-green leaves have no spines and are downy on the underside. The steel to dark mauve-blue flowers appear in mid to late summer and are up to 5cm (2in) across. 'Veitch's Blue' has richer blue flowers.

Cultivation
Plant from mid autumn to early spring in any ordinary well-drained garden soil. In windy situations, stake the tall stems to prevent them from toppling over. Cut the stems down to ground level in mid autumn.
Propagation Divide the roots during suitable weather from mid autumn to early spring.

Insert root cuttings in a box of sandy soil in late autumn to early winter and overwinter them in a cold frame. In the spring, transplant rooted cuttings to a nursery bed and plant them out in the autumn.

Echinops ritro 'Veitch's Blue'

Alternatively, sow seeds outdoors in mid spring in a sunny position. Prick out the seedlings into nursery rows, finally setting them out in their permanent positions in autumn.
Pests and diseases Generally trouble free.

Epimedium

barrenwort, bishop's hat

Epimedium × youngianum

- ☐ Height 23-30cm (9-12in)
- ☐ Planting distance 30-38cm (12-15in)
- ☐ Flowers mid spring to mid summer
- ☐ Moist, humus-rich soil
- ☐ Partial, cool shade
- ☐ Hardy, semi-evergreen or evergreen

In moist shady places *Epimedium* provides a lustrous carpet of richly tinted foliage. In spring the new leaves, heart-shaped and sometimes toothed, are fresh green, tinted red or pink. As summer advances a network of veins develops and the leaves deepen in colour, reaching the height of their beauty in autumn when they become suffused with superb yellow, red, orange and bronze tints. The plants make marvellous, year-round ground cover.

The spurred, saucer-shaped flowers are white, pink, carmine, violet, red or yellow, though in many species they are hidden within the carpet of leaves.

Popular species

Epimedium grandiflorum, syn. *E. macranthum*, a semi-evergreen up to 30cm (1ft) tall and wide, has long-spurred, white, pink, red or violet flowers up to 5cm (2in) across in mid summer. The young leaves are browny-beige.

Epimedium perralderianum, an evergreen up to 30cm (1ft) high and 38cm (15in) across, has bright green and bronze-red leaves turning copper-bronze in winter, and sprays of yellow flowers in mid summer.

Epimedium pinnatum, an evergreen 30cm (1ft) tall and wide, has mid green, hairy leaves tinted red in autumn. The bright yellow

Epimedium perralderianum

flowers, 18mm (¾in) wide, appear in late spring to mid summer. The variety *E. p. colchicum* has larger and more profuse flowers.

Epimedium × rubrum, semi-evergreen and 30cm (1ft) high and wide, has mid green, red-tinted young leaves turning orange and yellow in autumn. Crimson flowers appear in late spring.

Epimedium × versicolor 'Sulphureum', a semi-evergreen, 30cm (1ft), has mid green, toothed leaves and pendent, pale yellow flowers.

Epimedium × warleyense, a semi-evergreen up to 30cm (1ft) tall and wide, has mid green, red-marked, toothed leaves and copper-red flowers in mid to late spring.

Epimedium × youngianum, a semi-evergreen up to 20cm (8in) high and 30cm (1ft) across, has toothed mid green, red-marked young leaves, flushed orange-red in autumn. Pink flowers appear in mid to late spring. Varieties include 'Niveum' (pure white flowers) and 'Roseum' (lilac-pink).

Cultivation

Plant from early autumn to early spring in partial shade in moist,

Epimedium × rubrum

rich loam. Top dress with forest bark or leaf mould in early spring and remove old leaves. *Epimedium* grows well under trees.

Propagation Divide and replant from early autumn to early spring.

Sow seeds during mid to late summer in pans of seed compost in a cold frame. Prick off the seedlings into an outdoor bed. Transfer them to their final positions the following spring.

Pests and diseases Trouble free.

Eremurus
foxtail lily

Eremurus 'Shelford Hybrids'

Eremurus robustus

☐ Height 60cm-3m (2-10ft)
☐ Planting distance 60-120cm (2-4ft)
☐ Flowers late spring and early summer
☐ Well-drained rich soil
☐ Sunny site
☐ Hardy, herbaceous

Foxtail lilies are imposing plants for the back of borders. The spikes of star-shaped, pastel-coloured flowers, which open from the base upwards, look spectacular in formal flower arrangements. They rise above clumps of long, strap-shaped leaves that die down in summer.

Popular species

Eremurus elwesii grows 1.8-2.4m (6-8ft) tall and forms clumps of light green leaves above which rise elegant, yellow-green stems, as much as 1.2m (4ft) tall, of fragrant, soft pink flowers in late spring. The variety 'Albus' is pure white.

Eremurus himalaicus, an ultra-hardy species, is more accommodating, reaching a height of up to 1.2m (4ft). Spikes, 60cm (2ft) tall, of pure white flowers with orange anthers are borne in late spring.

Eremurus olgae, about 1.2m (4ft) in height, has very narrow, pale green leaf clumps. The white flower spikes, tinted pale pink, appear in early and mid summer.

Eremurus robustus is the tallest species, growing 2.8-3m (8-10ft) high and bearing narrow, bright green leaves, 1.2m (4ft) long, that die down before the flowers open in early summer. These are peach-pink, with brown and green markings, and borne in dense spikes up to 1.2m (4ft) long.

Eremurus 'Shelford Hybrids' produce sturdy stems up to 2m (7ft) tall above light green leaves. They flower in early and mid summer,

the spikes varying in colour from palest pink to glowing copper-orange.

Eremurus stenophyllus bungei is much shorter, up to 90cm (3ft), whose golden-yellow and orange flower spikes appear in early and mid summer.

Cultivation

All *Eremurus* species resent wetness around the roots. Plant them deeply in early to mid autumn, in humus-rich, well-drained soil. Set the crowns on a layer of sand. They require a sunny site, but one not exposed to early morning sun. Mulch the crowns annually in early autumn with leaf-mould or well-rotted manure. Stake tall species and cut all stems right down after flowering unless the seed heads are wanted for drying.

Propagation The brittle, fleshy roots resent disturbance and although the plants can be divided in early autumn, they may take several years to recover. The best means of increase is by ripe seed sown by late winter or early spring under glass. Grow the seedlings on in pots in a cold frame for two or three years before transplanting them to the flowering sites.

Pests and diseases Generally trouble free.

Erigeron

fleabane

Erigeron × hybridus 'Gaiety'

Erigeron × hybridus 'Felicity'

Erigeron mucronatus

- ☐ Height 25-60cm (10-24in)
- ☐ Planting distance 23-38cm (9-15in)
- ☐ Flowers late spring to late summer
- ☐ Moist, well-drained soil
- ☐ Sunny site
- ☐ Hardy, herbaceous

The pretty double or semi-double daisy-like flowers of *Erigeron*, set against mid green or grey-green narrow oval leaves, give it a delicate appearance, belied by the plants' hardiness, reliability and long flowering season.

The outer ring of florets surrounding the yellow centres can be white, pink, yellow, blue or shades of mauve. The plants may be tufted or mat-forming and are good subjects for herbaceous and mixed borders, with the shorter species suitable for front edging. The flowers, which measure up to 6cm (2½in) across, are excellent as cut flowers.

Popular species

Erigeron aurantiacus, often short-lived, forms a velvety mat with a maximum height and spread of 25cm (10in) and is decorated with orange-yellow flowers in early to late summer. The variety 'Sulphureus' is pale yellow. Both are ideal as edging to borders.

Erigeron × hybridus plants have been developed from the species *Erigeron speciosus* and its variety, *E. s. macranthus*. They are ultra-hardy and easy-growing, giving the best display for borders and cutting. They have strong, leafy stems, a profuse show of flowers up to 6cm (2½in) wide and usually have a maximum height of 60cm (2ft). Varieties include: 'Amity' (lilac-rose); 'Darkest of All' (deep violet-blue); 'Dignity' (violet-blue, 45cm/1½ft); 'Dimity' (pink, 25cm/10in high); 'Felicity' (light pink); 'Gaiety' (bright pink); 'Prosperity' (blue, semi-double); and 'Schwartzes Meer' (lavender-violet).

Erigeron macranthus is a tufted plant, with yellow-centred, purple-blue flowers in mid to late summer. The species has a maximum height of 60cm (2ft).

Erigeron mucronatus, syn. *E. karvinskianus*, up to 25cm (10in) high, has white to pale pink flowers. It is suitable for edging, but self-seeds freely and can become invasive.

Cultivation

Plant from mid autumn to early spring in a sunny position in any type of moist but well-drained soil. In exposed sites support the plants with twiggy sticks. Removal of dead flowers encourages further flowering later in the season. Cut the stems down to ground level in autumn.

Propagation Divide and replant the roots during suitable weather from mid autumn to early spring. This should be done every two or three years to prevent overcrowding.

Alternatively, sow seeds in mid to late spring in pots or boxes of

Erigeron macranthus

Eryngium
sea holly

Erigeron aurantiacus

seed compost in a cold frame. Prick out the seedlings into boxes of potting compost and when well developed, move them to a nursery bed. Transfer the young plants to their final positions in autumn and firm in well.

Pests and diseases Generally trouble free.

Eryngium alpinum

☐ Height 60cm-1.2m (2-4ft)
☐ Planting distance 30-60cm (1-2ft)
☐ Flowers mid summer to early autumn
☐ Ordinary, well drained soil
☐ Sunny position
☐ Hardy, herbaceous

Eryngium is much prized by flower-arrangers for its spiny leaves and teasel-like flower heads surrounded by a collar of prickly bracts.

The leaves of these stylish plants may be greyish-green, bluish-green or dark green; the flower heads are light blue. steely-blue or violet-blue. They are suitable both for cutting and for drying.

Popular species
Eryngium alpinum, up to 60cm (2ft) high, has dark green-blue, heart-shaped leaves and stout blue stems bearing metallic- blue flower heads with impressive finely divided violet-blue bracts from mid summer to early autumn.
Eryngium bourgatii, up to 60cm (2ft) tall, has crisp, grey-green, white-veined leaves divided into threes, and bluish flowers with

Eryngium bourgatii

narrow, steely-blue bracts in mid to late summer.
Eryngium giganteum, up to 1.2m (4ft) tall, has bluish, heart-shaped leaves and silvery-blue to greenish flowers with long bracts. This species flowers only once, then dies, but self-seeds readily.
Eryngium maritimum, true sea holly, is up to 45cm (1½ft) high

Eryngium giganteum

Eupatorium
hemp agrimony

Eupatorium purpureum

☐ Height 60cm-1.8m (2-6ft)
☐ Planting distance 60-90cm (2-3ft)
☐ Flowers mid summer to early autumn
☐ Any moist soil
☐ Sun or partial shade
☐ Hardy, herbaceous

Ideal for large borders and wild gardens, eupatoriums are tall, upright plants with slender, mid green leaves and rounded, fluffy heads of blue-purple, red-purple or white flowers which are produced from mid summer to early autumn.

Popular species
Eupatorium cannabinum (hemp agrimony) is up to 1.2m (4ft) tall, with reddish-purple flowers in mid summer to early autumn. The more widely grown variety 'Plenum' has double flowers.
Eupatorium coelestinum (mist flower) is up to 60cm (2ft) tall with blue, violet or white flowers in mid to late summer. Invasive.
Eupatorium purpureum (Joe Pye weed) is up to 1.8m (6ft) tall with vanilla-scented leaves and rose-purple flowers in mid to late summer. The variety 'Atropurpureum' has purple-green foliage and rosy-lilac flowers.

Cultivation
Plant from mid autumn to early spring in a sunny or partially shaded site in any reasonable moist soil.
Propagation Divide and replant from mid autumn to early spring.
Pests and diseases Generally trouble free.

with stiff, silvery-green, deeply cut leaves. Large silvery bracts surround steely-blue flowers on branching stems from mid summer to early autumn.
Eryngium × *oliverianum*, up to 1.2m (4ft) high, has deeply cut, blue-green leaves, bluish flowers and deep mauve-blue, narrow bracts throughout summer.
Eryngium planum, up to 90cm (3ft) tall, has dark green, heart-shaped leaves, light blue flowers and narrow blue-green bracts from mid to late summer.
Eryngium variifolium, an evergreen up to 75cm (2½ft) tall, has rounded dark green leaves with white marbling. The flower heads appear from mid to late summer and are blue with silver bracts.

Cultivation
Plant from mid autumn to mid spring in a sunny position in ordinary, well-drained soil. Slender plants need twiggy sticks for support in exposed positions.
Propagation Take root cuttings in late winter and root in boxes of compost in a cold frame. When young leaves are well developed, set the plants in nursery rows and plant out in their flowering positions from mid autumn to mid spring.
Pests and diseases Generally trouble free.

Euphorbia

spurge

Euphorbia myrsinites

Euphorbia griffithii 'Fireglow'

- ☐ Height 30cm-1.2m (1-4ft)
- ☐ Planting distance 38-60cm (15-24in)
- ☐ Flowers early spring to late summer
- ☐ Ordinary soil
- ☐ Sunny site
- ☐ Hardy, herbaceous or evergreen

Grown for their colourful bracts and foliage, and architectural appearance, spurges are excellent plants for poor soils. The narrow to lance-shaped leaves grow on strong stems topped by showy yellow, green-yellow or orange-red bracts surrounding insignificant flowers. The plants are bushy and may form a rounded clump, a group of columns or a low, trailing mat. The stems contain a milky sap which can be irritating to skin and eyes.

Popular species
Euphorbia characias, up to 1.2m (4ft) high, has column-shaped heads of pale yellow bracts held upright from early spring over grey-green, sometimes evergreen, foliage. The variety 'Margery Fish' is superior, with larger heads of sulphur-yellow bracts.
Euphorbia characias wulfenii is similar to *E. characias*, but with yellow-green bracts.
Euphorbia cyparissias (cypress spurge) has pale green, narrow leaves. Only 30cm (1ft) tall, it is useful for ground cover, spreading over an area 60cm (2ft) across. The bracts, which appear from mid to late spring are green-yellow, This species thrives in alkaline soils.
Euphorbia epithymoides, syn. *E. polychroma*, up to 45cm (1½ft) high, forms a compact evergreen dome of bright green leaves, reddish in autumn, with profuse bright yellow 7.5cm (3in) wide heads of bracts in late spring.
Euphorbia griffithii 'Fireglow', up to 75cm (2½ft) tall, has pink-veined bright green leaves and brilliant orange-red bracts in late spring and early summer.
Euphorbia myrsinites is only 15cm (6in) tall but trails over an area up to 40cm (16in) wide. It has fleshy blue-grey evergreen leaves, tightly packed and spiralled along the arching stems, which are topped with greenish-yellow bracts in spring.
Euphorbia palustris is up to 90cm (3ft) high with canary yellow bracts in early to mid summer. Yellow-orange foliage.
Euphorbia robbiae has upright heads of greenish-yellow bracts in early to mid summer and forms a dense, dark green evergreen mound up to 60cm (2ft) high and across. Thrives in shade.
Euphorbia sikkimensis, up to 1.2m (4ft) high, has mid green leaves which are bright red when young. Yellow bracts appear in summer.

Euphorbia robbiae

Euphorbia epithymoides

Euphorbia characias

Cultivation
Plant from early autumn to mid spring in a sunny position in any ordinary, well-drained soil.

Set out only small plants of *E. characias* as large specimens resent disturbance.

Propagation Sow seeds in early spring in a cold frame. Prick out into nursery rows and transplant to final positions in autumn.

Alternatively take 7.5cm (3in) long cuttings of basal shoots or propagate any division from early autumn to mid spring.

Pests and diseases Shoots damaged by cold winds or frosts may be infected by grey mould.

EVENING PRIMROSE – see *Oenothera*
EVERLASTING PEA – see *Lathyrus*
FALSE HELLEBORE – see *Veratrum*
FALSE INDIGO – see *Baptisia*
FALSE SOLOMON'S SEAL – see *Smilacina*
FALSE SPIKENARD – see *Smilacina*
FEATHER GRASS – see *Stipa*
FESCUE – see *Festuca*

Festuca

fescue

Festuca glauca

☐ Height 15-23cm (6-9in)
☐ Planting distance 15cm (6in)
☐ Flowers early to mid summer
☐ Light, well-drained soil
☐ Sunny site
☐ Hardy evergreen grass

Fescue (*Festuca glauca*, syn. *F. ovina glauca*) forms a dense, domed tuft of tough, blue-grey blades of grass 15-23cm (6-9in) tall. In early to mid summer the clumps sprout purplish tufted flower spikes, but these may be removed as the plant tends to loose its neat shape when in flower. The spikes later turn a sandy colour.

This plant is ideal for the front of a border, providing year-round foliage interest, and is useful for planting between conifers.

Cultivation

Plant from early autumn to mid spring in a sunny position, preferably in light, well-drained soil. In late spring the developing flower heads may be cut off if the plants are being used primarily for foliage interest. If the flower heads are left on, remove the dead flowers before they can shed their seeds.

Propagation Sow seeds in mid spring in light soil in the open. Prick off the seedlings in small groups of three or four when large enough to handle and set in nursery rows. Plant out in early autumn.

Alternatively, divide and replant from early autumn to mid spring.

Pests and diseases Generally trouble free.

FEVERFEW – see
Chrysanthemum

Filipendula

meadowsweet

Filipendula purpurea

☐ Height 60cm-2.4m (2-8ft)
☐ Planting distance 45-60cm (1½-2ft)
☐ Flowers early to late summer
☐ Any ordinary, well-drained soil
☐ Sunny or partially shaded site
☐ Hardy, herbaceous

Meadowsweet is a stately perennial with white or pink flower plumes rising over a lush mound of mid to dark green toothed, palmate leaves. The taller species stand elegantly at the back of borders and most species thrive by water, mingling well with other waterside plants. The plumes are also useful for flower arrangements.

Popular species

Filipendula kamtschatica has fragrant, fleecy white plumes of flowers in mid to late summer and mid green leaves divided like hands. It grows up to 2.4cm (8ft) high. The variety 'Rosea' has reddish pink flowers.

Filipendula purpurea, syn. *Spiraea palmata*, up to 90cm (3ft) tall, has hand-shaped dark green leaves with white hairs beneath. The flower plumes are rose-pink fading to pale pink or white, and are borne in airy clusters in mid summer.

Filipendula rubra 'Venusta', 90cm-2.1m (3-7ft) tall, has deep pink flowers on branching stems from mid to late summer, and lobed, mid green leaves.

Filipendula ulmaria is a fragrant species up to 90cm (3ft) high with

Filipendula ulmaria 'Aurea'

narrow dark green leaves, hairy beneath. Branching, flattened heads of creamy white flowers appear from early to late summer. The variety 'Aurea', 45cm (1½ft) high, has golden foliage.

Filipendula vulgaris 'Flore Pleno' (dropwort) is the double-flowered form of the wild species. Up to 60cm (2ft) high, it has a froth of creamy white flowers.

Cultivation

Plant from mid autumn to early spring in a sunny position or partially shaded position in any ordinary soil that does not dry out in summer. However, *F. vulgaris* thrives in full sun and prefers a well-drained, particularly alkaline soil. *F. ulmaria* 'Aurea' needs moist soil and partial shade.

Propagation Divide and replant the roots between mid autumn and early spring.

Alternatively, sow seeds in pots of seed compost in late winter to early spring at a temperature of 10-13°C (50-55°F). In early to mid summer set the seedlings in nursery rows; plant out in autumn.

Pests and diseases Powdery mildew may cause a white coating on the leaves.

FLAX – see *Linum*
FLEABANE – see *Erigeron*
FOAM FLOWER – see *Tiarella*
FOUNTAIN GRASS – see
Pennisetum
FOXGLOVE – see *Digitalis*
FOXTAIL LILY – see *Eremurus*
FRINGECUP – see *Tellima*

Gaillardia
blanket flower

Gaillardia aristata 'Mandarin'.

☐ Height 60-75cm (2-2½ft)
☐ Planting distance 45cm (1½ft)
☐ Flowers early summer to mid autumn
☐ Any well-drained soil
☐ Sunny or shaded site
☐ Hardy, herbaceous

Blanket flower (*Gaillardia aristata*, syn. *G.* × *grandiflora*), forms a clump of brilliantly coloured, many-petalled orange, red or bronze flowers. These are often bi-coloured, with a yellow, brown or purple central eye. The narrow leaves are grey-green and the plant is relatively short-lived.

Popular varieties include: 'Burgundy' (deep wine-red); 'Dazzler' (yellow, maroon centre); 'Goblin' (25cm/10in high, yellow and red); 'Mandarin' (orange-flame and red); and 'Wirral Flame' (browny-red and gold).

Cultivation
Plant blanket flowers from early to late spring in light, well-drained soil in a sunny site, though they will grow reasonably well in shade in most soils.
Propagation Sow seeds outdoors in late spring to early summer; prick off seedlings and grow on. Plant out in early to mid spring of the following year. Alternatively, sow seeds under glass in late winter or early spring at a temperature of 15°C (59°F). Prick off, harden in a cold frame and plant out.
Pests and diseases Downy mildew causes yellowing of the leaves.

Galax
galax

Galax urceolata

☐ Height 30-45cm (1-1½ft)
☐ Planting distance 30cm (1ft)
☐ Flowers early summer
☐ Lime-free soil
☐ Partially shaded site
☐ Hardy, evergreen

The intense red-bronze winter foliage of *Galax urceolata*, syn. *G. aphylla*, forms a glossy, eye-catching carpet for planting in moist shade, perhaps in a woodland setting. The leaves, which grow in rosettes, are broadly heart-shaped and dark green in summer, turning red in autumn. Slender spikes of tiny white flowers rise over the low-growing leaf clumps, in early summer.

Cultivation
Plant in mid autumn or early spring in acid, rich soil in partial shade.
Propagation Divide and replant from mid autumn to early spring.
Pests and diseases Generally trouble free.

Galega
Goat's rue

Galega officinalis

☐ Height 90cm-1.5m (3-5ft)
☐ Planting distance 60-75cm (2-2½ft)
☐ Flowers early to mid summer
☐ Well-drained soil
☐ Sunny or lightly shaded site
☐ Hardy, herbaceous

Goat's rue (*Galega officinalis*) is a vigorous, bushy plant for the back of a border. It looks particularly lovely in a wild garden.

The light green, deeply divided foliage forms a bush 90cm-1.5m (3-5ft) high and up to 75cm (2½ft) across. In early to mid summer, tiny round lilac-blue flowers gathered on 15-30cm (6-12in) spikes appear above the foliage. Varieties include 'Alba' (white); 'Her Majesty' (soft lilac-blue); and 'Lady Wilson' (mauve and cream).

Cultivation
Plant from mid autumn to early spring in sun or light shade in any well-drained soil. Goat's rue looks best planted in groups of three or more. In rich soil the plants may sprawl and should be supported with twiggy pea sticks.
Propagation Sow seeds in mid spring in a sunny position in the open. Prick out into a nursery bed when large enough to handle and plant out from mid autumn onwards; or propagate by division from mid autumn to early spring.
Pests and diseases Powdery mildew causes foliage to turn grey.

Galium

sweet woodruff, bedstraw

Galium odoratum

- ☐ Height 25cm (10in)
- ☐ Planting distance 90cm (3ft)
- ☐ Flowers late spring to early summer
- ☐ Light but moist soil
- ☐ Lightly shaded or sunny site
- ☐ Hardy, herbaceous

Sweet woodruff (*Galium odoratum* formerly called *Asperula odorata*) is a vigorous sweet-smelling ground cover plant which will spread over an area up to 90cm (3ft) wide. The deep green, bristle-tipped leaves grow in whorls in sets of six, seven or eight. Tiny white flowers, suitable for cutting, appear in small clusters at the end of each leafy stem in late spring and early summer.

Cultivation
Plant from mid autumn to early spring in well-drained, but moisture retentive soil, ideally in the light shade cast by overhead trees.
Propagation Divide and replant from mid autumn to early spring.
Pests and diseases Generally trouble free.

GARDENER'S GARTERS – see *Phalaris*
GAYFEATHER – see *Liatris*

Gaura

gaura

Gaura lindheimeri

- ☐ Height 90-120cm (3-4ft)
- ☐ Planting distance 45cm (1½ft)
- ☐ Flowers mid summer to mid autumn
- ☐ Well-drained soil
- ☐ Sunny site
- ☐ Hardy, herbaceous

A bushy and graceful plant, *Gaura lindheimeri* is useful in borders for its long flowering season which lasts from mid summer well into autumn. The thin but erect stems are sparsely clothed with narrow blue-green leaves and studded with delicate star-shaped flowers that open white from rose-pink buds. Extremely hardy, the plant is sometimes short-lived, especially in cold and wet soils, but is easily raised from seed, frequently flowering in the first year.

Cultivation
Plant in groups of three or more in mid spring in any light and well-drained soil and in full sun, preferably protected from strong winds. *Gaura* thrives in dry, sandy soils. Remove the faded flowering stems to encourage further blooms and cut all stems back to ground level in late autumn.
Propagation Sow seeds in mid spring where the plants are to flower and thin out the seedlings to 45cm (1½ft) spacings.
Pests and diseases Generally trouble free. Poor and yellowish growth indicates that soil and site are too cold and wet.

Gentiana

gentian

Gentiana lutea

- ☐ Height 60cm-1.5m (2-5ft)
- ☐ Planting distance 30-45cm (1-1½ft)
- ☐ Flowers in mid and late summer
- ☐ Deep, rich and moist soil
- ☐ Sunny or lightly shaded site

The trumpets of many gentians are favourites in rock gardens, but two species are more suitable for herbaceous and mixed borders, and much less demanding.

Popular species
Gentiana asclepiadea (willow gentian), up to 60cm (2ft) tall, has willow-like, glossy leaves and blue trumpet flowers in rows on long stems. 'Alba' is white.
Gentiana lutea, up to 1.5m (5ft) tall, has large ovate, veined leaves. Bright yellow, starry flowers grow in whorls on tall stems, followed by attractive seed heads.

Cultivation
Plant in early to mid spring in deep, rich soil. Gentians thrive in sun provided the soil is kept moist in summer, and *G. lutea* will grow in light shade.
Propagation Sow ripe seeds before mid autumn and place in a cold frame. Freezing often speeds germination. Prick out seedlings when large enough to handle and later pot them up singly. Keep the young plants in the frame, or plunge outdoors until they are ready to plant out. Alternatively, divide and replant in early spring.
Pests and diseases Generally trouble free.

Geranium

geranium, crane's-bill

Geranium grandiflorum 'Johnson's Blue'

☐ Height 10-75cm (4-30in)
☐ Planting distance 15-60cm (6-24in)
☐ Flowers late spring to mid autumn
☐ Any ordinary, well-drained soil
☐ Sunny or partially shaded site
☐ Hardy, herbaceous or evergreen

True geraniums – not to be confused with pelargoniums, their more tender cousins, which are usually grown in pots – are among the most charming and well-known garden plants with their simple saucer-shaped flowers held over a rounded, bushy mass of foliage.

These tough plants have palmate, sometimes deeply divided, leaves. Usually mid green, some species have dark green, grey-green or silver-green leaves.

The soft, long-lasting flowers, about 2.5-5cm (1-2in) wide, are saucer-shaped and always have five petals. They appear in informal clusters or in twos, threes or fours and may be in many different shades of pink, mauve, blue or white. Many species have pale flowers with deeper veining, while

others have flowers of a deeper hue, including an unusual and intense shade of magenta-pink. *G. phaeum* has almost black flowers. Partnered with care, such species can form part of an exciting association. The flowers are followed by seed heads shaped like a crane's bill, which gives the plant one of its common names.

Depending on height, geraniums can be grown in borders, beds or rock gardens. Some are excellent for neat ground cover and as edging while others thrive in the moist, shady conditions of open woodland.

Popular species

Geranium cinereum, up to 15cm (6in) high and 30cm (1ft) across, has tufts of downy, grey-green kidney-shaped leaves cut into five or seven wedge-shaped lobes. Profuse deep pink flowers, with a darker centre and stripes, appear from late spring until mid autumn. Varieties include: 'Apple Blossom' (pale pink); 'Ballerina'

Geranium endressii 'A.T. Johnson'

(lilac-pink, dark centre, red veins); and 'Laurence Flatman' (large pink flowers, heavily marked crimson).

Geranium dalmaticum, up to 15cm (6in) high and 60cm (2ft) across, forms a dense cushion of lobed, glossy mid green leaves, tinted red and orange in autumn. Dainty clusters of light pink flowers,

Geranium cinereum 'Laurence Flatman'

Geranium sylvaticum 'Wanneri'

Geranium pratense 'Kashmir White'

Geranium ibericum (G. × magnificum)

about 2.5cm (1in) across, appear from early to late summer. 'Album' has white flowers, tinged pink.

Geranium endressii, up to 45cm (1½ft) high, has mid green, palmate, deeply divided leaves, and is useful for ground cover. The pale pink flowers, lightly veined red, open from late spring to late summer. Varieties include: 'A.T. Johnson' (silvery-pink); 'Rose Clair' (rose-salmon veined purple); and 'Wargrave Pink' (clear salmon). Hybrids include: 'Claridge Druce' (vigorous, to 50cm (20in), with 5cm/2in wide lilac-pink flowers); and 'Russell Prichard' (prostrate, moderately hardy, grey-green leaves, carmine flowers).

Geranium grandiflorum has round, mid green leaves and forms clumps up to 30cm (1ft) high and 60cm (2ft) across. Violet-blue, red-veined flowers, 25-38mm (1-1½in) across, appear in early to mid summer. The variety 'Plenum', syn. 'Birch Double', has double flowers. 'Johnson's Blue', a hybrid, has dark-veined, bright lavender blue flowers.

Geranium ibericum The plant usually sold under this name is in fact a hybrid between *G. ibericum* and *G. platypetalum*, and should correctly be called *G. × magnificum*. Up to 60cm (2ft) high and across, it has seven-lobed mid green, upright leaves and glossy violet-blue, 2.5cm (1in) wide flowers from mid to late summer.

Geranium macrorrhizum, up to 30cm (1ft) high and 60cm (2ft) across, has semi-evergreen, five-lobed, mid green leaves which have a rose-like scent when crushed. This ultra-hardy species has dark magenta-pink flowers, 2.5cm (1in) wide, from late spring to mid summer. Popular varieties include 'Album' (nearly white) and 'Walter Ingwersen', syn. 'Ingwersen's Variety' (rose-pink).

Geranium phaeum (mourning widow), up to 60cm (2ft) high and 45cm (1½ft) across, has small deep maroon-purple to blackish nodding flowers, with backward-pointing petals. This species thrives in shade.

Geranium pratense (meadow crane's-bill) grows 60cm (2ft) or more high, with an equal spread. It bears mid green, long-stalked leaves with five to seven deeply

G. sanguineum 'Lancastriense Splendens'

divided lobes. Small red-veined blue-purple flowers appear from mid summer to early autumn. Varieties include: 'Album Plenum' (double, white, rare); 'Coeruleum Plenum' (pale blue, double); 'Flore Pleno' (blue, double); 'Kashmir White' (white, veined pink); 'Mrs. Kendall Clarke' (pearly-grey tinted pink); and 'Purpureum Plenum' (purple-blue, double).

Geranium psilostemon, syn. *G. armenum*, forms a bushy mound up to 90cm (3ft) high and 75cm

Geranium subcaulescens

(2½ft) across. It has palmate, five-lobed mid green leaves and a profuse show of black-centred, intense magenta-pink flowers from early to late summer. This species tends to flop over when in flower and needs deep humus-rich soil.

Geranium renardii has soft grey-green, puckered leaves forming a clump up to 23cm (9in) high and 60cm (2ft) across. Palest lavender flowers, veined violet, appear from late spring to mid summer. This species does best in poor soil.

Geranium sanguineum (bloody crane's-bill), up to 25cm (10in) high and 45cm (1½ft) across, has dark green foliage and 2.5cm (1in) wide magenta-pink flowers from early summer to early autumn. This vigorous species is excellent for ground cover. Varieties include: 'Album' (white) and 'Lancastriense Splendens' (rose-pink).

Geranium subcaulescens, syn. *G. cinereum subcaulescens*, is up to 15cm (6in) high and about 30cm (1ft) across, with round, lobed, grey-green leaves and profuse black-centred, magenta flowers from late spring to mid autumn.

Varieties include: 'Guiseppii' (strong crimson-purple); and 'Splendens' (salmon-pink).

Geranium sylvaticum, up to 75cm (2½ft) high and 60cm (2ft) across, has rounded, seven-lobed, silver-green leaves and white-centred violet flowers on hairy stems. Varieties include: 'Album' (white); 'Mayflower' (pale violet-blue); and 'Wanneri' (pink).

Geranium wallichianum, a semi-prostrate species up to 30cm (1ft) high and 60cm (2ft) across, has hairy stems and silky, light green leaves which are wedge-shaped and deeply toothed. White-centred light blue flowers appear from mid summer to early autumn. The variety 'Buxton's Blue' has clearer blue flowers with white centres.

Cultivation

Plant geraniums from early autumn to early spring in any ordinary, well-drained soil in sun or partial shade. *G. cinereum* is best planted in early spring unless the site is sheltered and sunny. Taller species, such as *G. pratense* and *G. psilostemon*, may need

Geranium psilostemon

twiggy sticks for support, particularly in exposed or shady sites.

Cut back old flowering stems almost to ground level to encourage new compact growth and a second flush of flowers.

Propagation By division; or seed sown from early autumn to early spring. Overwinter in a cold frame and plant the seedlings out in nursery rows for the summer, until moving them to permanent quarters in autumn.

Pests and diseases Mildew can stunt and discolour leaves.

Geum

avens

Geum × borisii

Geum chiloense 'Lady Stratheden'

☐ Height 30-45cm (12-18in)
☐ Planting distance 30-45cm (1-1½ft)
☐ Flowers late spring to early autumn
☐ Rich soil
☐ Sunny or partially shaded site
☐ Hardy, herbaceous

Avens is a cheerful, little clump-forming plant, decorated with bright long-lasting flowers and suitable for the front of borders.

The saucer or bowl-shaped single or double blooms are in brilliant shades of yellow, red or orange, set against hairy mid green, usually rounded leaves held in rosettes or grouped on stalks with one larger leaf at the tip. The flowers are good for cutting, particularly the blooms of varieties of *Geum chiloense*.

Popular species

Geum × borisii, up to 30cm (1ft) high and across, has bowl-shaped, orange-scarlet flowers 3cm (1¼in) wide set on branching stems. The rosettes of crinkly leaves are useful for ground cover. The hybrid 'Georgenberg' is similar with apricot flowers suffused red.

Geum chiloense (Chilean avens), up to 60cm (2ft) high, has bowl-shaped scarlet flowers about 2.5cm (1in) across. Varieties, which have larger flowers, are now more commonly grown, including: 'Fire Opal' (flame-red, semi-double); 'Lady Stratheden' (yellow, double); and 'Mrs. Bradshaw' (scarlet, semi-double).

Geum rivale (water or purple avens, Indian chocolate), up to 45cm (1½ft) high and across, has nodding, bell-like 3cm (1¼in) flowers with yellow-pink petals veined red-purple and purple sepals. The species thrives in wet soils and its roots can be used to make a chocolate-flavoured drink. Varieties include: 'Leonard's Variety' (coppery-pink flushed orange) and 'Lionel Cox' (gold).

Cultivation

Plant from early autumn to early spring in sun or partial shade. Geums will grow in any ordinary garden soil, but they do better in deep soil enriched with well-rotted farmyard manure. *G. rivale* also thrives in moist soil. In exposed sites, *G. chiloense* may need support. Cut the plant stems back to ground level after flowering.

Propagation Sow ripe seeds in a cold frame from early to late summer or in late winter to early spring. Prick off when large enough to handle. Overwinter seedlings of summer-sown plants in a cold frame and transfer to nursery rows in spring. Plant out from early autumn onwards. Plants sown in spring will be ready for nursery rows that summer and can be planted out from early autumn of the same year.

Named varieties do not breed true from seed and are best increased by division in early to mid spring.

Pests and diseases Trouble free.

GLOBE FLOWER – see *Trollius*
GLOBE THISTLE – see *Echinops*
!GOAT'S BEARD – see *Aruncus*
GOAT'S RUE – see *Galega*
GOLDEN-EYED GRASS – see *Sisyrinchium*
GOLDEN RAY – see *Ligularia*
GOLDEN ROD – see *Solidago*
GRANNY'S BONNET – see *Aquilegia*
GRASS WIDOW – see *Sisyrinchium*

GRACEFUL GRASSES

**Perennial grasses add grace and charm
to herbaceous and mixed borders, introducing air
and light to solid flower colours.**

The airy grace of ornamental grasses provides valuable contrast in herbaceous and mixed borders. It is their slender stems and arching leaves as much as their delicate flower sprays and plumes that make them ideal foils for brilliant flower colours and dark green foliage plants. The shorter types look good at the front of borders and as edging, while taller grasses make impressive specimen plants for a lawn.

Leaf colour is an important consideration in planning combinations of grasses in borders. Leaves are rarely grass-green, but often come in striking shades of yellow or gold, as in the bright yellow *Milium effusum* 'Aureum' or the golden sedge (*Carex stricta* 'Bowles' Golden'). Both of these grass types create pools of sun-light against purple leaves and strong flower colours. Fountain grass (*Pennisetum orientale*) and *Festuca glauca* are blue-green and look stunning against grey and silver-leaved plants such as woolly lamb's tongue (*Stachys lanata*).

For edging beds and borders, the Japanese sedge (*Carex morrowii*) forms evergreen arching mounds of bright green narrow leaves, striped white in 'Variegata' and golden in 'Evergold'.

Grasses should not, however, always be relegated to the background as foils for other border perennials. Some make excellent focal points in themselves, their impressive height and graceful outline adding architectural dimensions to planting schemes. Pampas grass (*Cortaderia sel-loana*) is ever popular, with its huge silken flower plumes in autumn, but it is not the only example. In moist soil, the 1.2m (4ft) tall *Carex pendula* is a striking specimen plant with broad golden-yellow leaves and drooping seed heads in autumn. In similar soil, silver grass (*Miscanthus* sp.) will reach 3m (10ft) in a single season, forming slender clumps of leaves striped yellow or white. In smaller gardens, feather grass (*Stipa* sp.) is particularly attractive, with its silver and brown plumes.

▼ Autumn plumes The creamy-white and silky plumes of the evergreen pampas grass make an eye-catching focal point in early autumn. They tower above the pale russet spikes of the herbaceous silver grass (*Miscanthus sinensis*).

▲ **Silver foil** Sheltered by silver grass, yellow-flowered rudbeckias stand out dramatically against the narrow-leaved *Miscanthus sinensis* 'Gracillimus'. It is accompanied by the popular, yellow-banded zebra grass (*Miscanthus sinensis* 'Zebrinus'). Both contrast well with the bronze leaves of the tender castor oil plant (*Ricinus communis*).

▶ **Feather tops** The dainty plumes of *Pennisetum villosum* tremble in the slightest breeze. They give an airy look to the flat, red flower heads of the late-summer perennial *Sedum* 'Autumn Joy' and are excellent for cutting and drying.

◀ **Feather grass** In late summer, the arching foliage and dainty silver-buff flower plumes of feather grass (*Stipa pennata*) introduce a delicate contrast to clumps of green hostas, golden rudbeckias and waving red spires of polygonum.

▼ **Zebra grass** A tall clump of yellow-speckled *Miscanthus sinensis* 'Zebrinus' dwarfs spires of pink phlox and a foreground planting of glossy round-leaved *Bergenia cordifolia*. Although herbaceous, the dead foliage can be left to provide winter colour and then cut down to the ground in early spring.

▲ Front edging The neat tufts of silver-blue fescues (*Festuca glauca*) form a low evergreen edging, topped in early summer with pale purple flower spikes.

◄ Border sedge The evergreen *Carex buchananii* grows only 30cm (1ft) tall and tolerates drier soil than most sedges. It is suitable for mixed borders and seen here with orange montbretia (*Crocosmia × crocosmiiflora*).

▼ Bottle brushes Also knownn as rose fountain grass, from its purplish flower spikes in early autumn, *Pennisetum alopecuroides* is long-lived if grown in a sheltered site and given some winter protection.

Gunnera

gunnera

Gunnera manicata

- ☐ Height 1.8-3m (6-10ft)
- ☐ Planting distance 3-4m (10-13ft)
- ☐ Flowers mid spring to mid summer
- ☐ Deep, moist soil
- ☐ Sunny or partially shaded site, sheltered from wind
- ☐ Near-hardy, herbaceous

Gunnera manicata is a magnificent waterside plant with enormous rhubarb-like, dark green leaves, up to 3m (10ft) wide, on thick, prickly stems. Green flowers, which turn brown, are massed in enormous cones and partially hidden by the foliage. Clusters of red fruits follow.

Gunnera is seen at its most dramatic in large gardens beside water.

Cultivation

Plant in mid to late spring in sun or light shade in deep, moist soil, preferably with shelter to protect the leaves from wind-damage. Do not disturb after planting. Protect the crowns in winter by covering with the plant's own leaves, weighed down with soil.

Propagation Sow seeds thinly in early to mid spring in boxes of seed compost at a temperature of 16°C (61°F). Pot on and overwinter in a frost-free greenhouse. Plant out in spring.

Alternatively, increase by division, using the small crowns that develop around the base and sides of old plants.

Pests and diseases Generally trouble free.

Gypsophila

baby's breath

Gypsophila paniculata

- ☐ Height 90cm (3ft)
- ☐ Planting distance 60-90cm (2-3ft)
- ☐ Flowers early to late summer
- ☐ Any well-drained soil
- ☐ Sunny site
- ☐ Hardy, evergreen

The tiny flowers of baby's breath, as delicate as their name, form a lovely cloud of white or pale pink over a bushy mound of narrow, grass-like grey-green leaves.

The slender, much-branched flower stems of *Gypsophila paniculata* are popular for floral displays and bridal bouquets, bringing a light cloudy effect to other flowers. The species sometimes known as chalk plant, grows up to 90cm (3ft) high and has grey-green lance-shaped leaves up to 7.5cm (3in) long and a profuse show of tiny white single flowers held in loose clusters from early to late summer. The best variety is 'Bristol Fairy' with double white flowers. Others include: 'Compacta Plena' (up to 45cm/1½ft high, double, white); 'Flamingo' (double, pale pink); 'Perfecta' (double, white); and 'Rosy Veil' (30cm/1ft high, double, very pale pink).

Cultivation

Baby's breath likes lime but will grow in any well-drained soil in a sunny position. Acid soils should be dressed with 50-100g (2-4oz) of lime per sq m/yd. Plant from mid autumn to early spring and provide twiggy support. The fleshy roots grow deep in the soil and resent disturbance once established.

Propagation Sow seeds in pans or boxes of seed compost in a cold frame in early spring. Prick off the seedlings into boxes and later transfer to nursery rows outdoors. Grow on until ready to plant out from mid autumn to early spring.

Alternatively, increase from 7.5cm (3in) long basal cuttings taken in mid to late spring. Insert in boxes or pots of a proprietary potting compost in a cold frame. Or take 5-7.5cm (2-3in) long lateral shoots in mid summer and root in the same way. In either case, pot up into 7.5cm (3in) pots. Cuttings taken in spring can be set in nursery rows in summer and will be ready to plant out that autumn or the following spring. Summer cuttings should be overwintered in a cold frame.

Pests and diseases Generally trouble free.

HARD FERN – see *Blechnum*
HART'S TONGUE FERN – see *Asplenium*
HAWKWEED – see *Crepis* and *Hieracium*

Helenium
sneezewort

Helenium autumnale 'Wyndley'

☐ Height 1.2-1.8m (4-6ft)
☐ Planting distance 30-45cm (1-1½ft)
☐ Flowers late summer to mid autumn
☐ Any ordinary soil
☐ Sunny position
☐ Hardy, herbaceous

A robust and striking border plant, sneezewort (*Helenium autumnale*) produces a mass of broad-petalled, daisy-like flowers with prominent central cones. The flowers, in shades of yellow, gold and red, are borne in tall, branching heads over lance-shaped leaves throughout late summer and autumn. Varieties, some of which start to bloom earlier, have now superseded the species.

These free-flowering plants produce long-lasting blooms for indoor floral arrangements.

Popular varieties
'Butterpat' has pure yellow flowers from late summer to early autumn.
'Coppelia' produces coppery orange flowers from mid to late summer.
'Moerheim Beauty' bears rich bronze-red flowers from mid summer to early autumn.
'Wyndley' produces yellow and orange flowers with brown centres from early to late summer.

Cultivation
Plant from mid autumn to early spring in a sunny position in any ordinary soil. In exposed positions support the plants with canes or stout pea sticks. Some early flowering varieties will produce a second crop of flowers if cut back as soon as the first flush has finished. Cut all stems back to ground level in late autumn.

Propagation Divide and replant every three years to maintain the quality and quantity of the flowers. Division can be done between mid autumn and mid spring; set each division in its permanent position.

Pests and diseases Stems, leaves and flowers may be eaten by slugs. Tortrix caterpillars spin the leaves together and eat them. A virus disease may turn the flowers green.

Helenium autumnale 'Coppelia'

Helianthus
sunflower

Helianthus decapetalus

☐ Height 1.2-2.4m (4-8ft)
☐ Planting distance 45-60cm (1½-2ft)
☐ Flowers mid summer to early autumn
☐ Well-drained garden soil
☐ Sunny position
☐ Hardy, herbaceous

Perennial sunflowers are smaller and bushier relatives of the giant annual, *Helianthus annuus*. They are useful at the back of borders and provide welcome colour in late summer and autumn. The daisy-like flowers are in shades of yellow, and many of the named varieties are double forms. They are all long-lasting as cut flowers.

Popular species
Helianthus decapetalus (syn. *H.* × *multiflorus*) grows up to 1.8m (6ft) tall and bears broadly ovate mid green leaves that are rough to the touch and sharply toothed. The species produces pale yellow flowers, 7.5cm (3in) across, from mid summer onwards. It is generally represented by such varieties as 'Capenoch Star' (lemon-yellow); 'Flore-Pleno' (double, clear yellow); 'Loddon Gold' (1.5m (5ft), fully double, golden yellow); and 'Soleil d'Or' (semi-double, golden-yellow).
Helianthus salicifolius (syn. *H. orgyalis*), up to 2.4m (8ft) high, has stout stems closely set with long,

Helichrysum
strawflower

Heliopsis
heliopsis

Helianthus decapetalus 'Loddon Gold'

Helichrysum orientale 'Sulphur Light'

Heliopsis scabra 'Ballerina'

mid green willow-like leaves. In early autumn it bears sprays of golden-yellow flowers about 38mm (1½in) wide.

Cultivation
Plant in any well-drained garden soil in a sunny position in mid to late autumn or mid spring. Support the stems with stakes or stout canes and cut them back to ground level when flowering has finished. Divide double varieties every third or fourth year or they may revert to single forms.
Propagation Sow seeds in early to mid spring in a sunny position in a nursery bed. Prick out the seedlings and transfer to their permanent positions in late autumn.
   Divide and replant between mid autumn and mid spring.
Pests and diseases Grey mould may cause the flowers to rot in wet weather.

☐ Height 30cm (1ft)
☐ Planting distance 30cm (1ft)
☐ Flowers late summer to early autumn
☐ Any ordinary, sharply drained soil
☐ Sunny position
☐ Moderately hardy, herbaceous

Strawflower (*Helichrysum orientale*) is grown for its narrow, grey-green woolly leaves, topped in late summer by 38mm (1½in) wide clusters of tiny round, fluffy yellow flowers. This soft-textured plant is only moderately hardy and needs a protected position, perhaps by a wall.
   The best variety is 'Sulphur Light' which has light yellow flowers.

Cultivation
Plant in any ordinary, sharply drained soil in a sunny position from late summer to early autumn or mid to late spring in a sheltered position or at the foot of a south-facing wall. In severe winters protect the roots with straw or bracken.
Propagation Take 5-7.5cm (2-3in) lateral shoot cuttings, preferably with a heel, in mid to late summer. Insert them in a proprietary potting compost in a cold frame. Pot on in the following spring. Plant out in the permanent site in autumn.
Pests and diseases Patches of white fungal growth on the undersides of the leaves are caused by downy mildew. Leaves may turn yellow and fall prematurely.

☐ Height 90cm-1.2m (3-4ft)
☐ Planting distance 45-60cm (1½-2ft)
☐ Flowers mid to late summer
☐ Any ordinary soil
☐ Sunny site
☐ Hardy, herbaceous

The stiff, upright stems and rough, mid green leaves of perennial heliopsis (*Heliopsis scabra*) set off a lush display of yellow to orange, rather dandelion-like flowers. These are single in the species, but varieties offer semi-double and double forms. The blooms are 7.5cm (3in) across and are excellent for cutting.

Popular varieties
'**Ballerina**' has warm yellow, semi-double flowers.
'**Desert King**' has single yellow flowers.
'**Golden Plume**' has double, rich yellow flowers,
'**Gold Greenheart**' has double, pale yellow flowers with the centre tinged green.
'**Incomparabilis**' has double orange-yellow flowers.
'**Patula**' has double, golden-yellow flowers.
'**Summer Sun**', shorter than the species, has double, golden-yellow flowers.

Cultivation
Plant from mid autumn to early spring in any ordinary garden soil in a sunny position.
Propagation Divide and replant the roots from autumn to spring.
Pests and diseases Trouble free.

HELLEBORE – see *Helleborus*
HELLEBORINE – see *Veratrum*

Helleborus

hellebore

Helleborus orientalis varieties

- ☐ Height 30-60cm (1-2ft)
- ☐ Planting distance 30-60cm (1-2ft)
- ☐ Flowers early winter to mid spring
- ☐ Deep, well-drained, moist soil
- ☐ Partially shaded site
- ☐ Hardy, evergreen or herbaceous

Hellebores are one of the few garden plants which are at their best in the winter when many gardens look dull and lifeless, the different species blooming in succession from early winter to mid spring. The most popular of these plants is the Christmas rose (*H. niger*) which is as much a symbol of Christmas as holly and ivy.

The flowers of hellebores, which are held singly or in clusters, can be either bell or cup-shaped and come in unusual shades of purple, green-yellow and white, decorated with yellow or gold anthers. They usually measure about 5cm (2in) across, though *Helleborus lividus* has slightly larger flowers, and *Helleborus foetidus* produces clusters of 3cm (1¼in) wide flowers. All are excellent for cutting.

The leaves are evergreen in most species and can be dark, mid or pale green or greyish.

Hellebores enjoy partial shade and are ideal for planting between shrubs. All parts of the plants are poisonous.

Popular species

Helleborus atrorubens, up to 30cm (1ft) high and 45cm (1½ft) across, has dark green, deeply lobed oval leaves. This species is deciduous except in mild climates. The cup-shaped, 5cm (2in) wide flowers, lasting from mid winter to early or mid spring, are bluish-maroon, turning violet.

Helleborus corsicus, syn. *H. argutifolius* (Corsican hellebore), is a moderately hardy evergreen up to

Helleborus lividus

Helleborus niger

Helleborus foetidus

60cm (2ft) high and across, with greyish, toothed leaves divided into three leaflets. Drooping cup-shaped 5cm (2in) wide yellowish-green flowers appear from early to mid spring.

Helleborus foetidus (stinking hellebore), up to 60cm (2ft) high and across, has narrow, deeply cut, shiny dark green evergreen leaves. Clusters of drooping, bell-shaped, pale green flowers, 3cm (1¼in) wide, appear from early to late spring, and are sometimes tipped with purple. The plant smells unpleasant.

Helleborus lividus is a semi to moderately hardy evergreen plant up to 45cm (1½ft) wide and 30cm (1ft) across. Pale green leaves with greyish veins are divided into three lobes, and the cup-shaped 6cm (2½in) wide flowers are yellowish green, lasting from early to mid spring.

Helleborus niger (Christmas rose), up to 45cm (1½ft) high and across, has dark green, leathery leaves, divided into seven to nine lobes. The white or pink-tinged, saucer-shaped, nodding flowers have golden anthers and appear from early winter to early spring. Varieties include: 'Lewis Cobbett' (flowers rose-pink outside bluish-pink, flushed green inside) and 'Potter's Wheel' (glistening white, 13cm/5in wide flowers).

Helleborus orientalis (Lenten rose), up to 60cm (2ft) high and 45cm (1½ft) across, has broad prostrate, dark green leaves. The cream to plum-coloured flowers, often flecked crimson, are 5-7.5cm (2-3in) wide and appear from late

winter to early spring. This species is evergreen in mild areas. Hybrids include: 'Heartsease' (maroon) and 'Winter Cheer' (flushed pink).

Helleborus purpurascens, an herbaceous species up to 30cm (1ft) high and 38cm (15in) across, has mid green, deeply lobed leaves. The 5cm (2in) wide nodding maroon flowers are greenish inside and appear from early to mid spring.

Helleborus viridis (green hellebore), an herbaceous species up to 30cm (1ft) high and 45cm (1½ft) across, has dull green leaves and cup-shaped 5cm (2in) wide, yellow-green flowers from late winter to early spring.

Cultivation

Plant in mid autumn in partial shade in deep, well-drained but moist soil. *H. foetidus* in particular thrives in shade. Once planted, hellebores should not be disturbed. Protect the opening blooms of *H. niger* with cloches from early winter onwards.

Propagation Sow seeds when ripe, usually in early to mid summer, in boxes or pans of compost in a cold frame. Prick off the seedlings into a nursery bed. They will be ready to plant out in their permanent positions in the autumn of the following year and should flower when they are two to three years old.

Pests and diseases Leaf spot may show as round or oval black blotches. Diseased leaves wither and die.

Helleborus atrorubens

Hemerocallis
day lily

Hemerocallis 'Pink Damask'

Hemerocallis 'Stafford'

□ Height 20cm-1.2m (8-48in)
□ Planting distance 30-90cm (1-3ft)
□ Flowers early to late summer
□ Any fertile soil
□ Sunny or lightly shaded site
□ Hardy, herbaceous

The lovely, but fleeting, flowers of day lilies last only one day, yet the plants produce so many blooms that as one dies a fresh one takes its place, providing a superb display throughout the summer.

Set against clumps of arching, strap-shaped pale to mid green leaves, the graceful flowers consist of five long petals, sometimes ruffled, forming a widely flared trumpet, with yellow or red anthers at the centre. The flowers come in many shades of gold, yellow, pink or red, sometimes with stripes on the petals or contrasting throats. They usually open from early to late summer, with a few varieties flowering in autumn. Numerous hybrids are available.

These plants make a fine display in borders but they are unsuitable for cutting.

Popular species
Hemerocallis citrina, up to 90cm (3ft) high, has slightly fragrant lemon-yellow flowers which open at night in mid to late summer. The blooms are 13cm (5in) wide.

Hemerocallis flava, up to 60cm (2ft) high, has clear yellow, scented flowers in early summer. *Hererocallis fulva*, up to 90cm (3ft) high, has rusty orange-red flowers about 9cm (3½in) wide in early to late summer.

Hemerocallis hybrids are generally 60-90cm (2-3ft) high and 45cm (1½ft) across. Dwarf varieties, less common than the tall types, are 20-45cm (8-18in) high and 30cm (1ft) across. The hybrids produce flowers in a wide range of shades of yellow, orange, apricot, red and pink. The flower's dominant colour may be suffused with another contrasting colour. This group includes a large number of varieties, some with large bold flowers as much as 15cm (6in) across, others with many small flowers only 5-7.5cm (2-3in) wide. Varieties include: 'Burning Daylight' (deep orange); 'Cartwheels' (yellow); 'Chicago Royal Robe' (deep purple, green throat); 'George Cunningham' (soft orange-pink); 'Golden Orchid' (golden-yellow); 'Hornby Castle' (dull, brick-red); 'Hyperion' (pure yellow); 'Kwanzo Flore Pleno' (double, dusky orange); 'Pink Damask' (pink, yellow throat); 'Stafford' (bronzy red); 'Stella d'Oro' (dwarf, canary-yellow).

Cultivation
Plant from mid autumn to mid spring in a sunny or lightly shaded position in fertile soil. After planting, leave them undisturbed. Cut the stems almost to ground level after flowering.
Propagation Divide and replant the tuberous roots, but only after five to six years, from mid autumn to early spring.
Pests and diseases Trouble free.

HEMP AGRIMONY – see *Eupatorium*
HERB CHRISTOPHER – see *Actaea*

Hemerocallis 'Cartwheels'

Hemerocallis 'Golden Orchid'

Hesperis
sweet rocket, damask violet

Hesperis matronalis

- ☐ Height 60-90cm (2-3ft)
- ☐ Planting distance 45cm (1½ft)
- ☐ Flowers early to mid summer
- ☐ Any moist soil
- ☐ Sunny site
- ☐ Hardy, herbaceous

The common name of sweet rocket refers to the fragrance of the flowers, especially noticable in the evening. *Hesperis matronalis* is an ultra-hardy, undemanding border perennial, the branching stems clothed with dark green narrow leaves above which rise, from early summer on, loose spikes of small, cross-shaped flowers that vary in colour from white to purple. Double flowered forms are occasionally seen. The plants can be short-lived but they self seed freely.

Cultivation
Plant in groups of three in good well-drained but moisture-retentive soil, in mid autumn or in mid spring. They thrive in full sun. Cut stems back to near ground level in autumn.
Propagation Sow seeds in an outdoor bed in mid spring; prick out the seedlings when they are large enough to handle and move to permanent sites in autumn. Alternatively, divide and replant the roots in autumn or spring.
Pests and diseases Trouble free.

Heuchera
coral flower

Heuchera sanguinea 'Red Spangles'

- ☐ Height 60-90cm (2-3ft)
- ☐ Planting distance 30cm (1ft)
- ☐ Flowers summer to autumn
- ☐ Light, well-drained soil
- ☐ Sunny or partially shaded site
- ☐ Hardy, semi-evergreen

The tiny bell-shaped flowers of coral flower are gathered in loose, graceful clusters on long, reddish stalks, forming a swathe of colour in shades of pink, red, white or greenish yellow. They rise over a dense mat of rounded, dark green leaves which are lobed and hairy.

Popular species
Heuchera cylindrica, up to 90cm (3ft) high, has spikes of creamy white to greenish yellow flowers. 'Greenfinch' has green flowers.
Heuchera sanguinea. up to 60cm (2ft) high, has bright coral-red flowers and the leaves are often marbled. Varieties include 'Bressingham Hybrids' (mixed white, pinks and reds); and 'Red Spangles' (crimson-scarlet).

Cultivation
Plant deeply from mid autumn to mid spring in a sunny or partially shaded site in light, well-drained soil. If the crowns of old plants rise out of the soil, mulch them. Or lift, divide and replant in autumn.
Propagation Sow seeds in early to mid spring in a cold frame. Prick off into boxes and later into a nursery bed. Plant out in autumn.
Pests and diseases Trouble free.

× Heucherella
heucherella

× Heucherella tiarelloides

- ☐ Height 30-45cm (1-1½ft)
- ☐ Planting distance 30-45cm (1-1½ft)
- ☐ Flowers late spring to mid summer
- ☐ Well-drained soil
- ☐ Sunny or partially shaded site
- ☐ Hardy, herbaceous

A hybrid of *Heuchera* and *Tiarella*, heucherella is rather similar in appearance to *Heuchera*. Its graceful sprays or spikes of tiny bell-shaped flowers are in shades of pink and are excellent for cutting. Dark or golden-green, rounded and lobed leaves form spreading ground cover.

Popular species
× Heucherella 'Bridget Bloom', up to 45cm (1½ft) high, has compact dark green foliage and sprays of pink flowers in late spring to mid summer.
× Heucherella tiarelloides is up to 45cm (1½ft) high with spreading golden-green leaves and spikes of salmon-pink flowers in spring.

Cultivation
Plant from mid autumn to mid spring in sun or light shade in any good well-drained soil.
Propagation Divide and replant the roots from mid autumn to mid spring.
Pests and diseases Trouble free.

Hieracium
hawkweed

Hieracium villosum

- ☐ Height 30-60cm (1-2ft)
- ☐ Planting distance 30cm (1ft)
- ☐ Flowers early to mid summer
- ☐ Any ordinary soil
- ☐ Sunny or partially shaded site
- ☐ Ultra-hardy, herbaceous

Though not the most glamorous of perennials, hawkweed is a useful plant, happy to grow in any soil, even a poor dry one. Its yellow dandelion-like flowers rise on stiff stems from rosettes of silvery, hairy leaves which are sometimes spotted purple.

Popular species
Hieracium maculatum (spotted hawkweed) has reddish flower stems and purple-spotted leaves.
Hieracium tomentosum, syn. *H. lanatum*, is grown for its densely silvered leaves which provide a better show if the flowers are removed.
Hieracium villosum (shaggy hawkweed) forms a clump of woolly, greyish leaves.

Cultivation
Plant from mid autumn to mid spring, in any kind of soil and in sun or partial shade.
Propagation Divide and replant between autumn and spring.
Pests and diseases Trouble free.

HIMALAYAN BLUE POPPY – see *Meconopsis*
HONESTY – see *Lunaria*

Hosta
hosta, plantain lily

Hosta × tardiana 'Halcyon'

- ☐ Height 25cm-1.2m (10-48in)
- ☐ Planting distance 25-75cm (10-30in)
- ☐ Flowers mid summer to autumn
- ☐ Well-drained, rich, moisture-retentive soil
- ☐ Partially shaded or sunny site
- ☐ Hardy, herbaceous

The outstanding feature of all hostas is their bold and textured foliage, sought after by flower arrangers and gardeners alike.

The plants form mounds or clumps of splendid heart of lance-shaped leaves creating a lush display throughout late spring, summer and into autumn.

The leaves are blue-green, grey-green or mid to dark green, often with yellow, white or silvery markings and are sometimes heavily veined or crinkled. In mid to late summer spikes or clusters of bell or funnel-shaped flowers, which may be white or shades of mauve and purple, rise over the leaves on straight stalks.

Provided the soil is kept moist, these reliable and adaptable plants provide excellent ground cover for borders, associating well with a wide range of foliage and flowering plants.

Popular species
Hosta albo-marginata, syn. *H. sieboldii*, up to 45cm (1½ft) high and across, has narrowish green 15cm (6in) long leaves with a narrow white edge. Lilac funnel-shaped flowers, striped violet, appear in mid to late summer.
Hosta crispula, up to 75cm (2½ft) high and 45cm (1½ft) across, has broad, long-pointed, waxy leaves about 20cm (8in) long, with prominent white edges. Deep lilac flowers appear in mid summer.
Hosta elata, syn. *H. fortunei gigantea* or *H. montana*, is up to 90cm (3ft) high and 75cm (2½ft) across. The wavy edged, dark green leaves are up to 25cm (10in) long and form glossy mounds. Loose clusters of white to deep lavender-blue flowers rise above the foliage on rigid stems in early to mid summer. The variety 'Aureomarginata' has leaves with wide yellow-cream edges.
Hosta fortunei, up to 75cm (2½ft) high and 60cm (2ft) across, has grey to sage-green heart-shaped, pointed leaves. They are about 12cm (5in) long, deeply veined and long-stalked and turn yellow in autumn. Spikes of lilac flowers are produced in mid summer. Popular varieties include: 'Albopicta' (creamy-yellow edged and striped pale green, fading to cream); 'Aurea' (yellow to green); 'Aureo-marginata' (green, edged yellow); 'Marginata-alba', syn. 'Albomarginata' (green edged white, green-grey beneath); and 'Obscura Marginata' (green edged creamy-yellow).
Hosta hybrids, usually 60-90cm (2-3ft) high and 60cm (2ft) across, offer still more choice of leaf form and colour. They include: 'Gold Standard' (upright, puckered blue-green leaves, broad gold-green centre); 'Honeybells' (light green wavy leaves up to 30cm/1ft long, lilac flowers striped violet);

Hosta sieboldiana

Hosta crispula

Hosta fortunei 'Albopicta'

'Krossa Regal' (25cm/10in long greyish-green, slightly wavy-edged leaves arching outwards, lavender flowers on 1.5m/5ft stems in late summer); 'Royal Standard' (heart-shaped, wavy and puckered green leaves, white flowers in late summer); and 'Thomas Hogg' (glossy dark green 20cm/8in leaves, edged cream; pale lilac flowers in early summer).

Hosta lancifolia, up to 60cm (2ft) high and 45cm (1½ft) across, forms a neat mound of narrow, lance-shaped glossy dark green leaves, about 12cm (5in) long. Pale lilac flowers appear in late summer.

Hosta rectifolia, up to 90cm (3ft) high and 45cm (1½ft) across, has upright, lance-shaped dark green leaves which can be as much as 30cm (1ft) long. Profuse violet-blue flowers, 5cm (2in) long, appear on slender spikes in late summer. 'Grandiflora' has longer, narrower flowers.

Hosta sieboldiana, syn. *H. glauca*, forms a mound up to 60cm (2ft) high and across. The glossy mid green leaves are heavily veined and up to 40cm (16in) long. Off-white flowers with a purplish tinge appear in late summer. The finest variety is 'Elegans' (blue-green leaves 30cm/1ft wide). Other

Hosta sieboldiana 'Frances Williams'

Hosta undulata

varieties include: 'Frances Williams', syn. 'Gold Edge' (mature leaves edged yellow), and 'Helen Doriot' (to 90cm/3ft, blue-green, puckered leaves).

Hosta × tardiana is a hybrid between *H. sieboldiana* 'Elegans' and *H. tardiflora*. It has bluish leaves and grows up to 40cm (16in) high and 25cm (10in) across. The variety 'Halcyon' has silvery-grey leaves and dense flower clusters of pale lilac.

Hosta tardiflora, syn. *H. japonica tardiflora*, is up to 25cm (10in) high and across. It forms a neat mound of mid green, glossy, lance-shaped leaves, topped with mauve flowers in early autumn.

Hosta undulata, up to 60cm (2ft) high and wide, has mid green, wavy, oblong leaves with white or silvery markings. Pale lilac flowers appear in late summer. Varieties include: 'Erromena' (to 1.2m/4ft, plain mid green leaves and slightly darker flowers) and 'Mediovariegata' (light green leaves, centre variegated yellow, 30cm/1ft, spikes of mauve flowers). *Hosta ventricosa*, syn. *H. coerulea*, is up to 90cm (3ft) high and 60cm (2ft) across. This vigorous species has grey, heart-shaped leaves, shiny underneath and about 20cm (8in) long. Violet-mauve flowers appear in mid to late summer. Varieties include: 'Aureomaculata' (to 75cm/2½ft, leaves splashed yellow) and 'Variegata' (dark green leaves with striking yellow edging).

Cultivation
Plant hostas during suitable weather from mid autumn to early spring, in light shade or dappled sun in any well-drained but moisture-retentive soil enriched with leaf-mould or well-rotted compost. Variegated plants retain their colouring best in light shade.
Propagation Divide and replant the crowns as new growth emerges in early spring.
Pests and diseases Slugs and snails may devour leaves, often destroying whole plants.

Hosta lancifolia

HOUND'S TONGUE – see
Cynoglossum

Incarvillea

incarvillea

Incarvillea delavayi

☐ Height 60cm (2ft)
☐ Planting distance 30cm (1ft)
☐ Flowers late spring to early summer
☐ Rich, well-drained soil
☐ Sunny, open position
☐ Hardy, herbaceous

Incarvillea delavayi is one of the beauties of the early summer garden. Rich, rose-pink flowers, shaped like funnels or trumpets cluster on stout stalks, the first few blooms on each plant often appearing before the generous tufts of deep green leaflets have fully developed.

Cultivation
Plant in early to mid spring in rich, well-drained soil in a sunny, open position. Set the fleshy-rooted crowns 7.5cm (3in) deep.

Renewed growth begins in late spring. To protect the crowns from accidental damage, mark established plants with sticks when the dead foliage is removed in autumn. A 2.5cm (1in) deep mulch of compost in autumn is beneficial and also helps to indicate the whereabouts of old plants.

Propagation Established plants may be divided and replanted in autumn, but the crowns are tough and difficult to split.

Alternatively, sow seeds thinly in a shallow drill outdoors in early to mid spring. Leave for a year, then transplant young plants to their permanent positions.

Pests and diseases Generally trouble free.

Inula

inula

Inula magnifica

☐ Height 60cm-1.8m (2-6ft)
☐ Planting distance 45-90cm (1½-3ft)
☐ Flowers mid spring to mid autumn
☐ Any moisture-retentive, fertile soil
☐ Sunny position
☐ Ultra hardy, herbaceous

Inulas are very hardy plants grown for their showy yellow, golden-yellow or greenish-yellow flowers set against mid green leaves. The blooms are daisy-like, but with thinner petals that give them a spidery appearance.

The different species vary widely in height.

Popular species
Inula ensifolia, up to 60cm (2ft) high, forms a clump of narrow pointed leaves with yellow flowers in mid summer.

Inula hookeri, up to 60cm (2ft) high and across, has a bushy mass of hairy oblong leaves and greenish-yellow flowers in late summer.

Inula magnifica, up to 1.8m (6ft) tall, has large leaves which are hairy underneath, and 15cm (6in) wide yellow flowers in late summer. It is suitable for growing at the back of borders or in waterside gardens.

Inula royleana, syn. *I. macrocephala* (Himalayan elecampane), is up to 60cm (2ft) high and across, with oval leaves on unbranched stems and orange-yellow flowers in late summer and autumn.

Cultivation
Plant from mid autumn to early spring in any moist fertile soil.

Propagation Divide and replant between autumn and spring.

Pests and diseases Trouble free.

JACOB'S LADDER – see *Polemonium*
JACOB'S ROD – see *Asphodeline*
JAPANESE ANEMONE – see *Anemone*
JOE PYE WEED – see *Eupatorium*
KING'S SPEAR – see *Asphodeline*
KNAPWEED – see *Centaurea*
KNOTWEED – see *Polygonum*

Kniphofia

red-hot poker, torch lily

Kniphofia 'Fiery Fred'

Kniphofia 'Gold Else'

☐ Height 60cm-1.8m (2-6ft)
☐ Planting distance 60cm (2ft)
☐ Flowers early summer to autumn
☐ Any well-drained soil
☐ Sunny site
☐ Hardy, herbaceous or evergreen

The unmistakable dense spikes of pendent tubular flowers, rising over clumps of grassy foliage, make red-hot pokers outstanding focal points for herbaceous and mixed borders.

Set on strong upright stems, the poker-like flower spikes are traditionally yellow with hot red or orange tips. But a wide range of hybrid varieties in colours, including cool creams, yellows, and greenish-yellows is now available.

The narrow leaves are mid to bright green or grey-green. A few are evergreen, but the majority are herbaceous.

Popular species/varieties

Early types, 60-100cm (2-3½ft) tall, bloom in early to mid summer. They include: 'Atlanta' (broad evergreen, grey-green leaves, red and yellow flowers); 'Candlelight' (clear yellow); 'Earliest of All' (flame-red); K. *primulina* (red and yellow, very early flowering); 'Gold Else' (soft yellow); and 'Tubergeniana' (creamy-yellow).

Mid season types, 90cm-1.5m (3-5ft) tall, flower in mid to late

Kniphofia rooperi

summer. They include: 'Fiery Fred' (burning orange); 'Gold Mine' (orange-yellow); 'Maid of Orleans' (cream); and 'Samuel's Sensation' (up to 1.5/5ft tall, scarlet).

Late season types, up to 1.8m (6ft) tall, flower in late summer to autumn. They include: 'Bressingham Cornet' (yellow and flame-red); K. *caulescens* (coral-red,

fading yellow; evergreen); 'C.M. Prichard' (bronze-orange); 'Cool Lemon' (60cm/2ft, lemon-yellow); K. *erecta* (thick orange spikes); K. *galpinii* and K. *rooperi* (short fat, pale yellow tipped rusty-orange spikes); 'Ice Queen' (creamy-white); and K. *uvaria* original red-hot poker, coarse evergreen leaves, orange to yellow flowers).

Kniphofia 'Atlanta'

Kniphofia erecta

Cultivation
Red-hot pokers like full sun and adapt to almost any well-drained soil. Plant in early to mid autumn or in mid spring in holes large enough to take the spread out roots. Winter mulch heavy soils.
Propagation Divide in spring.
Pests and diseases Thrips may cause a fine mottling and discolouring of the leaves and flowers. Slugs may damage buds.

LADY FERN – see *Athyrium*
LADY'S MANTLE – see *Alchemilla*
LADY ORCHID – see *Dactylorrhiza*
LAMB'S TAIL – see *Cotyledon*

Lamium
dead nettle

Lamium maculatum 'Beacon Silver'

☐ Height 15-60cm (6-24in)
☐ Planting distance 30-60cm (1-2ft)
☐ Flowers late spring to mid summer
☐ Any soil
☐ Sunny or shaded site
☐ Hardy, evergreen or herbaceous

To many gardeners dead nettle is little more than a rampant weed, but several ornamental types are suitable for cultivation and are particularly useful for gardens with poor soil. Some provide good, shade-tolerant ground cover with their nettle-like green, silver or golden leaves. The tubular, hooded flowers come in pretty shades of pink and yellow.

Popular species
Lamium galeobdolon (yellow archangel), up to 45cm (1½ft) high and 60cm (2ft) across, is correctly

Lamium maculatum 'Chequers'

known as *Lamiastrum galeobdolon*, syn. *Galeobdolon luteum*, and is suitable for wild gardens. 'Variegatum', up to 30cm (1ft) high, has silver-flushed leaves, tinted bronze in winter, and spikes of yellow flowers in summer. Though rampant, it is useful for ground cover.
Lamium maculatum, up to 30cm (1ft) high and 60cm (2ft) across, has mid green leaves with a central silver stripe, and pink flowers in late spring. Varieties include: 'Aureum' (semi-evergreen, golden leaves); 'Beacon Silver' (a good carpeting plant with silvery leaves); and 'Chequers' (up to 20cm/8in high with smaller leaves).
Lamium orvala (giant dead nettle) is an herbaceous, non-invasive species up to 60cm (2ft) high. It forms a clump of mid to deep green leaves with deep pink to purple flowers in late spring to early summer.

Cultivation
Plant in any soil in a shady site from mid autumn to early spring. *L. orvala* tolerates deep shade, and *L. maculatum* 'Aureum' needs moist, rich soil.
Propagation Divide and replant the roots from mid autumn to early spring
Pests and diseases Generally trouble free

Lathyrus
everlasting pea

Lathyrus latifolius 'White Pearl'

☐ Height 1.8-3m (6-10ft)
☐ Planting distance 45cm (1½ft)
☐ Flowers early summer to early autumn
☐ Any fertile, well-drained soil
☐ Sunny site
☐ Hardy, herbaceous

Perennial sweet pea or everlasting pea (*Lathyrus latifolius*) uses its clinging tendrils to scramble up trellises, wire fences or shrubs, covering them with colour.

Flowers open in clusters on long stalks, against a background of dull green leaves divided into two slightly pointed oval leaflets.

'Rose Queen' has pink flowers and 'White Pearl' is a good, profusely flowering white variety.

Cultivation
Plant from mid autumn to mid spring in any fertile, well-drained soil in full sun. Support against fences, pergolas or pea-sticks.

Dead-head unless seeds are required, and cut down the current year's growth to ground level in mid to late autumn.
Propagation Sow seeds in a cold frame in early spring. Prick out as soon as they are large enough to handle. Plant out in mid autumn.

Alternatively, divide and replant in autumn or spring.
Pests and diseases Aphids may infest plants.

LENTEN ROSE – see *Helleborus*
LEOPARD'S BANE – see *Doronicum*

Liatris
gayfeather, blazing star

Liatris spicata

Liatris callilepis 'Kobold'

☐ Height 90cm-1.8m (3-6ft)
☐ Planting distance 45cm (1½ft)
☐ Flowers late summer to early autumn
☐ Moist soil
☐ Sunny open site
☐ Hardy, herbaceous

Gayfeather's bristly looking, almost thistle-like flower heads are borne in tall dense spikes that weave in the breeze and provide good vertical interest in herbaceous and mixed borders. The spikes, which open from the top downwards, are excellent as long-lasting cut flowers and come in white, pink or mauve shades. They rise from clumps of narrow, grass-like and mid green leaves that arch gracefully.

Popular species
Liatris callilepis, up to 90cm (3ft) tall and spreading to 45cm (1½ft), is a particularly good species on poor soils. The fluffy flower spikes, borne on sturdy leafy stems, are lilac purple and up to 30cm (12in) long. They are borne from mid summer to early autumn. The variety 'Kobold' is similar but smaller (60cm/2ft).
Liatris graminifolia, up to 90cm (3ft) high, tolerates dry soil and has sparse narrow leaves and purple flower spikes.
Liatris scariosa, is up to 1.8m (6ft) high. Varieties include: 'September Glory' (deep purple flowers),

and 'Snow White' (up to 1.2m/4ft high with white flowers).
Liatris spicata, up to 90cm (3ft) high, thrives in boggy soil and has pink-purple flower spikes on stout leafy stems.

Cultivation
Plant all species in early to mid autumn or in early and mid spring, setting the tuberous roots in an open and sunny position. Most soils are suitable, provided they are moisture-retentive, but heavy soil may cause rotting of the roots. Mulch annually in spring to conserve moisture and water well during prolonged dry weather. The plants disappear completely below ground in winter; mark their positions to avoid damage during cultivation.
Propagation Divide and replant in spring every three or four years.

Sow seeds in early spring in a cold frame or greenhouse. Prick out and grow on in nursery rows until the autumn of the following year, then move the young plants to their flowering positions.
Pests and diseases Slugs may eat young shoots.

Ligularia
golden ray

Ligularia dentata and *L.d.* 'Desdemona'

- ☐ Height 90cm-1.8m (3-6ft)
- ☐ Planting distance 75-90cm (2½-3ft)
- ☐ Flowers mid to late summer
- ☐ Moist soil
- ☐ Partially shaded or sunny site
- ☐ Hardy, herbaceous

Ligularia is a striking border plant with a mound of large leaves and bright, showy flowers. These yellow or golden-yellow blooms are either large and daisy-like, held in sprays over the foliage, or packed into tall, upright spikes.

These perennials, formerly classified in the genus *Senecio*, thrive in moist or boggy soils, enjoying a waterside position, but adapt readily to ordinary soils.

Popular species
Ligularia dentata, syn. *Senecio clivorum*, is up to 1.5m (5ft) high. The deep green glossy heart-shaped leaves are sometimes flushed purple underneath, and form a large clump. Branched stems carry sprays of 7.5-10cm (3-4in) wide yellow daisy flowers in mid to late summer. Varieties include 'Desdemona' (orange-red flowers, leaves and stems heavily flushed purple); 'Gregynog Gold' (up to 1.8m/6ft high, huge spikes of orange flowers); and 'Othello' (orange-red flowers, stems and leaves strongly flushed with red-purple).
Ligularia (Senecio) przewalskii is up to 1.8m (6ft) high with rich green, irregularly toothed leaves which are roughly triangular. Numerous ragged yellow flowers are carried on purple-brown

Ligularia przewalskii 'The Rocket'

spikes rising up to 60cm (2ft) above the foliage from mid to late summer. The variety 'The Rocket' has bright yellow flowers on black stems above large toothed foliage.

Cultivation
Plant between mid autumn and mid spring. Boggy soil is preferable, but the plants tolerate ordinary soil provided this is kept moist.
Propagation Lift, divide and replant in mid to late spring.
Pests and diseases Slugs and snails may eat young plants.

LILY-TURF – see *Liriope* and *Ophiopogon*

Limonium
sea lavender

Limonium latifolium

- ☐ Height 45-60cm (1½-2ft)
- ☐ Planting distance 60-90cm (2-3ft)
- ☐ Flowers mid to late summer
- ☐ Any ordinary, well-drained soil
- ☐ Sunny site
- ☐ Hardy, evergreen

Perennial sea lavender's stiff-looking, rounded heads of bell-shaped pinkish or lavender-blue flowers rise over clumps of pointed, narrow, oblong leaves. They are suitable as cut or dried flowers.

Popular species
Limonium incanum is up to 45cm (1½ft) high. The flowers' outer ring of petals is red, and the inner ring white, giving a pinkish effect.
Limonium latifolium, up to 60cm (2ft) high, has lavender-blue flowers with white sepals on wiry stems. Varieties include 'Blue Cloud' (pale lavender-blue) and 'Violetta' (rich violet).

Cultivation
Plant in mid spring in ordinary, well-drained soil in a sunny site.
Propagation Sow seeds at a temperature of 13-16°C (55-61°F), prick out and harden off in a cold frame. Grow on until the autumn of the following year.

Or take root cuttings in spring and root in a cold frame. When the cuttings have developed three or four leaves, set out in a nursery bed and grow on until autumn of the following year.
Pests and diseases Grey mould causes rotting of the stems and flowers; powdery mildew shows as a white powdery coating.

Linaria

toadflax

Linaria purpurea

□ Height 90cm-1.2m (3-4ft)
□ Planting distance 45cm (18in)
□ Flowers early summer to early autumn
□ Any ordinary, well-drained soil
□ Sunny position
□ Hardy, herbaceous

The curious flowers of toadflax are said to resemble a dragon's open jaws. Held in sprays or on slender spikes, they may be pink, shades of purple, or yellow, and sometimes have patches of a contrasting colour. The narrow leaves are grey or mid green. The plants are often short-lived, but seed themselves freely.

Popular species

Linaria dalmatica up to 1.2m (4ft) high and 45cm (1½ft) across, has narrowly lance-shaped, mid green leaves and loose spikes of pale yellow flowers.
Linaria purpurea, up to 1.2m (4ft) high and 38cm (15in) across, has grey to mid green linear leaves and slender spikes of purple-blue flowers. 'Canon Went' has light pink flowers.
Linaria triornithophora, up to 90cm (3ft) high, has grey-green leaves and rosy-purple flowers. It is less hardy than the other species.

Cultivation

Plant from mid autumn to early spring in any ordinary, well-drained garden soil in sun. In cold gardens, protect *L. triornithophora* in winter.
Propagation Sow seeds thinly in late winter to early spring in a cold frame. Prick off the seedlings and plant out in mid to late spring. Alternatively, sow directly in the flowering site and thin the seedlings to the necessary spacings.
Pests and diseases Generally trouble free.

Linaria triornithophora

Linum

flax

Linum flavum 'Compactum'

□ Height 30-60cm (1-2ft)
□ Planting distance 23-30cm (9-12in)
□ Flowers late spring to late summer
□ Any ordinary, well-drained soil
□ Full sun
□ Hardy or moderately hardy, herbaceous

The wide-open, five-petalled flowers of perennial flax are most lovely when the sun shines full on them, bringing out their clear blues and yellows. Though the flowers are short-lived, they are produced in such profusion that the leaves are covered with blooms throughout summer.

Popular species

Linum arboreum, up to 30cm (1ft) high and across, is a moderately hardy, sub-shrubby perennial suitable for the front of a border in full sun and with some shelter. It bears triangular, mid green leaves and golden yellow flowers from late spring to early summer.
Linum austriacum, to 60cm (2ft) high and 30cm (1ft) across, is an ultra-hardy but often short-lived border plant. The lax, arching stems, set with narrow mid green leaves, carry soft blue flowers in mid summer. The variety 'Album' is pure white.
Linum campanulatum grows 30cm (1ft) high and across from a woody rootstock. The lance-shaped leaves are grey-green, and the pale yellow, orange-veined flowers are produced from early to late summer.
Linum flavum (golden flax), up to

Linum narbonense

Liriope
liriope, lily-turf

Liriope muscari

☐ Height 30-45cm (1-1½ft)
☐ Planting distance 30-38cm (12-15in)
☐ Flowers late summer to late autumn
☐ Light well-drained soil
☐ Sun or partial shade
☐ Hardy, evergreen

45cm (1½ft) high and 23cm (9in) across, is a hardy, sub-shrubby border plant with lance to spoon-shaped blue-grey to green leaves and golden yellow flowers from early to late summer. The variety 'Compactum' is smaller and neater than the species.

Linum narbonense, up to 60cm (2ft) high and 30cm (1ft) across, is a hardy border plant and the most popular of the perennial species. It has narrow lance-shaped grey-green leaves and bears loose sprays of rich blue flowers from early summer onwards. It is some-times evergreen in mild areas.

L. perenne, up to 45cm (1½ft) tall and 30cm (1ft) across, is a hardy if short-lived border plant. It bears narrowly lance-shaped, grey-green leaves and masses of sky-blue flowers throughout the summer months.

Cultivation
Plant in mid to late autumn or early to mid spring in any ordinary, well-drained soil. An open site in full sun is necessary to obtain the maximum effect from the brilliant flowers. Cut down dead growth in mid to late autumn.

Propagation Perennial flax is short-lived and needs frequent propagation. All species grow easily from seed, although named varieties do not come completely true to type. Sow seeds in early to mid spring in pots or boxes of John Innes seed compost in a cold frame. Prick out the seedlings into nursery rows when they are large enough to handle and grow on until mid autumn. Transplant to the flowering site.

Take 5cm (2in) cuttings of soft basal shoots in late spring and root in a cold frame. Move the rooted cuttings to an outdoor nursery bed and grow on until mid autumn or the following spring before trans-ferring them to their permanent positions.

Pests and diseases Generally trouble free.

LION'S HEART – see *Physostegia*

The closely packed, knobbly flower spikes of liriope rise on wiry stems from an arching clump of broad, glossy, grass-like deep green leaves. The bell-shaped flowers are mauve to lilac, though varieties offer white flowers and leaves variegated gold or yellow.

These useful, late-flowering plants are suitable for the front of a border.

Popular species
Liriope muscari, up to 45cm (1½ft) high, has violet flower spikes from late summer to late autumn. Varieties include: 'Silvery Sunproof' (leaves variegated gold); and 'Variegata' (leaves striped yellow). *Liriope spicata* (creeping lily-turf, up to 38cm (15in) high, has more upright leaves and bright lilac-mauve flowers from late summer to mid autumn. 'Alba' is white.

Cultivation
Plant in early to mid spring in any well-drained soil, ideally sandy loam, and in sun or partial shade. After flowering cut off the flower spikes; the leaves are attractive throughout the year.

Propagation Lift, divide and re-plant the fibrous matted roots in early to mid spring.

Pests and diseases Trouble free.

Lobelia

lobelia

Lobelia × vedrariensis

☐ Height 30cm-1.2m (1-4ft)
☐ Planting distance 30-38cm (12-15in)
☐ Flowers mid summer to mid autumn
☐ Rich, moist soil
☐ Sheltered, partially shaded site
☐ Moderately to ultra-hardy, herbaceous

The reds of perennial lobelias outshine other reds in the herbaceous border. Unlike low-growing annual lobelias, the perennials carry their distinctive tubular, lipped flowers, which also come in shades of blue and purple, on wand-like spikes, providing a vertical focal point for the middle of a border.

The lance-shaped leaves grow at the base of the plant and on the flower stems; they sometimes have purplish tints.

Popular species

Lobelia cardinalis is up to 75cm (2½ft) high. It is generally short-lived and not always reliably hardy. The stems, which are often purplish, carry lance-shaped, mid green leaves, with brilliant scarlet flowers from mid to late summer.

Lobelia fulgens is similar to *L. cardinalis*, but half-hardy. It forms basal rosettes of purple, ovate and toothed leaves from which rise thick branching stems bearing tapering flower spikes of bright scarlet. These open in late summer and continue well into autumn.

Lobelia × hybrida plants are generally hardy and 90cm-1.2m (3-4ft) tall with reddish to coppery tinted leaves. Varieties include: 'Bees Scarlet' (moderately hardy, large vivid scarlet flowers);

Lobelia fulgens

'Cherry Ripe' (cerise-scarlet); 'Dark Crusader' (velvety dark red); and 'Queen Victoria' (moderately hardy, deep plum-red leaves, vivid scarlet flowers).

Lobelia siphilitica, up to 90cm (3ft) high, is a hardy border plant with light green leaves and 75cm (2½ft) long spikes of clear blue flowers in mid to late summer. 'Alba' is white.

Lobelia × vedrariensis, up to 1.2m (4ft) tall, has dark green leaves and spikes of purple trumpet-shaped flowers from late summer to mid autumn.

Cultivation

Plant lobelias in mid spring in rich, moist soil in a sheltered and partially shaded position. Taller plants, especially *L. × vedrariensis*, may need to be staked.

Moderately hardy lobelias need winter protection. Cover the roots with leaves or lift in late autumn and store in boxes in a greenhouse or cold frame. When new growth begins in early to mid spring, separate the rosettes and pot them in compost. Plant out when renewed growth is well established.

Propagation Sow seeds in early spring at a temperature of 13-16°C (55-61°F), harden off and prick out into a nursery bed. Lift *L. cardinalis* from the nursery bed and overwinter in a cold frame. Leave other species in the nursery bed and plant out the following mid spring. Alternatively, increase by division in early spring.

Pests and diseases Damping off and root rot are usually caused by rhizoctonia, a virus disease; infected plants collapse. Stem rot shows as pale spots on leaves.

LOOSESTRIFE – see *Lysimachia* and *Lythrum*

Lunaria

perennial honesty

Lunaria rediviva

- ☐ Height 90-100cm (3-3½ft)
- ☐ Planting distance 60cm (2ft)
- ☐ Flowers in spring
- ☐ Light soil
- ☐ Partially shaded site
- ☐ Hardy, herbaceous

Perennial honesty (*Lunaria rediviva*)) looks quite lovely in spring with its branched clusters of starry four-petalled flowers in such a pale shade of mauve that they seem white from a distance. The flowers are later replaced by papery lance-shaped seed-heads which should be picked at the end of summer if they are to be dried for winter decoration.

The large, sharply toothed mid green leaves form a bushy mound about 90cm (3ft) high.

Cultivation

Lunaria grows best in light soil in a partially shaded site. Plant from early autumn to early spring.

Propagation Sow seeds in mid spring in a nursery bed. Thin out the seedlings, or transplant to 15cm (6in) spacings, and grow on. Plant out in early autumn.

Alternatively, lift and divide in early spring.

Pests and diseases Club root may distort the roots but the top growth is unaffected. No symptoms are seen until the plants are lifted. A virus disease causes white streaks on the flowers, which may be distorted.

LUNGWORT – see *Pulmonaria*
LUPIN – see *Lupinus*

Lupinus

lupin

Lupinus 'Inverewe Red'

- ☐ Height 60-1.2m (2-4ft)
- ☐ Planting distance 60cm (2ft)
- ☐ Flowers in early summer
- ☐ Well-drained neutral soil
- ☐ Sun or partial shade
- ☐ Hardy, herbaceous

Lupins' colourful, knobbly flower columns have made them one of the most popular and well-known perennials in Britain. The pea-like flowers, packed densely on strong, upright stems, come in shades of pink, blue, mauve, yellow, orange, red and white. They may be all one colour (self) or the lower petal and upper petals may contrast in colour (bicoloured).

The handsome leaves are mid green and deeply divided into a rough hand-shape.

Popular varieties

Russell hybrids (garden hybrids), derived mainly from *L. polyphyllus*, are usually up to 1.2m (4ft) tall and 60cm (2ft) across. Spikes up to 60cm (2ft) long are thickly packed in early summer with short-lived self of bicoloured flowers in shades of white, yellow, orange, red-purple and blue.

Named varieties include: 'Chandelier' (yellow shades); 'Dwarf Lulu' (up to 60cm/2ft high, mixed colours); 'Inverewe Red' (pink red); 'My Castle' (brick-red shades); 'Noble Maiden' (white

Lupinus 'Russell Hybrids' (bicoloured)

and cream); 'The Chatelaine' (pink and white); 'The Governor' (blue and white); and 'The Pages' (carmine-pink).

Cultivation

Plant in sun or light shade from mid autumn to early spring. Lupins like well-drained soil, neutral or slightly acid.

Propagation Propagate hybrids and named varieties from cuttings. In early to mid spring take 7.5-10cm (3-4in) cuttings close to the rootstock, preferably with a small piece of rootstock attached. Root in sandy soil in a cold frame. Pot up or transfer to nursery rows in late spring to early summer. Plant out in mid autumn.

Propagate species from seed. Named varieties do not come true and self-sown seedlings differ from the parents. Sow thinly in a cold frame in early spring. Prick out to 15cm (6in) apart in nursery rows and plant out in mid autumn. Remove the flower spikes for the first year to encourage well-rooted plants.

Pests and diseases Virus diseases cause symptoms such as mottled or yellowing leaves, light green spots turning brown in older leaves, upcurled or twisted leaflets, brown streaks on leaf stalks, or flowers with broken colouring. The plants may be attacked by blackfly, aphids, slugs or snails.

Modern seed strains are more resistant than Russell hybrids.

Lupinus 'Russell Hybrids' (bicoloured)

Lupinus 'The Governor'

Lychnis

campion

Lychnis chalcedonica

☐ Height 30-90cm (1-3ft)
☐ Planting distance 23-38cm (9-15in)
☐ Flowers late spring to late summer
☐ Any ordinary well-drained soil
☐ Sun or light shade
☐ Hardy, herbaceous

Though the pretty open flowers of campion are usually saucer-shaped, the plant has varying floral habits, giving the separate species quite different effects in bloom. The flowers may be held in sprays, clusters or tightly packed heads resembling large, flattened drumsticks, and are in shades of magenta, pink, red, orange, purple and white. Campions are good border plants, the shorter species sited at the front or as edging. All are excellent as cut flowers.

The leaves are usually lance-shaped and mid to dark green, sometimes flushed purple, or silvery-grey.

Popular species
Lychnis × arkwrightii, up to 30cm (1ft) high and across, has mid green, purple-flushed leaves. Scarlet-orange flowers with toothed petals open from early to late summer.
Lychnis chalcedonica (Maltese Cross or Jerusalem Cross), up to 90cm (3ft) high and 38cm (15in) across, has mid green leaves. Brilliant scarlet cross-shaped flowers are held in drumstick-like heads up to 13cm (5in) across in mid to late summer.

Lychnis viscaria 'Splendens Plena'

Lychnis (Agrostemma) coronaria, (rose campion or mullein pink), is up to 60cm (2ft) high and 30cm (1ft) across with woolly, silvery grey leaves. Sprays of magenta-pink flowers open from mid summer to early autumn. This species does well on poor, dry soils, but is often short-lived. Varieties include: 'Abbotswood Rose' (cerise-pink); 'Alba' (white); and 'Atrosanguinea' (deep red-pink).
Lychnis (Silene) dioica, syn. *Melandrium dioicum* (red campion), is a very hardy plant up to 50cm (20in) high and 40cm (16in) across. The hairy leaves form a rosette and the sprays of reddish purple or rose-pink flowers open from spring to mid summer: Varieties include: 'Rosea Plena' (double, pink); 'Rubra' (red); and 'Rubra Plena' (double, red).
Lychnis flos-jovis (flower of Jove) is a reliable border plant up to 60cm (2ft) high and 30cm (1ft) across. The silvery or grey hairy leaves form a dense tuft and loose rounded clusters of purple or red flowers appear from early to late summer. 'Alba' is a white-flowered variety.
Lychnis × haageana, up to 30cm (1ft) high and 20cm (8in) across, has mid green, occasionally purple-flushed leaves, and small clusters of orange or scarlet flowers in early to mid summer.
Lychnis viscaria, syn. *L. (Viscaria) vulgaris* (German catchfly), is up to 30cm (1ft) high and 30-38cm (12-15in) across. The leaves are tufted and grass-like and the dense oval

Lychnis coronaria 'Abbotswood Rose'

clusters of carmine flowers open from late spring to early summer. Varieties include 'Alba; (white) and 'Splendens Plena' (double carmine flowers, dark leaves)

Cultivation
Campions thrive in any ordinary, well-drained garden soil in sun or light shade. Plant from mid autumn to early spring, or in late spring if raised from seed sown early in the year. Taller plants in exposed sites may need twiggy sticks for support. Dead-head all species, particularly *L. coronaria*, to prevent self-seeding. Remove dead stems in autumn or spring and mulch annually in early spring with manure.
Propagation Sow seeds in a cold frame in late spring or early summer. Prick off seedlings into nursery rows and plant out in permanent positions from mid autumn onwards.

Alternatively, increase species, and especially named varieties, from cuttings taken in mid to late spring. Root 38-75mm (1½-3in) long basal cuttings in a cold frame.
Pests and diseases Aphids and froghoppers may damage flowering shoots. A virus disease may cause mottling on the leaves of *L. chalcedonica*.

Lysimachia
loosestrife

Lysimachia punctata

☐ Height 5-90cm (2-36in)
☐ Planting distance 23-45cm (9-18in)
☐ Flowers mid summer to early autumn
☐ Moist garden soil or pool margin
☐ Sun or partial shade
☐ Hardy, herbaceous

Lysimachia, one of many plants with the common name of loosestrife, is an easy-to-grow plant whose species vary in habit, though all are invasive. The three described below may all be grown in a border, though *L. nummularia* (moneywort or creeping Jenny) also thrives in waterside locations.

Popular species
Lysimachia clethroides, up to 90cm (3ft) high and 45cm (1½ft) across, has lance-shaped mid green leaves which may turn orange or red in autumn. Small white star-shaped flowers form

Lysimachia nummularia

Lysimachia clethroides

arching spikes up to 15cm (6in) long from mid summer to early autumn.
Lysimachia nummularia (moneywort or creeping Jenny) is an evergreen waterside plant which will also grow in ordinary soil. The rounded mid green leaves trail over an area up to 45cm (1½ft) across, and bright yellow cup-shaped flowers appear in early to mid summer. The species is good for ground cover. 'Aurea' has yellow leaves.
Lysimachia punctata (garden or yellow loosestrife), up to 90cm (3ft) high and 45cm (1½ft) across, has lance-shaped mid green leaves and whorls of bright yellow cup-shaped flowers on spikes up to 20cm (8in) long in early to late summer.

Cultivation
Plant from mid autumn to mid spring in any moist garden soil, in sun or partial shade.
  L. nummularia may also be grown at the edge of water where it needs soil 5cm (2in) deep. Set the plant a few inches from the pool's rim with the shoots growing towards the water.
  In rich soils the lower stems of tall species may need support.
Propagation Divide and replant between mid autumn and early spring.
Pests and diseases Generally trouble free.

Lythrum
loosestrife

Lythrum salicaria 'Robert'

☐ Height 60cm-1.5m (2-5ft)
☐ Planting distance 45cm (1½ft)
☐ Flowers early summer to early autumn
☐ Ordinary or wet soil
☐ Sun or semi-shade
☐ Ultra-hardy, herbaceous

This tough plant, also known as loosestrife, looks handsome in borders or near water with its spires of starry purple, pink or red flowers and lance-shaped mid green leaves.

Popular species
Lythrum salicaria is up to 1.5m (5ft) tall with red-purple flowers. Varieties include: 'Firecandle' (vivid rose-red); 'Lady Sackville' (rose-pink); and 'Robert' (rose-red).
Lythrum virgatum has narrower leaves than *L. salicaria* and violet-pink flowers. Varieties include 'The Rocket' (deep rose-pink).

Cultivation
Lythrum grows well in ordinary garden soil but thrives in damp or wet soils. Plant in sun or semi-shade in mid autumn or from late winter to mid spring.
Propagation Divide the roots of named varieties in autumn or spring. Sow seeds of the species in mid spring in a greenhouse at a temperature of 16°C (61°F). Prick off when large enough to handle and grow on until the following autumn.
Pests and diseases Trouble free.

Macleaya

plume poppy

Macleaya microcarpa

- ☐ Height 1.5-2.4m (5-8ft)
- ☐ Planting distance 90cm (3ft)
- ☐ Flowers mid to late summer
- ☐ Deep rich soil
- ☐ Sunny sheltered position
- ☐ Hardy, herbaceous

Plume poppy needs plenty of space to spread its plumes of tiny pink or whitish-buff flowers. The bronze, 20cm (8in) wide, lobed leaves are grey-white on the underside.

Popular species

Macleaya cordata, syn. *Bocconia cordata,* up to 2.4m (8ft) tall, has pearly-white flowers.
Macleaya microcarpa, syn. *Bocconia microcarpa,* is similar, but with buff flowers. 'Coral Plume' is rich pink.

Cultivation

Plant from mid autumn to early spring in rich deep soil in a sunny and sheltered site.
Propagation Divide and replant from mid autumn to early spring. Or detach outer shoots with root attached and replant.
Pests and diseases Trouble free.

MAIDENHAIR FERN – see *Adiantum*
MAIDENHAIR SPLEENWORT – see *Asplenium*
MALE FERN – see *Dryopteris*
MALTESE CROSS – see *Lychnis*

Malva

mallow

Malva alcea

- ☐ Height 60cm-1.2m (2-4ft)
- ☐ Planting distance 45-60cm (1½-2ft)
- ☐ Flowers early summer to mid autumn
- ☐ Ordinary garden soil
- ☐ Partial shade
- ☐ Very hardy, herbaceous

Mallow, closely related to the annual mallow of the genus *Lavatera,* has similar, deep cut, delicate looking foliage and pretty five-petalled flowers. It thrives in poor and inhospitable soils.

The leaves are light to mid green and the mauve to rose-pink or white funnel-shaped flowers are borne on spire-like, upright stems.

Popular species

Malva alcea, up to 1.2m (4ft) high, has light green lobed and toothed leaves. Mauve-pink flowers open from mid summer to mid autumn.
Malva moschata (musk mallow) is 60cm (2ft) high with deeply cut and lobed mid green leaves which give off a musky smell when crushed. Rose-pink flowers open from early summer to early autumn. 'Alba' has white flowers.

Cultivation

Plant from mid autumn to early spring in sun or a partially shaded site in any kind of soil.
Propagation Sow seeds in early to mid spring in a cold frame or greenhouse at a temperature of

Malva moschata 'Alba'

16°C (61°F). Prick out the seedlings and grow the young plants on in a nursery bed before planting out the following spring.

Alternatively, take 7.5cm (3in) long cuttings of basal shoots and insert in sandy soil in a cold frame in mid spring. Plant out the rooted cuttings in their flowering positions in autumn or spring.
Pests and diseases Rust may appear as orange pustules containing spores. The pustules, which appear on leaves, stems and fruits, later turn brown.

MARJORAM – see *Origanum*
MASTERWORT – see *Astrantia*

Matteuccia

ostrich fern, shuttlecock fern

Matteuccia struthiopteris

☐ Height 90cm-1.5m (3-5ft)
☐ Planting distance 90cm (3ft)
☐ Foliage plant
☐ Any moisture-retentive soil
☐ Partial shade
☐ Ultra-hardy, herbaceous

In spring the arching, golden green fronds of ostrich fern (*Matteuccia struthiopteris*, syn. *Struthiopteris germanica*), unfurl into the form of an elegant vase, later surrounding an inner shuttlecock-shaped circle of shorter, dark brown fertile fronds which give the plant one of its common names.

Ostrich fern is at its best in late spring, as the fronds tend to turn brownish by late summer. Like most ferns, it prefers moist soil, and will do well even in boggy conditions, perhaps under trees.

Cultivation
Plant ostrich fern from mid autumn to mid spring in any ordinary, moisture-retentive soil; on free-draining soils incorporate large amounts of organic materials. The plant likes partial shade, but tolerates sun. Give it plenty of space, preferably 90cm (3ft) or more for root development.
Propagation Remove offsets and replant in mid spring.
Pests and diseases Trouble free.

MAY APPLE – see *Podophyllum*
MEADOW CLARY – see *Salvia*
MEADOW RUE – see *Thalictrum*
MEADOWSWEET – see *Filipendula*

Meconopsis

meconopsis

Meconopsis × sheldonii

☐ Height 30cm-1.5m (1-5ft)
☐ Planting distance 30-60cm (1-2ft)
☐ Flowers early summer to early autumn
☐ Rich, well-drained but moist soil
☐ Semi-shaded and sheltered position or full sun
☐ Hardy, herbaceous

Meconopsis is one of the most beautiful genera of hardy perennials. The species include the sky-blue Himalayan poppy – considered by some gardeners to approach perfection in both colour and form in spite of its temperamental nature – the easy-going yellow or orange Welsh poppy, and many others.

The frail-looking five-petalled blooms are usually in shades of blue, yellow or orange with long golden anthers. They open from early summer to early autumn. The mid green leaves may be oblong, ferny or deeply cut.

Unfortunately, some species are short-lived and a few are monocarpic (they die after flowering once), but these lovely plants are well worth the effort of re-growing every few years.

The plants look superb as a showpiece in a border.

Popular species
Meconopsis betonicifolia, syn. *M. baileyi* (Himalayan blue poppy),

109

Meconopsis betonicifolia

Mentha

mint

Mentha × rotundifolia 'Variegata'

☐ Height 30cm-1.2m (1-4ft)
☐ Planting distance 60cm-1.2m (2-4ft)
☐ Flowers mid summer to early autumn
☐ Any moist soil
☐ Sunny or partially shaded site
☐ Hardy, herbaceous

Many people think of mint only in terms of its culinary use, confining it to the herb garden. But the genus includes several types with ornamental sometimes variegated foliage.

The pointed leaves are pale green, mid green or grey-green and are a broad lance shape. Popular varieties often have variegated leaves, with splashes of white or yellow. The hooded flowers, which are rather insignificant, are borne in short spikes and appear from mid summer to early autumn. They come in shades of purple, pink and white.

Mint is very easy to grow in moist soil, and can be used in borders, rock gardens and between paving stones. Some species are rampant, so they are best planted with the roots enclosed in a container.

Popular species
Mentha × *gentilis* (red or Scotch mint) is a hybrid of *M. arvensis* and *M. spicata*. Up to 45cm (1½ft) high and 90cm (3ft) across, it has red-purple stems and mid green leaves. Spikes of pale purple tubular flowers appear from mid summer to early autumn. The variety 'Variegata' (yellow-splashed leaves)

Meconopsis cambrica

90cm-1.5m (3-5ft) high, has hairy oblong leaves. The beautiful sky-blue flowers, up to 10cm (4in) wide, are carried in small clusters at the top of the stems in early to mid summer. This species may be monocarpic if allowed to flower in the first year. 'Alba' is white.
Meconopsis cambrica (Welsh poppy), 30-45cm (1-1½ft) high, has ferny, slightly hairy basal leaves and numerous lemon-yellow or orange flowers up to 5cm (2in) wide. Short-lived, it seeds itself freely.
Meconopsis regia, 90cm-1.5m (3-5ft) high and 60cm (2ft) across, has a rosette of large, deeply cut leaves up to 50cm (20in) long and covered with bronze hairs. The cup-shaped golden-yellow flowers are up to 10cm (4in) wide. This species is monocarpic.
Meconopsis × *sheldonii* 'Branklyn', up to 1.5m (5ft) high and 45cm (1½ft) across, has rich blue flowers sometimes measuring over 10cm (4in) across. Divide regularly to avoid deterioration.
Meconopsis villosa, up to 60cm (2ft) high and 30cm (1ft) across, has a rosette of hairy leaves and clear yellow, nodding, globular flowers about 5cm (2in) wide.

Cultivation
Plant in early to mid spring. Most species need rich soil that is moist but quick-draining, in a semi-shaded and sheltered site, but *M. cambrica* does well in any garden soil and in any position. Monocarpic species usually take two to four years before they flower and die.

Meconopsis needs plenty of water in summer, but as little as possible in winter. Dead-head regularly to prolong flowering. In wet regions, place cloches or panes of glass over *M. regia*.
Propagation Sow seeds as soon as ripe in a cold frame or greenhouse in late summer or early autumn. Prick out the seedlings into boxes and overwinter in a well-ventilated greenhouse or cold frame. Germination is slower in spring, but seeds may be sown in early to mid spring at a temperature of 13-16°C (55-61°F). Prick out the seedlings and grow on in nursery rows. Transfer the young plants to their permanent site in early to mid autumn. Named varieties do not come true to type.
Pests and diseases Downy mildew may show as furry grey patches on leaf undersurfaces.

Mertensia
Virginia cowslip

Milium
Bowles' golden grass

Mentha × gentilis 'Variegata'

Mertensia virginica

Milium effusum 'Aureum'

is the best ornamental form.
Mentha longifolia (horsemint) is a variable plant reaching a height of 30cm-1.2m (1-4ft) and 60cm (2ft) across. It bears grey-green foliage with large aromatic leaves up to 9cm (3½in) long, and 10cm (4in) spikes of pink, lilac or white flowers in mid summer.
Mentha × rotundifolia (apple mint), a hybrid of *M. longifolia* and *M. suaveolens*, is considered to have the best flavour of the culinary mints. Up to 90cm (3ft) high and 1.2m (4ft) across, it has hairy, pale green, rounded aromatic leaves. 'Variegata' (pineapple mint) is an ornamental variety with aromatic leaves edged and splashed with white.

Cultivation
Ornamental mint likes a sunny or partially shaded site in any ordinary garden soil, preferably one that remains moist in summer. Plant at any time from mid autumn to early spring with the roots restricted in sunken pots or containers.
Propagation Divide the roots at any time from mid autumn to early spring. Choose vigorous 15-23cm (6-9in) long rhizomes and replant directly in their permanent positions.
Pests and diseases Mint rust may cause the shoots and leaves to become swollen and distorted.

☐ Height 30-60cm (1-2ft)
☐ Planting distance 30cm (1ft)
☐ Flowers late spring
☐ Rich, moist soil
☐ Shady position
☐ Hardy, herbaceous

The pretty, easy-to-grow Virginia cowslip or Virginia bluebells (*Mertensia virginica*) has loose clusters of drooping bell-shaped flowers in a lovely shade of purple-blue and are suitable for cutting. They are borne at the top of upright stems, which bend over slightly under their weight. The blue-grey leaves are oval and sit in pairs along the stems. The floral display finishes by early summer, the foliage dying down completely by mid summer. The variety 'Rubra' is pink.

Cultivation
Plant in mid to late autumn or early to mid spring. Though a rich loamy soil in a moist shady position is ideal, the plants can adapt.
Propagation Divide and replant from mid autumn to early spring.
   Alternatively, sow seeds as soon as ripe, or in mid to late summer, in a cold frame or greenhouse. The following spring, prick the seedlings out into nursery rows.
Pests and diseases Trouble free.

MICHAELMAS DAISY – see *Aster*

☐ Height 45-60cm (1½-2ft)
☐ Planting distance 30cm (1ft)
☐ Foliage plant
☐ Moist soil
☐ Partial shade
☐ Hardy, herbaceous

Bowles' golden grass (*Milium effusum* 'Aureum') is a handsome foliage plant, brightening lightly shaded sites with its bright yellow and arching grassy leaves. Tufted but slender of habit, the grassy mounds are topped in summer with dainty, oat-like flower plumes of pale yellow. They are suitable for drying. Golden grass is ideal for highlights in herbaceous and mixed borders and for edging by trees and shrubs.

Cultivation
Plant in mid autumn or early spring, in any moisture-retentive soil and in light shade. Cut flower stems for drying before they begin to set seed and remove any remainder from the base in late autumn.
Propagation Sow seeds in the open in early to mid spring. The plant self-seeds freely and breeds true to type; remove unwanted seedlings while still small.
Pests and diseases Trouble free.

Mimulus

monkey flower

Mimulus guttatus

- ☐ Height 15-75cm (6in-2½ft)
- ☐ Planting distance 30-45cm (12-18in)
- ☐ Flowers mid spring to mid autumn
- ☐ Any moist soil
- ☐ Sun or light shade
- ☐ Hardy, herbaceous or evergreen

Monkey flowers are particularly appealing to children with their cheerful flowers in bright shades or red, pink, yellow and orange and white. These trumpet-shaped, lipped blooms often having striking blotches in contrasting colours and resemble snapdragon flowers. They usually appear in late spring, continuing their profuse display until early autumn.

The plants like moist, even boggy soil, bringing colour to waterside settings, but are adaptable enough to thrive in any moist soil in borders and beds.

Popular species

Mimulus × burnetti, 15-23cm (6-9in) high and 30cm (1ft) across, has coppery coloured flowers with yellow throats and spots.

Mimulus cardinalis (scarlet monkey flower) is an herbaceous species up to 60cm (2ft) high and 30cm (1ft) across. It has sticky, hairy, mid green, sharply toothed leaves and narrow scarlet to cerise yellow-throated flowers with prominent stamens. This species tolerates dryish soil, but requires a sheltered position.

Mimulus glutinosus (bush monkey flower), syn. *Diplacus glutinosus* of *M. aurantiacus*, is a semi-hardy evergreen sub-shrub up to

Mimulus × burnetii

45cm (1½ft) high and 38cm (15in) across. The sticky, lance-shaped leaves are mid to dark green, and the flowers are orange, salmon, pale crimson or white to buff coloured, appearing in succession from mid spring to mid autumn. This species may be grown as a pot plant indoors or in a cool greenhouse for an even longer floral display, where it will reach much larger proportions.

Mimulus guttatus (common monkey flower) is a very hardy herbaceous species which has become naturalized in Europe. Up to 60cm (2ft) high and 30cm (1ft) across, it has yellow flowers, blotched brown-purple.

Mimulus lewisii, up to 60cm (2ft) high and 30cm (1ft) across, is a very hardy, rather floppy plant with greyish, sticky hairy leaves and rose-pink flowers from mid summer to early autumn.

Mimulus ringens (Allegheny monkey flower), up to 75cm (2½ft) high and 23cm (9in) across, will grow in moist soil or water up to a depth of 15cm (6in). It has dark green, narrow leaves and blue flowers from late summer to early autumn.

Cultivation

Plant in spring in sun or shade in any ordinary moist garden soil or at pool margins. In cold districts, cover the plants with cloches.

Mimulus lewisii

Propagation Divide and replant in early to mid spring. Alternatively, in mid spring root 5cm (2in) cuttings in a cold frame in a proprietary cuttings compost.

Sow seeds in mid to late spring under-glass; prick out the seedlings singly into pots and grow on in a cold frame or transplant to nursery rows before moving to permanent sites in spring.

Pest and diseases Trouble free.

MIND-YOUR-OWN-BUSINESS
– see *Soleirolia*
MINT – see Mentha

Miscanthus

silver grass

Miscanthus sinensis 'Zebrinus'

Miscanthus sinensis 'Variegatus'

☐ Height 90cm-3m (3-10ft)
☐ Planting distance 90cm (3ft)
☐ Foliage plant
☐ Any moist soil
☐ Sunny site
☐ Hardy, herbaceous

The remarkable silver grass grows at a most astonishing rate. When established, it will reach a height of up to 3m (10ft) in one season, starting afresh each year.

The slender, upright but arching mid green leaves usually have a paler mid rib. Varieties offer a choice of yellow or white striped leaves and some have silky flower plumes.

Silver grass can be used as a screen, a windbreak or to provide shade for other plants. It thrives in moist soil and looks particularly attractive when planted by water. It is also popular as a specimen plant in lawns or grown in mixed borders.

The species and varieties described are particularly suitable for drying; cut down in late summer for this purpose. Otherwise, the foliage may be left on the plants continuing to provide a windbreak and foliage interest throughout the winter.

Popular species

Miscanthus sacchariflorus (Amur silver grass), 2.1-3m (7-10ft) high, has narrow arching mid green toothed leaves with paler mid ribs. This species is particularly useful for providing shade or as a windbreak. The variety 'Variegatus' has white striped leaves.

Miscanthus sinensis (eulalia), syn. *Eulalia japonica*, is a very hardy species from 90cm to 1.5m (3-5ft) tall. It forms a 90cm (3ft) wide clump of narrow blue-green leaves with a white mid rib. The lower leaves are hairy underneath. Varieties include: 'Giganteus' (the highest variety for screening);

'Gracillimus' (to 1.2m/4ft high, very narrow leaves); 'Purpureus' (leaves tinged purple); 'Silver Feather' ('Silberfeder', to 2.1m/7ft high, arching sprays of silky flower plumes in autumn); 'Variegatus' (to 1.8m/6ft high, leaves striped bright yellowish and silver-white); and 'Zebrinus' (zebra grass, to 1.2m/4ft high, striking yellow bands across the leaves).

Cultivation

Plant in early to mid spring in any moist garden soil and in a sunny position. Despite their height, these grasses do not need staking. The foliage may be cut during dry weather in late summer and hung up to dry, or it may be left on the plant over winter. If the foliage is left over winter, cut down all dead stems to ground level in late spring before new growth begins.

Propagation Divide and replant the roots during early to mid spring.

Pests and diseases On lower leaves, powdery mildew may show initially as white or brown patches of fungal growth. The leaves turn yellow and shrivel, and the trouble gradually spreads over the entire plant, leaving a grey-white coating on leaves and stems. Towards the end of the season, small black fruiting bodies develop on the diseased area.

MIST FLOWER – see *Eupatorium*

Monarda

Oswego tea, sweet bergamot

Monarda didyma 'Cambridge Scarlet'

- ☐ Height 60-90cm (2-3ft)
- ☐ Planting distance 23-45cm (9-18in)
- ☐ Flowers early summer to early autumn
- ☐ Moist soil
- ☐ Sun or partial shade
- ☐ Very hardy, herbaceous

Sweet bergamot (*Monarda didyma*) has dense flowers in shades of red, pink and purple or white. The hairy aromatic leaves, which may be used for herbal tea, are mid green and lance-shaped.

Varieties include: 'Adam' (cerise-scarlet); 'Cambridge Scarlet' (rich red); 'Croftway Pink' (rose-pink); 'Mahogany' (deep red); 'Prairie Night' (purple-violet); and 'Snow Maiden' (white).

Cultivation Plant groups of four to six plants in mid autumn or early to mid spring in any moist soil in sun or partial shade.
Propagation Divide the roots in early spring every two or three years. Plant out 5cm (2in) wide tufts, discarding the centre.
Pests and diseases Trouble free.

MONDO GRASS – see
Ophiopogon
MONEYWORT – see *Lysimachia*
MONKEY FLOWER – see
Mimulus
MONKSHOOD – see *Aconitum*
MOURNING WIDOW – see
Geranium
MULLEIN – see *Verbascum*
MUSK MALLOW – see *Malva*
NEEDLE GRASS – see *Stipa*

Nepeta

catmint

Nepeta × faassenii

- ☐ Height 30-90cm (1-3ft)
- ☐ Planting distance 30-45cm (1-1½ft)
- ☐ Flowers late spring to early autumn
- ☐ Any well-drained soil
- ☐ Sun or partial shade
- ☐ Ultra-hardy, herbaceous

Old-fashioned catmint has been used for hundreds of years for edging and ground cover in cottage gardens. It produces a cloud of tiny tubular, hooded flowers in shades of blue to violet, appearing from late spring to autumn.

The leaves, which are often aromatic, may be grey-green or mid green and are generally small and tapering.

Popular species
Nepeta × faassenii, up to 45cm (1½ft) high, has aromatic grey-green leaves and lavender-blue flowers from late spring. The variety 'Six Hills Giant' is up to 60cm (2ft) high. It is sometimes offered as *N. mussinii*.
Nepeta nervosa, up to 60cm (2ft) high, is a bushy plant with prominently veined, mid green leaves which are narrower than the other species. Clear blue flowers appear from mid summer.

Nepeta sibirica, syn. *N. macrantha*, up to 90cm (3ft) high, has violet-blue flowers on upright stems and aromatic leaves. Varieties include 'Blue Beauty' (to 45cm/1½ft), lavender-blue flowers).

Cultivation
Plant in a sunny or partially shaded position in ordinary, well-drained garden soil from mid autumn to early spring.
Propagation Divide and replant in early to mid spring. Or increase *N. nervosa* and *N. × faassenii* from 5-7.5cm (2-3in) basal cuttings in mid spring. Root in a cold frame, pot up and plunge outside. Plant out the following spring.

Sow seeds of *N. nervosa* in early to mid spring in a cold frame or greenhouse at a temperature of 16°C (61°F). Prick out and grow on.
Pests and diseases Powdery mildew may cause a white powdery coating on the leaves.

NEW ZEALAND FLAX – see
Phormium
OBEDIENT PLANT – see
Physostegia

Oenothera

evening primrose, sundrops

Oenothera missouriensis

- ☐ Height 10-90cm (4-36in)
- ☐ Planting distance 23-45cm (9-18in)
- ☐ Flowers early summer to early autumn
- ☐ Any well-drained garden soil
- ☐ Open sunny site
- ☐ Hardy, herbaceous

The faintly scented, gleaming cup-shaped blooms of evening primrose or sundrops look like numerous specks of sunlight shining against the foliage. Each flower may live for only a day but so many are produced in succession that the display lasts throughout the summer months. Unlike some wild species, most cultivated species have open flowers during the day – the outstanding O. missouriensis, for instance, has buds, sometimes spotted with red, which first unfurl in the evening but remain open for several days.

The leaves are generally narrow to lance-shaped, and pale, mid or dark green. Most species are upright and ideal for borders, while the mat-forming O. missouriensis is suitable for edging the front of a border or bed.

Popular species

Oenothera fruticosa, syn. O. linearis, 15-60cm (6-24in) high, is an ultra-hardy species with narrow, mid green leaves and yellow 2.5-4cm (1-1½in) wide flower from early to late summer.

Oenothera missouriensis (Ozark sundrops) is 10-15cm (4-6in) high and forms a 45cm (1½ft) wide mat

Oenothera fruticosa

of narrow mid to dark green leaves. Beautiful short-stemmed, pale yellow flowers, up to 10cm (4in) wide, open in the evening and last for several days throughout the summer months.

Oenothera perennis, syn. O. pumila (dwarf sundrops), up to 45cm (1½ft) high and 30cm (1ft) across, has pale to mid green lance-shaped leaves and loose leafy spikes of 2.5cm (1in) wide yellow flowers in mid summer.

Oenothera tetragona, syn. O. fruticosa youngii, or O. youngii, is an ultra-hardy plant up to 90cm (3ft) high and 30cm (1ft) across. It has dark green leaves and spikes of clear yellow flowers up to 4cm (1½in) wide, from early summer into autumn. Varieties, usually up to 60cm (2ft) tall and forming a neat mound, include: 'Fireworks' (golden-yellow); 'Highlight' (bright yellow) and 'Yellow River' (rich yellow).

Cultivation

Plant from mid autumn to mid spring in any ordinary, well-drained garden soil in an open sunny site. Water freely in dry weather. Cut faded flower spikes back to ground level in mid autumn.

Propagation Sow seeds in a cold frame in mid spring. Prick out the seedlings and grow on in nursery rows. Plant out in permanent positions in mid autumn.

Named varieties do not come true from seed. Divide and replant the roots in early to mid spring.

Pests and diseases Powdery mildew appears as a white powdery coating on the leaves. Root rot may occur on heavy, wet soils.

Onoclea

sensitive fern

Onoclea sensibilis

☐ Height 30-60cm (1-2ft)
☐ Planting distance 90cm (3ft)
☐ Foliage plant
☐ Moist soil
☐ Partially shaded site or sun
☐ Hardy, herbaceous

The long-stemmed, pale blue-green fronds of the sensitive fern (*Onoclea sensibilis*) wither and turn brown at the first touch of autumn frost. In spring, large sterile fronds with mainly triangular, scalloped leaflets unfurl from fat red buds and are joined in late summer by narrow fertile fronds that resemble strings of beads and last through the winter.

The sensitive fern spreads rapidly through underground runners and is ideal as ground cover for boggy banks and streamsides.

Cultivation
Plant in mid spring, setting the rhizomes just below the surface of any permanently moist soil. An open shaded site is ideal.
Propagation Divide the rhizomes in mid spring, making sure that each piece contains a growing point before planting them at least 90cm (3ft) apart.
Pests and diseases Trouble free.

Ophiopogon

lily-turf, mondo grass

Ophiopogon planiscapus 'Nigrescens'

☐ Height 30-60cm (1-2ft)
☐ Planting distance 30-60cm (1-2ft)
☐ Flowers mid summer
☐ Good, well-drained, but moisture-retentive soil
☐ Sun or shade
☐ Moderately hardy, evergreen

Lily-turf's clump of dark green grassy leaves almost conceals the short spikes of bell-shaped white, purple or purplish pink flowers, which are later replaced by blue berries. The plant is useful for all-year-round ground cover.

Popular species
Ophiopogon jaburan, up to 60cm (2ft) high and across, is clump-forming, with whitish flowers and violet-blue berries.
Ophiopogon japonicus (mondo grass), up to 30cm (1ft) high and 45cm (1½ft) across, spreads using stolons and is good for carpeting.
Ophiopogon planiscapus, up to 45cm (1½ft) high and across, has white or purplish-pink flowers. The low-growing 'Nigrescens' has purple-black leaves. The flowers are white to violet.

Cultivation
Plant in spring in fertile, well-drained but moist soil, in a sheltered, lightly shaded site.
Propagation Lift, divide and replant the fibrous roots.
Pests and diseases Trouble free.

ORCHIS – see *Dactylorrhiza*

Origanum

common or wild marjoram

Origanum vulgare 'Aureum'

☐ Height 30-45cm (1-1½ft)
☐ Planting distance 30cm (1ft)
☐ Flowers mid summer
☐ Ordinary, well-drained soil
☐ Sunny sheltered position
☐ Hardy, herbaceous

Though the fragrant-leaved common marjoram (*Origanum vulgare*) is usually grown as a culinary herb the ornamental variety *O. v.* 'Aureum' is more than suitable for decorative use in borders or as edgings. Rounded leaves, yellow when young and turning green later, grow in whorls on wiry stems, with clusters of rosy-purple flowers in mid summer.

Cultivation
Plant in early to mid spring in a sunny, sheltered position in ordinary, well-drained soil
Propagation Lift and divide in mid autumn or early spring.
Alternatively, take 2.5-5cm (1-2in) long cuttings of non-flowering basal shoots from mid summer to early autumn and root in a cold frame. Pot up and overwinter in the frame. Plant out the following early to mid spring.
Pests and diseases Generally trouble free.

ORNAMENTAL RHUBARB – see *Rheum*

Osmunda
royal fern

Osmunda regalis in spring

Osmunda regalis in summer

Osmunda regalis in autumn

□ Height 1.2-1.8m (4-6ft)
□ Planting distance 1.2-1.8m (4-6ft)
□ Foliage plant
□ Any moist humus-rich soil
□ Sun or partial shade
□ Ultra-hardy, herbaceous

The imposing royal fern (*Osmunda regalis*) is a giant among British native ferns and looks magnificent when grown in moist or boggy soils. Coppery young fronds unfurl from straight stalks in spring, turning a fresh green as the season progresses and the stalks blacken. The fertile fronds resemble dried flowers or dead astilbe blooms. In autumn the plant turns a rich brown.

Cultivation
Plant in early to mid spring in sun or partial shade in any moist, humus-rich soil. The crowns should be at soil level. Top-dress with humus or rotted manure in spring.
Propagation Sow fresh spores during summer in a greenhouse.
   Alternatively, lift and divide well-separated crowns in spring.
Pests and diseases Generally trouble free.

OSTRICH FERN – see *Matteuccia*
OSWEGO TEA – see *Monarda*

Paeonia
peony

Paeonia arietina

□ Height 45-90cm (1½-3ft)
□ Planting distance 60-90cm (2-3ft)
□ Flowers late spring to mid summer
□ Any moist, well-drained garden soil
□ Sun or partial shade
□ Moderately to very hardy, herbaceous

When peony's huge, often fragrant flowers first start to open, it is a sign that summer is near. These magnificent plants, one of the best loved and oldest genera of hardy perennials are invaluable for early summer colour in herbaceous and mixed borders. After planting, they may take three or four seasons before they flower, but once established and thriving, they will survive for 50 years or more.

The blooms, from the cup-shaped single flowers of the species to the bowl-shaped mass of petals of double-flowered varieties, measure 6-15cm (2½-6in) across and come in a vast range of colours. They are set on long stems against a neat bush of glossy mid, dark or grey-green foliage, attractive enough to hold its own in the border once the flowers have disappeared, usually before mid summer. The deeply cut leaves, often tinted red in spring, occasionally develop crimson tints in autumn. Unlike many herbaceous perennials, the foliage remains neat after the flowers fade. Some species have colourful seed heads in autumn.

Paeonia lactiflora 'Globe of Light'

Paeonia lactiflora 'Edulis Supreme'

Paeonia mlokosewitschii

Paeonia lactiflora 'Aureole'

Paeonia cambessedesii

Paeonia lactiflora 'White Wings'

Paeonia lactiflora 'Nancy Lindsay'

Popular species

Paeonia anomala, up to 60cm (2ft) high and across, has finely divided, dark green leaves and crimson-red, 7.5-10cm (3-4in) wide flowers with yellow stamens from late spring.

Paeonia arietina, up to 75cm (2½ft) high and 90cm (3ft) across, has mid to greyish green, finely divided leaves which are hairy underneath. Hairy stems carry fragrant rose to magenta-pink flowers up to 13cm (5in) across in late spring and early summer. The variety 'Northern Glory' is silky magenta-pink.

Paeonia cambessedesii, a moderately hardy species, is up to 45cm (1½ft) high and across. The leathery leaves are purple beneath and the deep rose-pink flowers, 6-10cm (2½-4in) wide, with red stamens and purple pistils, appear from late spring onwards.

Paeonia emodi, up to 90cm (3ft) high and across, has dark green leaves which are paler beneath, and fragrant, pure white, 7.5-10cm (3-4in) wide flowers with yellow stamens from late spring to early summer.

Paeonia lactiflora (Chinese peony), syn. *P. albiflora*, now rarely grown, is the main parent of hundreds of varieties and hybrids. These are generally 75-90cm (2½-3ft), high with 10-15cm (4-6in) wide flowers in late spring or early summer. They may be single, semi-double or fully double.

Single varieties, usually with golden or yellow stamens, include: 'Beersheba' (fragrant, rose-pink); 'Countess of Altamont' (fragrant, flesh pink to near white); 'Krin-kled White' (very large, crêpe-like white petals); 'Nancy Lindsay' (yellowish cream); 'Scarlett O'Hara' (warm red); and 'White Wings' (white).

Semi-double, 'Japanese' and anemone-flowered varieties include: 'Aureole' (pink, cream centre); 'Bowl of Beauty' (fragrant, deep pink, creamy white centre); 'Bridal Veil' (light pink, centre creamy white and pink); 'Chocolate Soldier' (fragrant, purple-red, centre mottled yellow); 'Globe of Light' (fragrant, rose-pink, gold centre); and 'Pink Lemonade' (strongly fragrant, pink, centre pink, yellow and cream).

Double varieties include: 'Agida' (carmine-red, tipped silvery pink); 'Blush Queen' (large, creamy white); 'Border Gem' (white, deep pink outer petals); 'Claire Dubois' (very fragrant, satiny pink); 'Edulis Superba' (fragrant, rosy lilac); 'Edulis Supreme' (vivid pink); 'Felix Crousse' (fragrant, carmine-red); 'Festiva Maxima' (fragrant, white flecked crimson); 'Martin Cahuzac' (dark crimson-maroon); 'Monsieur Jules Elie' (fragrant, silvery rose-pink); 'President Poincare' (fragrant ruby-red); and 'Sarah Bernhardt' (fragrant, apple-blossom pink).

Paeonia lobata, syn. *P. peregrina*, is a very hardy, spreading species up to 60cm (2ft) high and across. The deeply cut leaves are shiny and mid green above, and greyish green and slightly hairy underneath. Cup-shaped, deep red flowers, up to 10cm (4in) wide, appear from late spring to early

Paeonia officinalis 'Rubra Plena'

summer. Varieties include: 'Fire King' (brilliant crimson-scarlet and 'Sunshine' (salmon-scarlet).

Paeonia mlokosewitschii, a very hardy species up to 60cm (2ft) high and 90cm (3ft) across, has soft grey-green leaves with downy undersides, and 7.5-10cm (3-4in) wide lemon-yellow flowers with golden stamens in mid to late spring. The red seed pods are particularly striking in autumn.

Paeonia obovata 'Alba' is up to 60cm (2ft) high and across with dark green leaves and pure white 7.5cm (3in) wide flowers with golden stamens in late spring. The variety 'Grandiflora' has larger creamy white flowers.

Paeonia officinalis has been superseded by its varieties which are generally up to 75cm (2½ft) high and 90cm (3ft) wide. They include: 'Liza Van Veen' (double white,

Paeonia lactiflora 'Festiva Maxima'

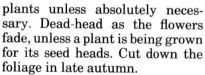
Paeonia anomala

Paeonia lactiflora 'Countess of Altamont'

Paeonia mlokosewitschii (seed pods)

flushed pink); 'Rosea Superba' (double, bright pink); and 'Rubra Plena' (double, deep crimson).

Paeonia × smouthii, up to 60cm (2ft) high and across, has finely dissected dark green leaves and crimson 7.5cm (3in) wide flowers from late spring on.

Paeonia tenuifolia (fern-leaved peony), up to 45cm (1½ft) high and across, has dense, very finely cut fern-like foliage and shiny, deep crimson flowers up to 7.5cm(3in) wide with golden stamens. Varieties include: 'Plena' (double) and 'Rosea' (pink).

Cultivation

Grow peonies in any moist, well-drained soil in sun or partial shade. The site should be shaded from early morning sun.

Plant 2.5cm (1in) deep in mild weather from early autumn to early spring. After planting, lightly fork a handful of bonemeal into the soil.

Water freely during dry weather and mulch annually on light soils. Avoid disturbing the plants unless absolutely necessary. Dead-head as the flowers fade, unless a plant is being grown for its seed heads. Cut down the foliage in late autumn.

Peonies may need support, particularly in exposed positions; use twiggy sticks, metal-link stakes or wire-ring supports.

When cutting flowers, take only a few stems from each plant. To prevent the petals from dropping, cut the blooms as they begin to open and lay them flat in a cool, dry place for 24 hours. Then trim 12mm (½in) from the stems and place in deep water.

Propagation All peonies can be raised from seed, although named varieties and hybrids do not come true. Sow seeds in early autumn in a cold frame and prick out into a nursery bed the following late spring. Grow on for three or four years, then plant out from early autumn to early spring, or divide and replant in early autumn. Cut the tough crowns with a sharp knife, ensuring that each piece has roots and dormant buds.

Pests and diseases

Peonies may be affected by several pests and diseases.

Swift moth caterpillars may eat roots and crowns.

Peony wilt affects the base of the shoots which turn brown and die. Brown angular patches form on leaves of other shoots, and the flower buds may turn brown, shrivel and die off.

A grey velvety fungal growth may show on the flower buds and stem bases. When similar symptoms occur late in the season they are often caused by grey mould fungus.

A physiological disorder, causing the flower buds to remain small and hard and fail to open, may be due to frost damage, over-dry soil, malnutrition, too deep planting or root disturbance.

A virus disease shows as a yellow mosaic of irregularly shaped patches or rings on the leaves.

PAMPAS GRASS – see *Cortaderia*

Papaver

oriental poppy

Papaver orientale 'Harvest Moon'

Papaver orientale 'King George'

☐ Height 60-90cm (2-3ft)
☐ Planting distance 60cm (2ft)
☐ Flowers early summer
☐ Ordinary, well-drained soil
☐ Sunny position
☐ Ultra-hardy, herbaceous

Despite the delicate, crêpe-papery appearance of its fine flowers, oriental poppy (*Papaver orientale*) is an ultra-hardy plant, thriving in the hottest sun and poor, dry soils.

The spectacular flowers appear at the very end of spring or the beginning of summer. The typical bloom of the poppy species has five thin, slightly overlapping petals of bright scarlet, with prominent black stamens in the centre, and usually a large black blotch at the base of each petal. The large seed pods are suitable for drying.

Named varieties of the oriental poppy measure up to 12cm (5in) across and come in scarlet, orange, red and shades of pink as well as pure white. Some have ruffled or frilled petals and a few are semi-double.

The flowers of all are short-lived, but with regular dead-heading there is sometimes a second flush later in the season. The blooms are borne singly on rather hairy stems which are usually floppy and need staking; they rise above spreading clumps of deeply cut, coarse and hairy, mid to deep green leaves which usually die down by late summer.

Oriental poppies provide a colourful early-season show for borders and look charming in a wild garden.

Popular varieties

'Black and White' has white flowers with a black central zone.

'Blue Moon' has mauve-pink flowers up to 25cm (10in) across with a black-marked throat.

'Curlilocks' has serrated, frilly vermilion petals with a black throat. Semi-erect.

'Fireball', syn. *P. o. nanum plenum*, is only about 30cm (1ft) high, with double, orange-scarlet flowers.

'Glowing Embers' is a strong grower of upright habit and more than 1m (3½ft) tall, with ruffled and glistening orange-red blooms.

'Goliath' has blood-red flowers.

'Harvest Moon' has deep orange, semi-double flowers that tend to fade in strong sun.

'King George' has orange-vermilion, serrated petals with black blotches.

'Ladybird' is vermilion-red.

'Marcus Perry' has deep scarlet flowers.

'Mrs. Perry' has salmon-pink flowers.

'Perry's White' has off-white flowers.

'Picotee' has salmon-pink and white flowers with fringed petals.

'Redizelle' has a compact growth habit and the deep scarlet, black-throated flowers appear late.

'Salmon Glow' has rich salmon-pink double flowers.

'Sultana' has glistening pink flowers.

'Turkish Delight' has flesh-pink flowers.

Papaver orientale 'Ladybird'

Papaver orientale 'Perry's White'

Cultivation

Plant in mid autumn or early to mid spring in ordinary, well-drained soil and in a sunny position. The plants need staking as they grow. Dead-head after flowering.

In mild weather, oriental poppy and its varieties sometimes produce a few more flowers in autumn if the first flower stems are cut down.

Propagation Divide and replant the roots in early to mid spring. Or take root cuttings and root in a cold frame in winter.

Alternatively, sow seeds in pots or pans of seed compost and place in a cold frame or greenhouse in mid spring. Prick out in nursery rows when the plants are big enough to handle, and plant out from mid autumn to mid spring.

Named varieties do not come true from seed.

Pests and diseases Yellow blotches on the leaves are caused by downy mildew.

PEARLY EVERLASTING – see *Anaphalis*

Peltiphyllum

umbrella plant

Peltiphyllum peltatum

☐ Height 60-90cm (2-3ft)
☐ Planting distance 90cm (3ft)
☐ Flowers in early spring
☐ Moist soil
☐ Sun or shade
☐ Hardy, herbaceous

The umbrella plant (*Peltiphyllum peltatum*) takes its name from the elegant leaves – circular discs, up to 30cm (1ft) across, with lobed edges, bright green in colour and held on long stalks. In autumn the foliage turns an eye-catching bronzy-pink. In early spring, before the leaves begin to unfold, thick bare flower stems push up through the ground and are topped with large rounded heads of white or pink flowers.

Grown primarily for its foliage effect, the umbrella plant makes handsome ground cover on moist banks or by pools and streams, but it is invasive and not recommended for small gardens.

Cultivation
Plant the rhizomes in mid autumn, in rich and permanently moist soil in full sun or light shade. Tidy the site of dead leaves during the winter.
Propagation Lift, divide and replant rhizomes, 90cm (3ft) apart, during suitable weather between late autumn and early spring.
Pests and diseases Trouble free.

Pennisetum

fountain grass

Pennisetum villosum

☐ Height 30-90cm (1-3ft)
☐ Planting distance 30-60cm (1-2ft)
☐ Flowers early summer to mid autumn
☐ Ordinary, well-drained garden soil
☐ Sunny sheltered position
☐ Half-hardy, herbaceous

Pennisetum's graceful narrow leaves and feathery flower plumes tremble and waver in the slightest breeze, giving the grass a delicate, misty look.

The arching leaves are mid green, grey-green or blue-grey. They surround narrow stalked, cylindrical flower plumes in gentle shades of yellow, purple, pink and brown or white; these may be used in fresh arrangements or dried for winter decoration.

P. alopecuroides may be grown as a specimen plant while *P. orientale* and *P. villosum* look lovely planted in drifts.

Popular species
Pennisetum alopecuroides (Chinese pennisetum or rose fountain grass) is a good specimen plant up to 90cm (3ft) high and 60cm (2ft) across, with grey-green leaves and tawny yellow or purplish flower plumes in autumn. The variety 'Woodside' produces more flowers than the species.
Pennisetum orientale, up to 45cm (1½ft) high and 30cm (1ft) across, has hairy blue-grey leaves and bristly brown-green or silvery pink flower spikes. This species may be grown as an annual.
Pennisetum villosum (feathertop), up to 60cm (2ft) high and 30cm (1ft) across, has arching, mid green leaves and white or brownish purple flower spikes. This species is usually grown as an annual.

Cultivation
Plant in mid spring in any ordinary, well-drained garden soil in a sunny, sheltered position. In warm sheltered areas, protect the plants during winter with bracken, coarse sand or weathered ashes. In colder areas, lift the plants in mid autumn and over-winter in pots in a cool greenhouse. Plant out in spring, after the last frost.

Flower plumes required for winter decoration should be cut when fully developed and hung upside down to dry.
Propagation Divide and replant perennial species in mid spring.

Germinate seeds of species to be treated as annuals in early to mid spring under glass at a temperature of 15-17°C (59-63°F). When the seedlings are large enough to handle, prick them off into boxes; plant out in late spring after the last frost.
Pests and diseases Trouble free.

Penstemon

penstemon

Penstemon × gloxinioides 'White Bedder'

☐ Height 45-90cm (1½-3ft)
☐ Planting distance 45-60cm (1½-2ft)
☐ Flowers early summer to autumn
☐ Any ordinary, well-drained garden soil
☐ Sunny position
☐ Hardy, herbaceous

Penstemon's bright spikes of long-lasting snapdragon-like flowers fill the border with colour from early summer, repeat-flowering until autumn if dead-headed regularly.

The trumpet-shaped flowers come in shades of pink, red, blue and purple and sometimes white. The leaves are usually lance-shaped and may be mid or grey-green.

Popular species

Penstemon barbatus, syn. *Chelone barbata*, is an ultra-hardy species up to 90cm (3ft) high and 60cm (2ft) across. It has mid green leaves and spikes of 2.5cm (1in) long rosy red flowers with bearded lips. Varieties come in shades of pink, scarlet and purple, or white.
Penstemon fruticosus is a very hardy, sub-shrubby border species up to 60cm (2ft) high and 38cm (15in) across with profuse lavender-purple flowers. 'Catherine de la Mare' is lilac-blue.
Penstemon × gloxinioides, syn. *P. × hybridus*, is a moderately hardy border hybrid, best treated as a tender bedding perennial or a half-hardy annual. It is up to 90cm

Penstemon hartwegii 'Myddleton Gem'

(3ft) high and 45cm (1½ft) across with densely set spikes of 5cm (2in) long flowers and mid green leaves. Varieties include 'Garnet' (very hardy, deep red); 'King George' (crimson-scarlet, marked white); 'Monarch Strain' (mixed colours); 'Snowstorm' (white, compact, 75cm/2½ft tall); 'Sour Grapes' (purple); and 'White Bedder' (white, pink in bud).
Penstemon hartwegii is a moderately hardy border species up to 60cm (2ft) high and 40cm (16in) across. It has rich green leaves and bright scarlet, 5cm (2in) long flowers. 'Myddleton Gem' has intensely pink flowers.
Penstemon heterophyllus, a moderately hardy sub-shrubby species, is up to 45cm (1½ft) high and across. It has narrow grey-green leaves on rather woody stems and blue, pink-flushed flowers in short spikes. 'Blue Gem' has pure blue flowers. Both are suitable for the front of sunny sheltered borders.

Cultivation

Penstemons like any ordinary well-drained garden soil in a sunny position and will not tolerate wet conditions round the roots. Plant perennial species in early to mid spring; cut them down to ground level after flowering and protect the crowns of moderately hardy types with cloches or a deep mulch in winter.

Penstemon fruticosus

Propagation Take 7.5cm (3in) long cuttings of non-flowering side-shoots in late summer to early autumn and root in a cold frame. Plant out the following spring when all danger of frost has passed.

Named varieties do not come true from seed, but several good strains of mixed colours are available. In late winter to early spring, germinate seeds under glass at a temperature of 13-18°C (55-64°F). Prick out into boxes and harden the seedlings off in a cold frame. Plant out in late spring.
Pests and diseases Trouble free.

PEONY – see *Paeonia*
PERENNIAL PEA – see *Lathyrus*

Perovskia

Russian sage

Perovskia atriplicifolia

- ☐ Height 90cm-1.5m (3-5ft)
- ☐ Planting distance 45cm (1½ft)
- ☐ Flowers late summer to early autumn
- ☐ Any well-drained soil
- ☐ Sun
- ☐ Hardy, herbaceous

Russian sage (*Perovskia atriplicifolia*) is a very hardy perennial of shrubby habit that thrives especially in seaside gardens. The downy branching stems are clothed with small grey-green, coarsely toothed leaves which smell of sage. In late summer and early autumn, the plant is enveloped in daintily branched flower spikes bearing tubular flowers of violet blue. The variety 'Blue Mist' is earlier flowering, with light blue flowers; and 'Blue Spire' has blooms of a richer blue than the species, and finely lobed leaves.

Cultivation
Plant from late autumn to mid spring in any light and well-drained soil; Russian sage does particularly well on chalky soils and needs full sun. Leave the faded stems to overwinter on the plant, before cutting them back to about 45cm (1½ft) in early spring.
Propagation Take cuttings, 7.5cm (3in) long, from side-shoots in mid summer and root in a cold frame. Plant the rooted cuttings in their permanent sites the following spring.
Pests and diseases Trouble free.

Phalaris

gardener's garters, ribbon grass

Phalaris arundinacea 'Picta'

- ☐ Height 60cm-1.5m (2-5ft)
- ☐ Planting distance 60cm (2ft)
- ☐ Flowers early to mid summer
- ☐ Any ordinary, well-drained garden soil
- ☐ Sun or partial shade
- ☐ Hardy, herbaceous

Gardener's garters (*Phalaris arundinacea* 'Picta') is a handsome grass which retains its striking appearance throughout the winter, ensuring year-round interest.

The spear-like leaves, vertically striped green and cream-white, are brightest in spring. In early to mid summer there is a profuse, but insignificant, display of green or purple flower plumes. The leaves turn yellow in autumn.

In rich, moist soil the plant will grow to 1.5m (5ft) and can be invasive. In drier soils it may reach only half that height, but is more manageable.

Cultivation
Plant from mid autumn to mid spring in any ordinary, well-drained garden soil in a sunny or partially shaded site. Restrict the spreading rhizomes by replanting every two or three years, or plant the roots in a pot and sink into the ground. Alternatively, surround the plant with vertical slates.
Propagation Divide and replant the roots from mid autumn to mid spring during suitable weather.
Pests and diseases Trouble free.

Phlomis

phlomis

Phlomis samia

- ☐ Height 60-120cm (2-4ft)
- ☐ Planting distance 60cm (2ft)
- ☐ Flowers early to mid summer
- ☐ Any ordinary soil
- ☐ Sun
- ☐ Hardy, herbaceous

Phlomis species are excellent border plants, valued for their bushy growth habit and abundance of attractive, oval to heart-shaped and downy leaves. The perennial species are related to Jerusalem sage, an evergreen shrub, but they are generally hardier and less fussy regarding soil as long as they are grown in full sun. The erect flower stems are set at regular intervals with densely packed whorls of tubular and hooded flowers, each 2.5cm (1in) or more long.

Popular species
Phlomis russeliana (syn. *P. viscosa*) grows 75-120cm (2½-4ft) high and bears large and wrinkled, ovate mid green leaves. In early and mid summer, the sturdy stems are studded with tiers of clear yellow flowers.
Phlomis samia, 60-90cm (2-3ft) tall, has heart-shaped leaves, mid green above and grey and woolly on the undersides. Whorls of creamy-yellow flowers, from late spring to early summer, have faint green and pink markings inside.
Phlomis tuberosa, an ultra-hardy species, grows 90cm-1.5m (3-5ft) tall from tuberous roots. It blooms

Phlomis russeliana

in early summer with pink to rose-purple flowers.

Cultivation
Plant in any kind of soil from mid autumn to mid spring, in a sunny position. Cut faded stems back to near ground level in mid autumn.
Propagation Divide and replant the roots of established plants in mid autumn or early spring. Alternatively, sow seeds in mid spring in a cold frame or greenhouse at a temperature of 15-18°C (59-64°F). Prick off the seedlings into individual pots of a proprietary potting compost when they are large enough to handle. Plant out in permanent sites in autumn; in cold areas, overwinter the young plants in a cold frame and set them out in mid spring.
Pests and diseases Generally trouble free.

Phlox
phlox

Phlox paniculata 'Eva Cullum'

☐ Height 30cm-1m (12-40in)
☐ Planting distance 45cm (18in)
☐ Flowers early summer to early autumn
☐ Any fertile, well-drained garden soil
☐ Sun or partial shade
☐ Hardy, herbaceous

One of the great beauties of the flower garden, phlox provides elegant and indispensable features for the back of herbaceous borders carrying massed heads of blooms on upright, leafy stems; they are excellent as cut flowers. The colours range from pastel shades of pink, blue, mauve and white to richer shades of salmon-pink and violet. The lance-shaped leaves are usually mid green.

Popular species
Phlox divaricata (blue phlox), syn. *P. canadensis*, is a spreading border species up to 30cm (1ft) high and 45cm (1½ft) across. Violet-blue to lavender and pink flowers are borne in loose heads in early summer. This species is suitable for edging.

The variety 'Laphamii' has blue flowers. Hybrids, which are all free-flowering, include: 'Anja' (purple); 'Hilda' (lavender, pink eye); 'Lisbeth' (lavender-blue); and 'Susanne' (white, red eye).

Phlox maculata, a border species up to 90cm (3ft) high and 45cm (1½ft) across, has mid green leaves and mauve-spotted stems. Slightly tapering heads of fragrant mauve-pink flowers appear from mid summer to early autumn. Varieties include: 'Alpha', (pink); 'Miss Lingard' (white); and 'Omega' (white, tinged violet).

Phlox paniculata (garden phlox) has dense, oval heads of scented flowers. The species has been superseded by numerous varieties, usually up to 1m (40in) high, with white, pink, red or purple

Phlox paniculata 'Glamis'

Phlox paniculata 'Alba'

Phlox paniculata 'Prospero'

Cultivation

Plant in groups of three or five, in a sunny or partially shaded position in mid autumn, late winter or early spring. The soil should be fertile and moist but well-drained. Water copiously during prolonged dry spells. Mulch annually in spring with well-rotted farmyard manure or with compost.

Older perennial phlox plants produce numerous shoots. Thin out the weaker ones in spring to leave about six healthy shoots on each plant. In exposed sites, support the plants with pea-sticks. In mid autumn cut all flower stems down to ground level.

Propagation Divide old, healthy clumps in mid autumn or early spring; replant only sections from the sides of the clump and discard the old wooden centre. Or, in late winter or early spring, slice off the crown, leaving only the roots in the soil. In spring or early summer, dig up and replant the young plantlets which appear from the roots.

Alternatively, take 7.5-10cm (3-4in) base stem cuttings in early spring and root in a cold frame. Or take 12mm (½in) root cuttings in late winter or early spring and root at a temperature of 13°C (55°F). When the shoots are 5-7.5cm (2-3in) high, harden off in a cold frame and later plant out in nursery rows. Plant out in permanent position after 18 months.

flowers, sometimes with contrasting eyes, from mid to late summer. They include: 'Alba' (pure white); 'Balmoral' (rosy lavender); 'Border Gem' (violet-blue); 'Cherry Pink' (bright carmine-rose); 'Dresden China' (shell pink); 'Endurance' (salmon-orange); 'Eva Cullum' (pink, red eye); 'Excelsior' (lilac-pink, darker eye); 'Glamis' (cerise-pink); 'Harlequin' (violet-purple, with cream-variegated leaves); 'Franz Schubert' (lilac); 'Fujiyama' (white); 'Paul Hoffman' (deep pink); 'Prince of Orange' (orange-salmon); 'Prospero' (pale lilac); 'Sandringham' (pink, darker eye); 'Starfire' (deep red); and 'White Admiral' (pure white).

Phlox paniculata 'Cherry Pink'

Pests and diseases Phlox may be affected by several pests and diseases.

Stem eelworm and bulb eelworm may invade tissues. The shoots become twisted and distorted. Dig up and burn affected plants and avoid planting phlox in the same spot for several years.

Leaf spot shows as brown spots with pale centres which eventually join up.

Leafy gall may show as a mass of abortive shoots at ground level.

A physiological disorder, usually due to an irregular supply of moisture in the soil, causes the leaves to turn yellow or brown.

Powdery mildew shows as a white powdery coating.

Phormium
New Zealand flax

Phormium tenax 'Variegatum'

☐ Height 90cm-3m (3-10ft)
☐ Planting distance 60cm-1.5m (2-5ft)
☐ Flowers mid summer to early autumn
☐ Deep moist soil
☐ Sunny position
☐ Moderately hardy, evergreen

With its bold clump of large strap-shaped leaves, New Zealand flax is a striking and dominant specimen plant for the lawn or as the centre-piece in a bed of annuals.

Though it is grown chiefly for its foliage, the plant sometimes produces tall spikes of tubular flowers which shoot up over the foliage in summer, followed by seed pods which are curved in shape, rather like scimitars.

Popular species
Phormium cookianum (syn. *P. colensoi*) up to 1.5m (5ft) high and 60cm (2ft) across, has brown flowers and twisted nodding seed pods. The arching green leaves are more lax than *P. tenax.*

Phormium tenax, up to 3m (10ft) high and 1.5m (5ft) across, has stiff, rough and leathery olive-green leaves. The rusty red flowers, in late summer, have purple stems and are followed by thick seed pods that are held erect. Varieties, grown for their foliage, include: 'Dazzler' (to 50cm/20in, red-brown striped carmine leaves); 'Purpureum' (leaves bronze-purple); and 'Variegatum' (dark green leaves, striped yellow).

Cultivation
Plant in late spring in deep moist soil in a sunny site. Protect the plants in winter with straw. Remove all dead flower stems, starting from late summer onwards.

Propagation Germinate seeds in spring at a temperature of 15-18°C (59-64°F). Prick off into boxes when the seedlings are large enough to handle, then harden off. Transplant to a cold frame until spring of the following year. Named varieties do not breed true. Increase by division in mid to late spring.

Pests and diseases Trouble free.

Phygelius
phygelius

Phygelius aequalis

□ Height 60-90cm (2-3ft)
□ Planting distance 60cm (2ft)
□ Flowers mid summer to mid autumn
□ Light soil
□ Sunny, sheltered site
□ Moderately hardy, herbaceous

Phygelius is a colourful and attractive evergreen shrub from South Africa, treated in Northern climates as an herbaceous perennial that is hardy in average winters.

The narrow tubular flowers, in shades of pink and creamy yellow or white, dangle prettily from the sparse branches rather like Christmas tree ornaments, providing valuable late season colour.

Popular species
Phygelius aequalis, up to 75cm (2½ft) high, has toothed, lance-shaped, mid green leaves and panicles up to 23cm (9in) long of buff-red flowers. Varieties include: 'African Queen' (deep salmon, yellow throat); 'Alba' (white); and 'Yellow Trumpet' (creamy yellow).

Phygelius capensis, up to 90cm (3ft) high, has mid to dark green oval leaves and 30cm (12in) long panicles of coral-red flowers. It may also be grown as a wall shrub, in which case it can reach a height of 1.8m (6ft) or more.

Cultivation
Plant in mid spring in a sunny sheltered position, preferably in light soil. Trim to ground level in spring.

Phygelius does not need staking if it is grown as a border plant, though *P. capensis* should be secured to a trellis or similar support if it is grown as a wall plant.
Propagation Divide and replant the roots in early to mid spring.

Sow seeds in a cold frame in mid spring. Prick out seedlings when they are large enough to handle. Pot up or plant out in nursery rows until mid autumn. Overwinter the plants in a cold frame and plant out the following spring.
Pests and diseases Trouble free.

Physalis
Chinese lantern, bladder cherry

Physalis alkekengi

□ Height 30-45cm (1-1½ft)
□ Planting distance 45cm (1½ft)
□ Fruits late summer to early autumn
□ Any well-drained garden soil
□ Sunny site
□ Hardy, herbaceous

Grown for its bright orange, swollen seed cases, Chinese lantern (*Physalis alkekengi*) brings oriental splendour to the garden.

Unbranched stems carry mid green, oval leaves and insignificant white flowers, followed by dangling, papery lantern-shaped seed cases which are often dried for winter decoration.

P. a franchetii is up to 60cm (2ft) high with larger leaves and seed cases.

Cultivation
Plant in early to mid spring in a sunny site in well-drained, ordinary garden soil. The plants' invasive underground runners should be dug out and cut off in autumn.
Propagation In early to mid spring, lift, divide and replant.

Sow seeds in mid spring and transplant the seedlings to a nursery bed when large enough to handle. Set out in autumn.
Pests and diseases Trouble free.

PINK – see *Dianthus*

Physostegia

obedient plant, lion's heart

Physostegia virginiana 'Vivid'

- ☐ Height 30cm-1.2m (1-4ft)
- ☐ Planting distance 60cm (2ft)
- ☐ Flowers mid to late summer
- ☐ Ordinary garden soil
- ☐ Sun or partial shade
- ☐ Ultra-hardy, herbaceous

Physostegia virginiana was given the name obedient plant because if a flower is pushed to one side, it stays where it is put.

These tubular, lipped, mauve-pink flowers are closely set on upright, leafy spikes from mid to late summer. The lance-shaped leaves are mid green.

Good border varieties include: 'Rose Bouquet' (pink); 'Summer Snow' (white); and 'Vivid' (to 50cm/20in, rose-pink, later flowering than the others).

Cultivation

Plant in mid autumn or spring in ordinary garden soil in sun or partial shade. Mulch in spring and keep moist in dry weather.
Propagation Divide in mid autumn or early spring. Replant only the vigorous outer roots.

Alternatively, take 5-7.5cm (2-3in) cuttings of young shoots in early to mid spring; root in a cold frame and plant out in mid autumn.
Pests and diseases Trouble free.

Phytolacca

poke weed, red-ink plant

Phytolacca americana

- ☐ Height 1-3m (3-10ft)
- ☐ Planting distance 90cm (3ft)
- ☐ Flowers in summer
- ☐ Moist soil
- ☐ Sun or partial shade
- ☐ Hardy, herbaceous

The American poke weed *Phytolacca americana*, syn *P. decanda*) is chiefly grown for its foliage and berries which add interest to the autumn garden.

The stems are sparsely set with mid green ovate leaves, 20cm (8in) or more long; they take on red and purple tints in autumn. From early summer onwards, tiny flowers, star-like and greenish-white, are borne in dense upright spikes; they mature to a reddish-brown and are followed by poisonous blue-black berries.

Cultivation

Plant in mid autumn or mid spring, in any moisture-retentive soil and in sun or light shade.
Propagation Divide and replant the fleshy roots in autumn or spring. Or sow seeds outdoors in mid spring; prick out the seedlings into a nursery row and plant out the following autumn.
Pests and diseases Trouble free.

PIGGY-BACK PLANT – see *Tolmiea*
PINCUSHION FLOWER – see *Scabiosa*
PINKS – see *Dianthus*
PLANTAIN LILY – see *Hosta*

Platycodon

balloon flower

Platycodon grandiflorum 'Apoyama'

- ☐ Height 30-60cm (1-2ft)
- ☐ Planting distance 38cm (15in)
- ☐ Flowers early to late summer
- ☐ Ordinary, well-drained soil
- ☐ Sunny position
- ☐ Hardy, herbaceous

The clustered, swollen buds of *Platycodon grandiflorum*, which comes from China, are held at the top of leafy stems like a bunch of balloons. In early summer they open into delightful pale blue, saucer-shaped flowers with pointed petals, set against a clump of greyish, toothed, oval leaves.

A long-lived plant, balloon flower is suitable for the front of borders. The species itself is rarely grown, having been superseded by numerous varieties, including: 'Album' (pure white); 'Apoyama' (deep mauve); 'Mariesii' (to 45cm/1½ft, blue, early flowering); 'Mother of Pearl' (pale pink, semi-double); and 'Plenum' (light blue, semi-double).

Cultivation

Plant in mid autumn or early spring in ordinary, well-drained soil in a sunny site. The fleshy roots resent disturbance.
Propagation In early spring, divide and replant any plants over three or four years old. They are slow to re-establish, and propagation by seed is preferable; sow under glass in early spring and prick out the fragile seedlings carefully. Grow on until planting out the following spring.
Pests and diseases Trouble free.

Podophyllum
podophyllum

Podophyllum emodi

☐ Height 30-45cm (1-1½ft)
☐ Planting distance 45cm (1½ft)
☐ Flowers late spring and early summer
☐ Rich moist soil
☐ Shade
☐ Hardy, herbaceous

Podophyllums are useful, if poisonous, plants for shady moist borders and woodland areas where the creeping rootstocks form attractive ground cover. The flowering season is comparatively short, but the foliage holds interest for many months: near-circular leaves, lobed and often sharply toothed, are spotted and edged with coppery brown when young. Five-petalled, saucer-shaped and waxy flowers are followed by conspicuous fruits.

Popular species
Podophyllum emodi (syn. *P. hexandrum*) grows 30cm (1ft) high and has mid green lobed leaves marbled with brown when young. The white flowers, with golden stamens, appear in early summer and are followed by bright red fruits up to 5cm (2in) long. The variety *Podophyllum emodi chinensis* is smaller, with more boldly patterned leaves and flowers delicately flushed with pink. The hybrid 'Majus', white-flowered, grows to 45cm (1½ft) tall.
Podophyllum peltatum (May apple) is ultra-hardy and 45cm (1½ft) high and wide. The lobed leaves, as much as 30cm (1ft) in diameter, are bright green. Creamy-white flowers are borne during late spring and early summer; the lemon-shaped fruits are golden-yellow.

Cultivation
Plant in early to mid spring, setting the rhizomes just below ground level, in moist soil containing plenty of humus. A partially shaded site is preferred.
Propagation Divide the rhizomes of established plants in spring, replanting at a distance of 45cm (1½ft). Sow seeds in a cold frame in early spring from fruits harvested in summer. Prick out the seedlings when large enough to handle and grow on in a nursery bed before planting out a couple of years later. Hybrid varieties do not come true to type.
Pests and diseases Trouble free.

POKE WEED – see *Phytolacca*

Podophyllum emodi chinensis

Polemonium
Jacob's ladder

Polemonium foliosissimum

☐ Height 45-90cm (1½-3ft)
☐ Planting distance 30-45cm (1-1½ft)
☐ Flowers mid spring to early autumn
☐ Ordinary garden soil
☐ Sun or partial shade
☐ Hardy, herbaceous

Jacob's ladder is a colourful, light-textured plant, once popular in cottage gardens. Its long-lasting flowers form a cloud of gentle colour over the finely divided, ferny leaves.

The flowers, which grow in loose clusters, are cup or saucer-shaped and come in shades of blue, lavender and pink, with some white and yellow varieties.

The mid green or dark green leaves are deeply divided into lance-shaped leaflets, arranged in pairs on a long midrib. They are borne upright on arching stems or form tufted mounds.

Jacob's ladder is a useful, easy-to-grow plant, adapting well to any ordinary soil. But it is happiest in rich, moist soils, perhaps by a pond or stream, where it will flower most profusely.

Popular species
Polemonium caeruleum, up to 60cm (2ft) high and 30cm (1ft) across, has tufts of arching mid green leaves. Loose clusters of lavender-blue flowers appear on upright, branched stems from mid spring to mid summer, or later. This species, which is also known as Greek valerian, self-seeds readily. 'Album' is white.
Polemonium carneum is a moderately hardy species about 45cm (1½ft) high and across. The

133

Polemonium caeruleum 'Album'

spreading, many-branched stems form a dome of mid green leaves, and profuse pink cup-shaped flowers appear from mid spring to mid summer. Varieties offer purplish pink, yellow and blue flowers.

Polemonium foliosissimum, up to 90cm (3ft) high and 45cm (1½ft) across, has abundant dark green leaves on upright stems and clusters of cup-shaped lavender-blue flowers with yellow centres from early summer to early autumn. A long-lived species, it rarely if ever self-seeds.

Cultivation

Plant from mid autumn to early or mid spring in sun or partial shade. Jacob's ladder grows in any soil but flowers more profusely in deep rich, loamy soil as the fibrous roots quickly exhaust the soil. Cut back faded flower stems to basal leaf growth as soon as flowering is over. On exposed sites, support the plants with canes or pea sticks; mulch light soils annually in spring.

Propagation Divide and replant older plants from mid autumn to early spring. Or sow seeds in a cold frame in spring; prick out the seedlings when large enough and grow on in a nursery bed before transplanting the following spring.

Pests and diseases Generally trouble free.

POLYANTHUS – *Primula*

Polygonatum
Solomon's seal

Polygonatum odoratum thunbergii 'Variegatum'

- ☐ Height 60cm-1.8m (2-6ft)
- ☐ Planting distance 30-75cm (1-2½ft)
- ☐ Flowers late spring to early summer
- ☐ Any well-drained but moisture-retentive soil
- ☐ Partial shade or sun
- ☐ Ultra-hardy, herbaceous

The slender, graceful stems of Solomon's seal arch away from the centre of the plant, carrying pairs of upward-curving leaves and, from late spring, small clusters of hanging narrow bell flowers.

The oval leaves are pale to mid green, the flowers white with green tips and the berries blue or black. These plants enjoy the dappled shade and leafy soil of woodland, though they will cope with most soils in shady conditions.

Popular species

Polygonatum commutatum, syn. *P. giganteum*, grows up to 1.8m (6ft) high in rich moist soil. It has narrow oblong leaves.

Polygonatum × hybridum, about 90cm (3ft) tall, has oblong, glossy leaves on arching stems bearing pendent flowers in early summer.

Polygonatum odoratum thunbergii is up to 60cm (2ft) high. 'Varie-

Polygonatum × hybridum

gatum' has white-edged leaves.

Cultivation

Plant from early autumn to early spring in well-drained but moist humus-rich soil in partial shade. *P. × hybridum* will tolerate sun. Mulch annually in spring.

Propagation Divide and replant in mid autumn or early spring.

Sow seeds, which may take 18 months to germinate, in a cold frame before mid autumn.

Pests and diseases Sawflies damage the leaves.

Polygonum

knotweed

Polygonum amplexicaule 'Atrosanguineum'

Polygonum bistorta 'Superbum'

Polygonum vaccinifolium

☐ Height 15cm-1.2m (6in-4ft)
☐ Planting distance 30-75cm (2-2½ft)
☐ Flowers early to late summer
☐ Any soil
☐ Sun or partial shade
☐ Hardy, herbaceous

With its dense flower spikes rising firmly over strong clumps of foliage, knotweed is a bold and popular plant for borders, ground cover and for trailing over walls. The genus includes several rampant climbers.

The tiny pink to dark red or white flowers are bell-shaped and borne in succession throughout summer.

Popular species

Polygonum affine, up to 23cm (9in) high, forms a mat up to 45cm (1½ft) across. The lance-shaped leaves are rusty brown in winter. Varieties include: 'Darjeeling Red' (deep pink, leaves dark green); 'Dimity' (dwarf, light pink, leaves bright green); and 'Donald Lowndes' (rose-red).

Polygonum amplexicaule, up to 1.2m (4ft) high and 75cm (2½ft) across, has deep green, heart-shaped leaves Varieties include: 'Album' (white); 'Arum Gem' (hanging tassels of bright pink flowers); 'Atrosanguineum' (crimson); 'Firetail' (scarlet); and 'Inverleith' (to 45cm/1½ft, red).

Polygonum bistorta 'Superbum' (snakeweed), up to 90cm (3ft) high and 60cm (2ft) across, forms a mat of light green leaves and 15cm (6in) spikes of clear pink flowers.

Polygonum campanulatum, up to 90cm (3ft) high and 75cm (2½ft) across, is bushy and spreading with pointed mid green leaves and loose heads of pink flowers.

Polygonum vaccinifolium, up to 15cm (6in) high and 60cm (2ft) across, has leathery leaves and rose-pink flowers.

Cultivation

Plant from mid autumn to early spring in any soil in sun or partial shade; *P. campanulatum* is best in light shade. Pinch out ground cover plants two or three times in summer to encourage side branches.

Propagation Divide and replant in early spring or in mid autumn.

Pests and diseases Trouble free.

Polypodium
common polypody

Polypodium vulgare

- ☐ Height 15-38cm (6-15in)
- ☐ Planting distance 38cm (15in)
- ☐ Foliage plant
- ☐ Rich, well-drained soil
- ☐ Partial shade or sun
- ☐ Ultra-hardy, evergreen

A creeping fern, common polypody (*Polypodium vulgare*) spreads over the ground, forming a thick evergreen carpet of mid green, elegantly drooping fronds.

New growth starts in mid to late spring and the plant retains its fresh colour until late winter.

Common polypody is ultra-hardy and easy to grow in dry, stony soil and wall crevices; it provides year-round foliage interest on tree trunks and on banks in chalk and limestone areas.

Popular varieties include: 'Cornubiense' ('Elegantissimum', lacy fronds); *P. v. interjectum* (broader fronds, tolerates wet soil); and 'Pulcherrimum' (fronds deeply and finely cut, vigorous).

Cultivation
Plant in partial shade or sun in mid to late spring when the new fronds are just appearing. Humus-enriched soil containing plenty of stones is best. Set the rhizomes just beneath the surface of the soil and anchor with stones or staples of bent wire.

Propagation Divide and replant in mid to late spring.

Pests and diseases Rust may show as scattered or loosely grouped brown spore pustules on the undersurface of the fronds.

Polystichum
shield fern

Polystichum setiferum

- ☐ Height 60-90cm (2-3ft)
- ☐ Planting distance 30cm-1.5m (1-5ft)
- ☐ Foliage plant
- ☐ Rich, moist soil
- ☐ Shady site
- ☐ Hardy, evergreen or semi-evergreen

Shield fern is an important and popular woodland fern that thrives in chalk or limy soil, provided it is moist and humus rich.

This large group of evergreen ferns includes several hardy garden types, as well as others suited for indoor cultivation. The stiff and leathery leaf fronds, glossy and dainty in some species, are popular in flower arrangements.

Popular species
Polystichum aculeatum (prickly or hard shield fern), up to 90cm (3ft) high and 75cm (2½ft) across, is an evergreen fern with deep green, glossy and leathery fronds. The stalks and midribs are covered with brown scales. Varieties in-

Polystichum setiferum 'Herenhausen'

Polystichum aculeatum

clude: 'Pulcherrimum' (silky, finely divided fronds) and 'Pulcherrimum Gracillimum' (very long, thin, tasselled pinnae).

Polystichum setiferum (soft shield or hedge fern), to 90cm (3ft) high and 1.5m (5ft) across, is evergreen in mild winters. It has mid green, gently arching fronds with scaly stems. The many popular varieties include: 'Acutilobum' (pointed pinnules with bristles at the ends, fronds prostrate in winter); 'Divisilobum' (finely divided fronds); 'Herenhausen' (slightly glossy); 'Iveryanum' (finely divided, crested); 'Plumosodivisilobum' (finely divided, overlapping fronds); 'Proliferum' (narrow, finely divided fronds with plantlets); and 'Plumosum' (semiprostrate, dense, feathery fronds).

Cultivation
Plant in mid spring in shade in humus-rich, moist soil. All thrive in woodland conditions.

Propagation Sow spores in early spring at a temperature of 10°C (50°F).

Divide the multiple crowns in early to mid spring. Or detach the fronds bearing bulbils (small, pea-like bulbs on the undersurface of the fronds) in early to mid autumn. Fill boxes with a potting compost and peg the fronds on to the surface. Pot up the young plants when they are well-developed.

Pests and diseases Trouble free.

POPPY – see *Papaver*

Potentilla
potentilla, cinquefoil

Potentilla atrosanguinea 'Gibson's Scarlet'

☐ Height 4-60cm (1½-24in)
☐ Planting distance 15-60cm (6-24in)
☐ Flowers late spring to early autumn
☐ Ordinary, well-drained garden soil
☐ Full sun
☐ Hardy, herbaceous

Potentillas are delightful plants with brightly coloured, saucer-shaped flowers held above attractive foliage.

The flowers are generally in shades of red, pink and bright yellow. The taller types are suitable for herbaceous and mixed borders while the mat-forming and creeping types make excellent ground cover in sunny sites; they can also be grown in raised beds and rock gardens.

The flowers are generally in shades of red, pink and bright yellow and may be single, semidouble or double.

Popular species
Potentilla atrosanguinea is the main parent of many hybrids, usually 45-60cm (1½-2ft) high and across with grey-green strawberry-like leaves and profuse 4-5cm (1½-2in) wide flowers borne in loose sprays from early summer to early autumn. They include: 'Blazeaway' (to 40cm/16in, single, suffused orange-red); 'Flamenco' (single, intense scarlet); 'Gibson's Scarlet' (to 30cm/1ft, single, brilliant scarlet); 'Glory of Nancy'

Potentilla atrosanguinea 'Yellow Queen'

(semi-double, orange-brown and coral-red); 'M. Rouillard' (mahogany); 'William Rollison' (semidouble, orange-red, yellow reverse); and 'Yellow Queen' (to 40cm/16in, semi-double, bright yellow, early).

Potentilla aurea forms a carpet 5-15cm (2-6in) high and 30cm (1ft) across. It has bright green silky leaves and clusters of bright yellow 1-2cm (¼-¾in) wide flowers. Suitable for edging.

Potentilla cinerea, up to 7.5cm (3in) high and 45cm (1½ft) across, is a spreading plant with small, incut, grey-green leaves and bright yellow flowers in summer.

Potentilla cinerea

Potentilla crantzii, syn. *P. alpestris*, up to 15cm (6in) high and across, has tufted deep green leaves and yellow, blotched orange 2.5cm (1in) wide flowers.

Potentilla nepalensis, up to 60cm (2ft) high and 40cm (16in) across, has deep green toothed leaves and very profuse branching sprays of rose-red flowers up to 4cm (1½in) wide. Hybrids include: 'Firedance' (salmon shading to scarlet at the centre); 'Miss Wilmott' (cherry pink, darker shading); and 'Roxana' (pink to rosy orange).

Potentilla nitida forms a mat up to 7.5cm (3in) high and 30cm (1ft) wide. It has silvery, hairy leaves and 2.5cm (1in) wide pale pink

Potentilla atrosanguinea 'William Rollison'

flowers in mid and late summer. 'Rubra' is deep pink.

Potentilla tabernaemontani, syn. *P. verna*, forms a mat up to 20cm (8in) high and 60cm (2ft) across. The leaves are dark green and divided; the flowers are yellow and appear in late spring.

Cultivation

Plant from mid autumn to early spring in ordinary well-drained soil and full sun. *Potentilla nepalensis* and its varieties are short-lived and exhaust themselves with profuse flowering. Cut them hard back after flowering and replace them every three or four years.

Propagation Divide and replant named varieties in mid autumn or early spring.

Sow seeds of the species in a cold frame in early to mid spring. When the seedlings are large enough to handle, prick them off and later transplant to a nursery bed. Plant out in mid autumn.

Alternatively, take 5-7.5cm (2-3in) basal cuttings in mid spring and root in a cold frame. Treat as for seedlings.

Pests and diseases Trouble free.

Potentilla nepalensis 'Roxana'

PRIMROSE – see *Primula*

Primula

primula

Primula sieboldii

Primula nutans

☐ Height 7.5cm-1.2m (3in-4ft)
☐ Planting distance 15-38cm (6-15in)
☐ Flowers mid winter to mid summer
☐ Moist or well-drained fertile soil
☐ Sun or partial shade
☐ Hardy, herbaceous

With its soft yellow flowers and dense clusters of leaves, the primrose (*Primula vulgaris*) is one of the first signs that the dull days of winter are over.

Other primulas have many different flower types, from the perfectly round heads of the drumstick primula to the nodding bell flowers of the sikkimensis section and the single, profuse blooms of the *P. × juliana* hybrids. The flowers always have five petals and come in an unusually wide range of colours, from white to yellow, orange, red, cerise, pink, purple and even blue. The leaves may be held in ground-hugging rosettes or loose clusters.

Most species prefer moist soil, and look their best in the informal setting of woodland or spring bulb associations. The low-growing alpine primulas are suitable for the edging of borders and beds and for growing in rock gardens. Border primulas require more moisture than alpine types and many thrive by the waterside, notably candelabra primulas.

Alpine types
Auricula primulas have rounded clusters of flowers in spring and fleshy, often farinose (coated with a white mealy powder) leaves.
Primula auricula (auricula, dusty miller), 15cm (6in) high and across, has pale to grey-green often farinose leaves and bright yellow scented flowers. Varieties include: 'Blue Fire' (blue); 'Old Yellow Dusty Miller' (farinose leaves, yellow flowers); 'Red Dusty Miller' (farinose leaves, red flowers); 'Willowbrook' (yellow).
Primula marginata, up to 10cm (4in) high and 23cm (9in) across, has farinose, grey-green, silver-edged and toothed leaves. The scented flowers are pale lavender to violet.
Primula × pubescens is usually 10cm (4in) high and 15cm (6in) across, with mid green, farinose leaves. Varieties include: 'Alba' (white); 'Argus' (purple, white eye); 'Faldonside' (bright crimson); and 'Mrs. J.H. Wilson' (violet, white eye).
Cortusoid types have clusters of flowers above lobed and toothed, crinkled and hairy leaves. They need moist, but well-drained, humus-rich soil in partial shade.
Primula sieboldii, up to 23cm (9in) high and 30cm (1ft) across, has tufts of pale green, prominently lobed and toothed leaves and white, red or purple flowers in late spring to early summer. 'Chinese Mountains' has white flowers and 'Lavender Girl' has magenta-purple flowers.
Farinose types have clusters of dainty flowers in early to mid

Primula × pubescens

spring and rosettes of farinose leaves. They like cool, moist soil in partial shade.
Primula farinosa (bird's-eye primrose), up to 15cm (6in) high and across, has rosettes of silvery leaves and yellow-eyed, pink, rosy lilac or purple flowers.
Primula frondosa is similar to *P. farinosa*, but sturdier. The larger flower clusters are rose-lilac.
Primula rosea is a showy species up to 30cm (1ft) high, with tufts of green, toothed leaves. The flowers are intense rose-pink. Varieties include: 'Delight' (large, deep carmine-pink flowers) and 'Grandiflora' (very large deep pink flowers). Prefers boggy soil.
Muscarioid primulas include *Primula vialii*, syn. *P. littoniana*, which is up to 30cm (1ft) high with dense spikes of flowers and tufted, slightly powdery pale green leaves. The early summer flowers

Primula denticulata

Primula florindae

are lavender-blue, but crimson in bud. It likes lime and a well-drained, dryish position in a rock crevice or cool, partial shade.

Nivalis types have clusters of flowers on tallish stems and strap-shaped, leathery leaves. They thrive in very well-drained, moist soil in cool semi-shade.

Primula chionantha is about 30cm (1ft) high with white, yellow-eyed flowers in late spring.

Petiolaris primulas have tight clusters of flowers on very short stems in spring, set among dense rosettes of leaves. They need protection from winter wet and thrive in well-drained, rich soil in cool shade.

Primula gracilipes, 7.5cm (3in) high and up to 30cm (1ft) across, has serrated, mid green leaves and profuse lavender-pink flowers with white eyes in mid spring.

Primula whitei, up to 10cm (4in) high, has toothed leaves and blue flowers with white eyes in spring.

Soldanelloid primulas have tight heads of bell-shaped, usually pendent flowers and soft, hairy leaves. Acid, gritty, moist soil in cool semi-shade is best.

Primula nutans, up to 30cm (1ft) high and across, has rosettes of

rather upright, grey-green velvety leaves up to 20cm (8in) long, and scented lavender to violet flowers in early summer.

Vernalis types have single, typical primrose flowers borne in profusion. The leaves are often crinkled and hairy. They thrive in cool, humus-rich soil in light shade and need to be divided regularly.

Primula × juliana hybrids are 7.5-15cm (3-6in) high with mid green leaves and flowers of various colours from mid winter to spring. Varieties include: 'Ariel' (blood-red flecked white); 'Blue Riband' (blue); 'Garryarde Guinevere' (sometimes sold as *P. × garryarde*, bronze leaves, soft pink flowers); 'Gigha White' (white); 'Kinlough Beauty' (salmon-pink striped cream); and 'Wanda' (wine-red).

Primula vulgaris (English primrose), syn. *P. acaulis*, is up to 15cm (6in) high with rosettes of bright green leaves and profuse pale yellow flowers with a darker centre in early spring. Varieties include: 'Alba Plena' (double, white) and various mixtures.

Border types
Candelabra primulas have tiered whorls of flowers on tall

stems above generally upright, toothed leaves up to 30cm (1ft) long. Mainly summer-flowering.

Primula aurantiaca, up to 45cm (1½ft) high and 20cm (8in) across, has ragged, mid green, red-ribbed leaves and yellow-orange flowers on brownish-red stems.

Primula beesiana, up to 60cm (2ft) high and 30cm (1ft) across, has light green, rough-textured and slightly farinose leaves and lilac flowers with a yellow eye.

Primula bulleyana, up to 75cm (2½ft) high and 30cm (1ft) across, has dark green leaves with a reddish midrib and golden yellow to light orange-red flowers.

Primula japonica (Japanese primrose); up to 75cm (2½ft) high and 30cm (1ft) across, has reddish purple flowers with a yellow eye from late spring to mid summer. Varieties include: 'Miller's Crimson' (crimson) and 'Postford White' (white, yellow eye).

Primula pulverulenta, up to 60cm (2ft) high and 30cm (1ft) across, has pale green, wrinkled leaves and wine-red to crimson flowers with a darker eye on farinose stems. Varieties include: 'Bartley Strain' (shell pink); 'Inverewe' (vivid orange-scarlet) and 'Rowal-

Primula pulverulenta 'Inverewe'

Primula × juliana 'Gigha White'

Primula vialii

lane' (salmon-pink) are both sterile and can be propagated only from cuttings.

Drumstick primulas include *Primula denticulata* which produces compact ball-shaped clusters of flowers on upright stalks from early to late spring, with rosettes of leathery leaves thinly coated with farina. The flowers are pale lilac to deep purple and the leaves are up to 20cm (8in) long. This species is often treated and an annual or biennial. Varieties include: 'Alba' (white); 'Bressingham Beauty' (powder blue); and 'Ruby' (red shades).

Sikkimensis primulas have large clusters of nodding, bell-shaped flowers on tall stems in mid summer, and long-stalked leaves.

Primula florindae (giant cowslip), up to 1.2m (4ft) high and 39cm (15in) wide, has clumps of heart-shaped, mid green leaves, each up to 25cm (10in) long. The scented flowers are pale yellow, or occasionally orange to blood-red. This species thrives in shallow water.

Primula sikkimensis (Himalayan cowslip), up to 60cm (2ft) high and 30cm (1ft) across, has pale green, wrinkled leaves and fragrant pale yellow flowers.

Cultivation

Plant alpine primulas from early autumn to early spring in sun or partial shade. Most like well-drained gritty, humus-rich soil.

Border primulas thrive in full sun or partial shade in any fertile

Primula frondosa

garden soil that does not dry out in spring and summer. Most will tolerate even quite boggy soil beside a water garden. Plant from mid autumn to early spring.

Propagation Most primulas can be divided after flowering.

Dwarf, tufted or mat-forming species are more easily increased from 2.5-5cm (1-2in) cuttings in summer and rooted in a cold frame. Pot up and plant out the following spring or autumn.

Alternatively, sow seeds in a cold frame or in a sheltered spot in the garden as soon as ripe (usually from late spring to early autumn). Keep the compost moist and prick off the seedlings singly into pots. Plunge outdoors and plant out in autumn or the following spring.

Pests and diseases

Aphids may cripple flowering shoots.

Caterpillars may eat the leaves.

Cutworms and **vine weevils** may attack the roots, causing collapse of the plants.

Brown core causes roots to rot back from the tips.

Crown rot, foot rot, and **root rot** may blacken and rot the underground tissues.

Virus diseases may cause various problems: stunted plants, leaves turning white, leaf veins turning brown, inferior, white-flecked flowers and distorted and mottled leaves with dark green blisters. Destroy affected plants.

Leaf spot shows as small brown circular spots. It may develop on older plants, or on the leaves of plants lacking in vigour.

Rust may show on the underside of *P. vulgaris* leaves as orange spore-bearing pustules, later turning brown, then black.

Primula vulgaris

Pulmonaria
lungwort

Pulmonaria officinalis

□ Height 30cm (1ft)
□ Planting distance 30cm (1ft)
□ Flowers early to late spring
□ Any ordinary garden soil
□ Partially shaded position
□ Hardy, herbaceous or evergreen

Grown for its superb foliage, as well as its flowers, lungwort forms an ornamental leafy carpet, often beautifully spotted or marbled.

The plant starts off in spring with a show of tubular flowers carried in small clusters. Their colour changes from pink to blue as they age, and depends on the soil type. As they die down the foliage thickens and spreads out, developing its full beauty. The leaves are oval or lance-shaped and plain mid green or marked with silver or white spots or marbling.

Pulmonarias are often evergreen, though *P. angustifolia* and its varieties may die down in winter.

Lungwort provides good ground cover in shady sites.

Popular species
Pulmonaria angustifolia (blue-eyed cowslip) has unspotted, lance-shaped leaves and sky-blue flowers in mid spring. 'Azurea', 'Mawson's Variety' and 'Munstead Blue' have deeper blue flowers.
Pulmonaria officinalis has several common names: Jerusalem cowslip, Jerusalem sage, soldiers and sailors or spotted dog. It has white-spotted, narrow oval, green leaves and purple-blue flowers in mid to late spring.
Pulmonaria saccharata (Bethlehem sage) has narrow oval leaves

Pulmonaria saccharata

with dense silver marbling. The flowers, which appear in early to mid spring, are pink when they open, changing to sky blue. Varieties include: 'Argentea' (silvery white leaves); 'Highdown' (rich blue flowers); 'Margery Fish' (leaves mottled silver and green); 'Pink Dawn' (pink flowers) and 'Sissinghurst White' (white flowers, green leaves).

Cultivation
Plant from mid autumn to early spring in any ordinary garden soil in a partially shaded site. Keep the roots moist during the growing season by watering and mulching.
Propagation Divide and replant the roots in mid autumn or early spring. Seeds may be sown outdoors in mid spring, but they often produce inferior plants.
Pests and diseases Sawfly larvae may eat the leaves.

Pyrethrum
pyrethrum, painted daisy

Pyrethrum roseum 'Brenda'

□ Height 75-90cm (2½-3ft)
□ Planting distance 38-45cm (15-18in)
□ Flowers early and mid summer
□ Light, well-drained soil
□ Open, sunny position
□ Ultra-hardy, herbaceous

With their clear, bright colours and simple daisy flowers, pyrethrums (*Pyrethrum roseum*, syn. *P. × hybridum*, or *Chrysanthemum coccineum*) are cheerful additions to a sunny border.

The flowers, which appear in early summer, may be single or double and measure 5-6cm (2-2½in) across. They are borne on upright stems and come in a wide range of reds and pinks, as well as white, all with prominent gold centres. The feathery foliage is bright green.

Pyrethrum has an old-fashioned cottage-garden charm and the flowers are excellent for cutting.

Popular varieties
Single varieties include: 'Avalanche' (white); 'Brenda' (cerise-pink); 'Eileen May Robinson'; (clear pink); 'Evenglow' (salmon); 'Kelway's Glorious' (crimson); 'Progression' (pink); 'Silver Challenger' (white); and 'Taurus' (blood-red).

Double varieties include: 'Aphrodite' (white); 'Helen' (light pink); 'J.N. Twerdy' (deep velvety-red); 'Lord Rosebery' (red); 'Mont Blanc' (white); 'Princess Mary' (deep pink); 'Prospero' (salmon); 'Red Dwarf' (to 30cm/1ft, carmine-red); 'Senator' (red flecked silver); and 'Vanessa' (pink flushed gold).

Ranunculus
buttercup

Pyrethrum roseum 'Eileen May Robinson'

Ranunculus acris 'Flore Pleno'

Cultivation

Plant pyrethrums in early spring in any light and well-drained soil in an open, sunny position. Stake with pea sticks in mid to late spring.

Water freely during the growing season, and cut back all stems as soon as the flowers are over. Young plants may flower again in early autumn.

Propagation Pyrethrums are best left undisturbed for three or four years before being increased.

Divide more mature roots in early spring or in mid summer, after flowering, when new basal growth has started; discard old woody root portions before replanting the divided rootstock.

Sow seeds in early spring under glass at a temperature of 16°C (61°F), though seedlings seldom come true to type.

Pests and diseases Generally trouble free.

□ Height 30-75cm (12-30in)
□ Planting distance 30-45cm (1-1½ft)
□ Flowers late spring to late summer
□ Any ordinary, moist garden soil
□ Sun or partial shade
□ Hardy, herbaceous

The yellow or white flowers of buttercups shine out against green foliage, making them attractive early summer plants for borders.

The flowers vary from the wild six-petalled species to double flowered forms and pompons.

Popular species

Ranunculus aconitifolius 'Flore Pleno', up to 60cm (2ft) high and 45cm (1½ft) across, has mid green palmate leaves with deeply toothed lobes, and bears profuse double white shining flowers from late spring to early summer.

Ranunculus acris 'Flore Pleno', up to 75cm (2½ft) high and 45cm (1½ft) across, is the double form of common meadow buttercup. It has deeply cut, lobed palmate leaves. The double flowers are bright yellow and shiny and appear from early to late summer.

Ranunculus ficaria (lesser celandine) is up to 30cm (1ft) high and has marbled heart-shaped glossy leaves and shiny golden-yellow flowers up to 5cm (2in) across. Varieties, more compact than the species, include: 'Albus' (white); 'Aurantiacus', syn. 'Cupreus' (coppery-orange); 'Flore Pleno' (double, yellow); and 'Primrose' (creamy-yellow).

Ranunculus gramineus, a compact plant up to 30cm (1ft) high and 30cm (1ft) across, has grassy leaves and sprays of glistening yellow flowers in late spring.

Cultivation

Plant from early autumn to mid spring in any ordinary, moist soil in sun or partial shade.

Propagation Divide and replant in mid autumn or early spring. Sow seeds of *R. gramineus* in late winter or early spring in a cold frame. Prick out the seedlings when they are large enough to handle. Pot up and plunge outside. Plant out in the permanent site from mid autumn to early spring.

Pests and diseases Trouble free.

RED-HOT POKER – see
Kniphofia
RED-INK PLANT – see
Phytolacca
RED VALERIAN – see
Centranthus

Pyrethrum roseum 'Vanessa'

Ranunculus aconitifolius 'Flore Pleno'

Rheum

ornamental rhubarb

Rheum palmatum

- ☐ Height 90-2.4m (3-8ft)
- ☐ Planting distance 60-120cm (2-4ft)
- ☐ Flowers late spring to early summer
- ☐ Rich moist soil
- ☐ Sunny site
- ☐ Hardy, herbaceous

Ornamental rhubarb is a striking and unusual – and very large – specimen plant, thriving in waterside gardens and in sunny borders where the soil is rich and moist.

Great glossy leaves unfurl in spring to form a huge round clump. Tall spikes carry loose sprays of bead-like flowers, sometimes concealed by large papery bracts.

Bear in mind that the stems of ornamental rhubarb are not edible. The leaves, like those of rhubarb, are poisonous.

Popular species

Rheum alexandrae, up to 90cm (3ft) high, has mid green leaves

Rheum alexandrae

Rheum palmatum 'Atrosanguineum'

and cream bracts resembling long drooping tongues.

Rheum palmatum, up to 2.4m (8ft) high, has deeply cut purple-red leaves which turn green when the pinkish-red flowers have finished. The variety 'Atrosanguineum', syn. 'Rubrum', has cerise-crimson flowers and exceptionally vivid red young leaves.

Cultivation

Plant from late autumn to late winter in ordinary garden soil in sun. Ornamental rhubarb gives a good display of leaves in ordinary garden soil, but the plants flower best in rich, moist soil. Water freely in summer, especially in periods of drought, and feed occasionally with liquid manure. Cut out the flower spikes when flowering has finished.

Propagation Lift and carefully divide old plants from late autumn to late winter, ensuring that each division has a dormant crown bud.

Sow seeds outdoors in early to mid spring. Prick out the seedlings when they are large enough to handle, grow in a nursery bed and plant out in the permanent site in late autumn of the following year.

Pests and diseases Trouble free.

RIBBON GRASS – see *Phalaris*

Rodgersia

rodgersia

Rodgersia sambucifolia

Rodgersia pinnata 'Superba'

☐ Height 90cm-1.8m (3-6ft)
☐ Planting distance 60-75cm (2-2½ft)
☐ Flowers early to mid summer
☐ Moist soil
☐ Partially shaded site, sheltered from wind
☐ Hardy, herbaceous

Rodgersia is a striking border plant with large clumps of outstanding foliage, often tinted bronze, and strong, upright plumes of numerous tiny creamy or pink flowers rising gracefully to a height of up to 1.8m (6ft).

The mid to deep green leaves may be held in a fan, rather like horse chestnut foliage, or divided into a string of leaflets. Rodgersias grow from rhizomatous roots and may take a couple of years to become established. Once growing strongly, they make superb specimen plants in the right situation and are ideal in the moist, semi-shaded and sheltered setting of a semi-wild garden with other foliage plants.

Popular species

Rodgersia aesculifolia, up to 1.8m (6ft) high, has glossy, bronze, toothed horse chestnut-like leaves, each leaflet almost 30cm (1ft) long. The showy erect and much branched plumes of star-shaped, white or pink flowers in mid summer are 45cm (1½ft) tall

and are followed by reddish seed heads.

Rodgersia pinnata, up to 1.2m (4ft) high, has deep green, sometimes bronzed leaves divided into leaflets that are prominently veined. It bears white to pink-red flower plumes, 30cm (1ft) long. Varieties include 'Elegans' (creamy-white); 'Irish Bronze' (bronze leaves, creamy-white flowers); and 'Superba' (bronze-purple leaves, pink flowers in plumes up to 50cm (20in) long.

Rodgersia podophylla, up to 1.2m (4ft) high, has heavily veined, lobed-tipped horse chestnut-like leaves which are bronzed when young, turning mid green in summer and then coppery. The branched, loose flower sprays, up to 45cm (1½ft) long, are pale buff to creamy-white.

Rodgersia sambucifolia, up to 90cm (3ft) high is compact of habit, with leaves divided into leaflets; the flat-topped flower heads are creamy-white.

Rodgersia tabularis, syn. *Astilboides tabularis*, up to 90cm (3ft) high, has long-stalked and scalloped bright green leaves in an almost circular umbrella-like shape up to 90cm (3ft) wide. The creamy-white flower plumes are about 25cm (10in) long and feathery.

Cultivation

Rodgersias like a partially shaded site, sheltered from wind. Plant the fleshy roots 2.5cm (1in) deep in moist soil containing decayed vegetable matter in early to mid spring. Rodgersias will also grow in ordinary soil in wide herbaceous and mixed borders though height will be less than in moist conditions. Water freely during the growing season; cut out faded flower stems unless the seed heads are wanted for drying.

Propagation Division is the most reliable method of increase; dig up the roots of established plants in early to mid spring, just as new growth begins to show. Cut the rhizomes into sections, each with a growing point, and replant 2.5cm (1in) below the soil surface.

Sow seeds in early spring in a cold frame and prick out the seedlings when they are large enough to handle. Set out in a nursery bed when the danger of frost has passed and plant out in the permanent site in spring two years later. Named varieties do not come true to type and are best propagated by division.

Pests and diseases Trouble free.

Rodgersia podophylla

Romneya
tree poppy

Romneya coulteri

☐ Height 1.3-1.8m (4-6ft)
☐ Planting distance 1.2-1.5m (4-5ft)
☐ Flowers mid summer to early autumn
☐ Well-drained, humus-rich soil
☐ Sunny and sheltered site
☐ Moderately hardy, herbaceous

Tree poppies are sub-shrubby perennials that die back to the ground in late autumn. They can be invasive and spread quickly through underground runners, but are reliably hardy only in southern gardens.

The brilliant white flowers, with pleated petals surrounding a prominent centre of golden stamens, resemble poppies and are up to 15cm (6in) across. They are short-lived but produced in succession over several summer months. Tree poppies are suitable for the back of borders or as specimen plants in sheltered sites.

Popular species
Roymneya coulteri grows 1.2-1.8m (4-6ft) tall, with a similar spread. It bears blue-green, broadly ovate and deeply lobed leaves and pure white flowers.
Romneya trichocalyx is similar to *R. coulteri* and possibly a natural variety of that species. It is slightly smaller in all its parts and can be distinguished by its rounded flower buds covered with bristly hairs.

Cultivation
Romneyas resent root disturbance; set out young pot-grown plants with the root ball intact, in mid to late spring. Deep rich soil that is well-drained gives the best results, and a sunny position sheltered from strong winds is essential. In mid to late autumn cut all stems down to just above ground level and apply a protective winter mulch or weathered ashes over the base of the plants.
Propagation Romneyas can be increased from seed or root cuttings, but the latter method may involve permanent damage to the parent plant, and seed propagation is preferable. Sow seeds in late winter or early spring at a temperature of 13-16°C (551°F). Prick the seedlings single into small pots of well-drained compost and grow them on under glass until roots fill the pots. Repot the young plants and overwinter them in a cold frame before planting out in permanent sites the following late spring.

Alternatively, dig up and replant in late spring any well-grown suckers that have appeared a good distance from the parent.
Pests and diseases Wilting shoots and yellowing leaves are usually caused by unsuitable growing conditions.

Roscoea
roscoea

Roscoea cautleoides

☐ Height 38-45cm (15-18in)
☐ Planting distance 30cm (1ft)
☐ Flowers mid to late summer
☐ Any ordinary moisture-retentive soil
☐ Sun or partial shade
☐ Moderately hardy, herbaceous

The handsome roscoea lies dormant until late spring, when its lance-like leaves suddenly appear, quickly followed by a fine show of elegant orchid-like flowers.

The leaves, up to 20cm (8in) long, are mid to bright green and the flowers, on strong upright stems, are in shades of yellow and purple.

Popular species
Roscoea beesiana, up to 40cm (16in) high, has yellow flowers with buff and lilac-purple tips.
Roscoea cautleoides, up to 45cm (1½ft) high, has soft yellow flowers in early summer.
Roscoea purpurea, up to 45cm (1½ft) high, is rich purple.

Cultivation
Plant in early spring in any ordinary, moisture-retentive soil in sun or partial shade. Set the fleshy roots 7.5-10cm (3-4in) deep.
Propagation Roscoea may be divided and replanted in early spring. Alternatively, sow seeds in a cold frame in late summer to early autumn. Prick out the seedlings when they are large enough to handle and grow on in a nursery bed for two seasons.
Pests and diseases Trouble free.

ROYAL FERN – see *Osmunda*

Rudbeckia

coneflower

Rudbeckia laciniata 'Goldquelle'

☐ Height 60cm-2.1m (2-7ft)
☐ Planting distance 45-60cm (1½-2ft)
☐ Flowers mid summer to early autumn
☐ Any good, well-drained garden soil
☐ Open, sunny site
☐ Hardy, herbaceous

Famous for their brilliant golden yellow blooms, coneflowers are excellent long-lasting perennials for both borders and cut flowers. In rich soils, they often spread to wide clumps.

The species have an open leafy form, bearing numerous daisy-like flowers with a prominent central brown or greenish cone. The mid green leaves are oblong, lance-shaped, deeply cut or divided into leaflets.

Varieties offer single and double forms in shades of yellow and orange.

Popular species

Rudbeckia fulgida, up to 90cm (3ft) high, is a bushy species with mid green leaves. Yellow to orange brown flowers with purple-brown cones appear from mid summer to late autumn. The species is rarely grown being replaced by varieties, usually with 7.5-10cm (3-4in) wide flowers, including: 'Deamii" (yellow); 'Goldsturm' (narrow-petalled, yellow); and 'Speciosa' (orange).

Rudbeckia laciniata, up to 2.1m (7ft) high, has deeply divided leaves and yellow 7.5-10cm (3-4in) wide flowers with a greenish cone from late summer to early autumn. Varieties include: 'Golden Glow' (double); 'Goldquelle' (to 90cm/3ft double); and 'Herbstsonne' ('Autumn Sun', green cone).

Rudbeckia maxima, reaching

Rudbeckia fulgida 'Deamii'

90cm-1.5m (3-5ft) high and 60cm (2ft) or more across, is a moderately hardy species with grey-green leaves. Its yellow flowers are 12-15cm (5-6in) across.

Rudbeckia subtomentosa, with a height of 90cm (3ft) and a spread of 45cm (1½ft), has oval mid green leaves which are finely covered in grey hairs. Its yellow flowers, 7.5cm (3in) across, appear from mid summer to early autumn and have a button-like disc – rather than a cone – at the centre.

Cultivation

Plant in mid autumn or early to mid spring in any well-cultivated, well-drained garden soil in a sunny, open site. The plants need staking in exposed positions. On dry soils mulch with decayed manure in early spring, unless height restriction of taller plants is required.

Propagation Sow seeds in early to mid spring or in late summer to early autumn in a cold frame. Prick out the seedlings when large enough to handle; grow on in nursery rows and plant out in mid autumn.

Varieties grown from seed do not come true to type: divide and replant the roots from mid autumn to early spring, replanting only strong outer shoots.

Pests and diseases Slugs and snails may be troublesome.

RUSSIAN SAGE – see *Perovskia*
SAGE – see *Salvia*

Salvia

sage, clary

Salvia fulgens

☐ Height 30cm-1.5m (1-5ft)
☐ Planting distance 45-60cm (1½-2ft)
☐ Flowers early summer to mid autumn
☐ Any fertile, well-drained garden soil
☐ Sunny site
☐ Moderately or very hardy, herbaceous

Planted in groups, perhaps in a long swathe at the front of a border, sage is a spectacular sight. The lower third of the strong upright stems is covered in a bushy mass of leaves, while the upper section carries dense, richly coloured spikes of flowers in shades of purple, blue, red and pink. They are borne in long succession and are good for cutting.

Popular species

Salvia fulgens (cardinal sage) is a half-hardy to moderately hardy sub-shrubby perennial. Up to 90cm (3ft) high and 60cm (2ft) across, it has leaves up to 7.5cm (3in) long, and spikes of vivid red flowers opening from purplish red bud cases in summer and autumn. Protect the crowns and root areas with a deep winter mulch.

Salvia haematodes, up to 90cm (3ft) high and 60cm (2ft) across, is a rather short-lived plant. It has a branching, upright habit. The slightly grey-green, oval leaves have a corrugated surface and the purple flowers appear from early summer to early autumn.

Salvia pratensis (meadow clary) is an ultra-hardy perennial, 30cm-1.2m (1-4ft) high and 60cm (2ft) across. Clump-forming, with

Salvia × superba

Sanguisorba
burnet

Sanguisorba obtusa 'Albiflora'

☐ Height 90cm-1.5m (3-5ft)
☐ Planting distance 60-75cm (2-2½ft)
☐ Flowers in summer and autumn
☐ Any moist soil
☐ Sun or partial shade
☐ Ultra-hardy, herbaceous

aromatic leaves up to 15cm (6in) long, it bears branched spikes of pink, lavender, blue or violet-purple flowers in early summer.

Salvia × superba is a very hardy hybrid, often sold incorrectly as *S. nemorosa*. It is a bushy plant, up to 90cm (3ft) high and 45-60cm (1½-2ft) across, with aromatic grey-green, narrow oval leaves and spikes of violet-blue flowers with crimson-purple bracts in mid summer to autumn. Varieties and related hybrids include: 'East Friesland' (up to 75cm/2½ft high); 'Indigo' (to 1m/3½ft), deep blue, branching spikes); 'Lubeca' (to 75cm (2½ft); and 'May Night' (to 40cm/16in, dark violet, very early flowering).

Salvia uliginosa (bog sage) is a moderately hardy species up to 1.5m (5ft) high and 45cm (1½ft) across, with branching spikes of sky-blue flowers in autumn. This species thrives in moist soil and needs support.

Cultivation
Plant from mid autumn to early spring in any ordinary, well-drained garden soil, preferably enriched with well-rotted compost or manure. A sunny site is best, with shelter for *S. fulgens*.

S. haematodes and *S. uliginosa* need staking with twiggy sticks or canes. Cut down all plants to ground level in late autumn.

Propagation Divide and replant *S. × superba* from early autumn to early spring. Other species are best raised from seed. Sow seeds in a cold frame in mid spring. When the seedlings are large enough to handle, prick them off into boxes and then into nursery rows. Overwinter moderately hardy plants in the cold frame. Hardy species may be planted out in their permanent sites from autumn to spring.

Pests and diseases Yellowed foliage and stunted growth on young plants are due to a physiological disorder, caused by too low temperatures.

Burnets are easy, long-lived and accommodating perennials suitable for borders with moisture-retentive soil and ideal for waterside planting. The bottle-brush-like flowers are good for cutting.

Burnet's elegant and abundant foliage is divided into numerous fine leaflets, sometimes with toothed or ragged edges.

Popular species
Sanguisorba canadensis grows 1.5m (5ft) tall and spreads to about 60cm (2ft). The erect stems are clothed with pale green leaves and topped, from late summer until the autumn, with 15cm (6in) tall white flower spikes.

Sanguisorba obtusa (Japanese burnet) is about 90cm (3ft) tall and has pale green, finely divided leaves up to 45cm (1½ft) long), with blue-green undersides. The wiry stems bear arching rose-pink flower spikes from early to late summer; the extraordinary long stamens give the flowers a fluffy appearance. The variety 'Albiflora' has white flowers.

Sanguisorba tenuifolia, up to 1.2m (4ft) high, resembles *S. canadensis* but with shorter red, sometimes white flower spikes that are produced in early and mid summer.

Salvia haematodes

Sanguisorba canadensis

Saponaria
bouncing Bet, soapwort

Saponaria officinalis 'Rosea Plena'

Scabiosa
scabious, pincushion flower

Scabiosa caucasica 'Clive Greaves'

Cultivation
Plant sanguisorbas from mid autumn to early spring in any kind of soil provided it does not dry out. Choose a sunny or lightly shaded site and provide twiggy supports for the taller-growing species. Water freely during the growing season and cut all stems back to ground level in late autumn.

Propagation Divide and replant the roots in early or mid spring. Alternatively, sow sees in spring in a cold frame. Prick out the seedlings, when large enough to handle, into boxes and grow on in the open. Transplant the young plants to permanent sites in mid autumn of the following year.

Pests and diseases Trouble free.

☐ Height 30-90cm (1-3ft)
☐ Planting distance 60cm (2ft)
☐ Flowers mid summer to early autumn
☐ Any fertile garden soil
☐ Sun or partial shade
☐ Hardy, herbaceous

Related to the popular creeping and trailing soapworts of rock gardens, the taller growing bouncing Bet (*Saponaria officinalis*) is suitable for an herbaceous border and for naturalizing in semi-wild gardens. It grows up to 90cm (3ft) high, spreading to 60cm (2ft) or more across, often being invasive. The erect stems bear pale green narrowly lance-shaped leaves.

The species itself has small clusters of single, five-petalled flowers that resemble shaggy carnations, but it is rarely grown having been superseded by double-flowered forms, such as 'Alba Plena' (white) and 'Rosea Plena' (pink).

Cultivation
Plant saponaria from early autumn to early spring in any fertile garden soil in sun or partial shade. Provide sticks for support and dead-head to prolong flowering. Cut all stems down to ground level in late autumn. During winter fork out the spreading underground runners.

Propagation Divide and replant the roots from mid autumn to early spring. Seeds may be sown in spring, but seedlings seldom come true to type.

Pests and diseases Trouble free.

☐ Height 60-90cm (2-3ft)
☐ Planting distance 45-60cm (1½-2ft)
☐ Flowers early summer to early autumn
☐ Any well-drained soil
☐ Hardy, herbaceous or evergreen

Related to the wild scabious that flourishes in chalk and limestone grassland, garden forms of the perennial scabious have for centuries been valued for their charm and ease of cultivation. Daisy-type flowers, with overlapping and frilled petals surrounding a prominent yellow-green pincushion-like centre, are produced over several months and are ideal for cutting; the silky seed heads can be dried for winter arrangements.

Suitable for herbaceous and mixed borders, scabious thrive on limy soils but are just as happy on neutral soils given good drainage.

Popular species
Scabiosa caucasica, the most popular of perennial species, grows 60-90cm (2-3ft) high and forms a ground-hugging clump of herbaceous, mid green lance-shaped leaves deeply divided into narrow segments. Leafless flower stems rise above the leaf mounds from early summer onwards, bearing clear lavender blue flowers, 7.5cm (3in) or more wide. The species itself is rarely seen having been superseded by numerous varieties including the popular 'Clive Greaves' (rich lavender-blue); 'Miss Willmott' (white); 'Moerheim Blue' (deep violet-blue); and the recent 'Mount Cook' (white).

Scabiosa columbaria, up to 75cm (2½ft) tall, has evergreen basal leaves, grey-green and lance-shaped while the stem leaves are

Scabiosa (mixed)

Sedum

sedum, stonecrop

Sedum roseum

- ☐ Height 25-60cm (10-24in)
- ☐ Planting distance 30-60cm (1-2ft)
- ☐ Flowers early summer to mid autumn
- ☐ Any ordinary well-drained soil
- ☐ Full sun
- ☐ Hardy, herbaceous or evergreen

Well-known for their dense heads of flowers in shades of rust to red, pink and yellow or white, sedums are outstanding garden plants.

The numerous species, varieties and hybrids include hardy and half-hardy annuals and herbaceous or evergreen perennials. Some are too tender for growing outdoors, while the hardy but small mat-forming types are best grown in rock gardens, on walls and in paving crevices. Those described here are all hardy herbaceous plants suitable for borders where the shape, texture and colours of the fleshy foliage add contrast to more soft-leaved, all green plants.

Popular species

Sedum aizoon, up to 30cm (1ft) high and across has lance-shaped shiny, mid green coarsely toothed leaves and golden yellow flower heads in mid summer.

Sedum 'Autumn Joy' is an herbaceous hybrid with a height and spread of 60cm (2ft). It has ovate pale grey-green leaves and the flower heads, up to 20cm (8in) wide, are borne on thick, fleshy stems; they are pink when they first open in late summer or early autumn, deepening to copper-red by mid autumn.

Sedum maximum, syn. *S. telephium maximum* has been superseded by varieties. 'Atropurpureum' up to 60cm (2ft) high, has purple-red stems and leaves; the pink flower heads, up to 15cm (6in)

finely divided. Lilac-blue flowers with dark purple bristly centres are borne on hairy stems in summer and early autumn.

Scabiosa ochroleuca grows to 75cm (2½ft) tall, the erect flower stems rising from evergreen clumps of deeply divided, silver-hairy leaves. The flowers, up to 10cm (4in) wide, are pale yellow. This species self-seeds freely.

Cultivation

Plant in early to mid spring in any fertile and well-drained soil and in full sun. Scabious thrive in coastal gardens but may need staking on windy sites. Regular dead-heading ensures a continuous floral display; cut all stems down to ground level in late autumn.

Propagation All scabious can be increased by seed sown in an outdoor bed in spring, but seedlings do not come true to type and division in mid spring is preferable. It is a good idea to divide and replant large clumps every three or four years.

Pests and diseases Slugs and snails feed on young basal leaves. On poorly drained soils, root rot may lead to the collapse of plants,

and excessively dry soils can encourage powdery mildew which shows as a white coating on the leaves.

SEA HOLLY – see *Eryngium*
SEAKALE – see *Crambe*
SEA LAVENDER -see *Limonium*
SEDGE – see *Carex*

Sidalcea

chequer mallow

Sedum 'Autumn Joy'

Sidalcea malviflora

☐ Height 75cm-1.4m (2½-4½ft)
☐ Planting distance 45-60cm (1½-2ft)
☐ Flowers early summer to early autumn
☐ Ordinary garden soil
☐ Sunny site
☐ Hardy, herbaceous

Chequer mallow (*Sidalcea malviflora*) is a graceful plant with tall branching spikes of silky flowers rising from clumps of leaves throughout summer.

The funnel-shaped flowers are in shades of pink and the leaves are mid green. The lower leaves are rounded, while the stem leaves are lobed and divided into segments.

Varieties, generally up to 1.1m (3½ft), include: 'Croftway Red' (deep pink-red); 'Loveliness' (shell pink); 'Oberon' (rose-pink); 'Rose Queen' (1.2m/4ft, rose-pink); and 'William Smith' (salmon-pink).

Cultivation

Plant in mid autumn or early spring in ordinary garden soil in a sunny position. After flowering, cut the stems down to 30cm (1ft).
Propagation Lift, divide and re-plant in early spring, discarding the centre of the clump.

Sow seeds in a cold frame in early spring, though named varieties do not come true to type. Pick out the seedlings and grow on in a nursery bed. Set out in mid autumn.
Pests and diseases Rust may show on the leaves and stems as raised orange pustules.

---

across, appear in early and mid autumn. 'Variegatum', 30cm (1ft) tall, has yellow and cream variegated leaves and bears bronze-red flower heads.

Sedum roseum (rose-root), syn. *S. rhodiola* or *Rhodiola rosea*, up to 30cm (1ft) high and across, has strap-shaped closely packed blue-grey leaves on thick stems, and 7.5cm (3in) wide pale yellow flower heads opening from coppery buds from late spring. The roots are rose-scented when dry.

Sedum 'Ruby Glow' is up to 25cm (10in) high and 30cm (1ft) across and suitable for the front of a border. It has blue-green ovate leaves and bright ruby-red flower heads up to 10cm (4in) wide in mid to late summer.

Sedum spectabile, up to 45cm (1½ft) high and across, has pale grey-green leaves and fluffy pink flower heads up to 15cm (6in) wide from early to mid autumn. Varieties include: 'Brilliant' (deep rose-pink); 'Carmen' (bright carmine-pink); and 'Meteor' (carmine-red).

Sedum 'Vera Jameson', up to 25cm (10in) high and 30cm (1ft) across, has arching stems with deep purple leaves and dusty-pink flower heads in mid summer.

Cultivation

Plant sedums in full sun from mid autumn to mid spring. *S. maxi-* *mum* needs moisture-retentive soil. All other species thrive in any ordinary, well-drained garden soil and are generally drought resistant.
Propagation Sow seeds in a cold frame in early to mid spring. When the seedlings are large enough to handle, prick them off and later pot them up singly. Plunge outside until mid autumn, then plant out. Named varieties do not come true from seed.

All species may be divided and replanted from mid autumn to early spring.

Or, take 2.5-7.5cm (1-3in) long stem cuttings from early spring to mid summer and root outdoors.
Pests and diseases Aphids may eat stems and leaves and make the plants sticky and sooty. Slugs may eat leaves and stems and check early growth. Crown or root rot may occur in over-wet soil.

SENSITIVE FERN – see *Onoclea*
SHASTA DAISY – see *Chrysanthemum maximum*
SHIELD FERN – see *Polystichum*
SHUTTLECOCK FERN – see *Matteuccia*
SIBERIAN BUGLOSS – see *Brunnera*

SILVER GRASS – see *Miscanthus*

Sisyrinchium

sisyrinchium

Sisyrinchium striatum

Sisyrinchium californicum

☐ Height 30-45cm (1-1½ft)
☐ Planting distance 30cm (12in)
☐ Flowers early spring to early autumn
☐ Well-drained, humus-rich soil
☐ Sunny site
☐ Hardy, herbaceous or evergreen

The elegant sisyrinchiums are low of stature and best grown in rock gardens although those described below are suitable for the front of sunny herbaceous borders. They bear erect spikes of satiny flowers, rising over a clump of grassy leaves. The flowers, usually star-shaped, come in shades of yellow to cream or blue to purple-violet.

Popular species

Sisyrinchium angustifolium (blue-eyed grass), syn. *S. gramineum*, grows up to 30cm (1ft) high and 23cm (9in) across. It bears violet-blue flowers from late spring until early autumn.

Sisyrinchium bermudiana, up to 30cm (1ft) high and 23cm (9in) across, has blue flowers on branched stems in early summer. It is often confused with *S. angustifolium*, but the light blue, satiny flowers are prominently marked with yellow at the base of the petals.

Sisyrinchium californicum (golden-eyed grass), up to 30cm (1ft) high and 15cm (6in) across, is herbaceous. It has yellow flowers from late spring to early summer.

Sisyrinchium douglasii (grass widow), syn. *S. grandiflorum*, grows up to 25cm (10in) high and 15cm (6in) across. It has nodding and bell-shaped, purple flowers with a satiny sheen in early spring.

Sisyrinchium striatum, an ever-green up to 45cm (1½ft) high and 30cm (1ft) across, has grey-green, sword-shaped leaves, and pale or cream-yellow flowers from early summer to early autumn. The variety 'Variegatum' has leaves striped cream and green. The species and its variety may be short-lived unless divided every three years, but the plants often self-seed.

Cultivation

Grow sisyrinchiums in well-drained soil containing plenty of humus. Plant in a sunny site from early autumn to early spring. Remove faded flower stems and dead leaves in autumn.

Propagation Sisyrinchiums often self-seed. Otherwise, germinate seeds in a cold frame in autumn or early spring. Prick out the seedlings, when large enough to handle, into boxes and later transfer them to an outdoor nursery bed. Grow on for a year before moving them to their permanent flowering sites.

Alternatively, divide and re-plant established clumps in early autumn or spring. Some of the species resent root disturbance and may take a couple of years to recover.

Pests and diseases Generally trouble free.

SCULPTURAL PLANTS

Bold leaves, architectural shapes and unusual textures are spectacular qualities that add a new dimension to the garden.

Striking foliage is important in the overall appearance of a garden. In beds and borders, foliage effects can be achieved by small-scale plants such as ferns or herbs. At the other end of the scale are dramatically shaped plants that are most impressive as isolated specimens. In between are plants which give a sense of form and structure against gently bobbing border perennials and provide a background for low-growing plants.

Many fine foliage plants thrive in shade, notably the hostas whose bold leaves are as striking in texture as in shape, colour and size. Some, such as the arching clumps of 'Blue Umbrella' or the ruffled golden blades of 'Piedmont Gold', merit a focal position of their own.

Also for semi-shade are the gigantic ornamental rhubarbs. They have incomparable sculptural beauty as the great glossy leaves unfurl to green and purple-red and the cerise or cream flower spikes rise majestically to several metres in height.

Graceful grasses, elegant bamboos, the bold shapes of many euphorbias and the velvety leaf candelabras of some verbascums are just some of the choices that add a sculptural dimension to the garden picture, creating a lasting pleasure for those who see it.

▼ **Heart-shaped hosta** A recent American introduction, *Hosta fortunei* 'Francee' is an outstanding specimen plant for sun or shade. The broad and quilted, rich green leaves are edged with white to complement the white to pale lavender flower spikes.

► **Ornamental rhubarb** As a specimen feature on a large expanse of lawn, or in the shelter of tall trees, few plants can rival the imposing *Rheum palmatum*. The furled leaves that push up in spring unfold to giant, jagged-edged umbrellas as much as 90cm (3ft) across. They are flushed with red, but turn bright green around the time the enormous stems branch into fluffy clusters of crimson.

▼ *Moisture lovers* In rich soil with plenty of moisture at the roots, two majestic foliage plants, *Rheum palmatum* (ornamental rhubarb) and the horse chestnut-like *Rodgersia* (left), create a decorative leaf canopy in early summer. In its dappled shade thrive primulas and the golden orbs of *Trollius* (globe flower).

▲ New Zealand flax Looking not in the least like a flax, the New Zealand plant of that name (*Phormium tenax*) forms a striking clump, up to 3m (10ft) high, of stiff, sword-shaped leaves. Of truly sculptural effect, the yellow and pale green stripes of 'Yellow Waves' shine against the red blades of its companion 'Purpureum' and a footing of crane's-bill (*Geranium endressii*).

◄ Giant reed A tall and sturdy, elegant grass, the giant reed (*Arundo donax*) flourishes in a sheltered site at the edge of the water. It will grow over 3m (10ft) high, bearing broad, grey-green leaves and producing silky flower plumes that unfold red in late summer, fade to buff-white in autumn and last throughout winter.

Primeval spurge The evergreen *Euphorbia characias wulfenii* bears huge club-like flower panicles.

Smilacina

false Solomon's seal

Smilacina racemosa

☐ Height 45-90cm (1½-3ft)
☐ Planting distance 45-60cm (1½-2ft)
☐ Flowers late spring to early summer
☐ Deep, rich, moist soil
☐ Partially shaded site
☐ Hardy, herbaceous

An unusual and elegant woodland plant, false Solomon's seal's graceful, arching stems carry double rows of glossy, broadly lance-shaped leaves and fluffy plumes of cream or white flowers, followed later by red berries.

Popular species
Smilacina racemosa (false spikenard), up to 90cm (3ft) high and 45cm (1½ft) across, has closely set, light green leaves. It bears dense sprays of fragrant cream-white flowers and red berries.
Smilacina stellata (star-flowered lily of the valley), up to 60cm (2ft) high and 30cm (1ft) across, has sprays of white starry flowers and dark red berries.

Cultivation
Plant from mid autumn to early spring in deep, rich soil in a partially shaded, moist position. The rhizomatous roots spread slowly and should not be disturbed for several years after planting.
Propagation Lift and divide old plants in mid autumn.
Pests and diseases Trouble free.

SNAKEWEED – see *Polygonum*
SNEEZEWORT – see *Achillea* and *Helenium*

Soleirolia

mind-your-own-business

Soleirolia soleirolii

☐ Height 2.5-7.5cm (2-3in)
☐ Planting distance 60cm (2ft)
☐ Foliage plant
☐ Light, well-drained, humus-rich soil
☐ Cool, moist shade
☐ Moderately, hardy, evergreen

Mind-your-own-business (*Soleirolia soleirolii*, syn. *Helxine soleirolii*), also known as baby's tears, forms a carpet of tiny leaves, each no more than 6mm (¼in) across.

The flowers are insignificant and the plant is grown solely for its bright green, rounded leaves. These provide foliage interest throughout the year, unless a sharp frost cuts it back.

Mind-your-own-business self-roots, spreading quickly to form low ground cover; it is particularly easy to propagate, though it can be invasive. It looks well growing in cool, moist shade, perhaps carpeting the ground beneath trees or shrubs.

Varieties include: 'Argentea' (leaves variegated silver) and 'Aurea' (yellow-green leaves).

Cultivation
Plant in spring in light, well-drained, humus-rich soil in a cool, moist, shady position.
Propagation Detach portions of the parent and replant.
Pests and diseases Generally trouble free.

Solidago

golden rod

Solidago 'Goldenmosa'

Solidago 'Golden Dwarf'

☐ Height 30cm-1.8m (1-6ft)
☐ Planting distance 38-75cm (15-18in)
☐ Flowers mid summer to mid autumn
☐ Ordinary garden soil
☐ Sun or partial shade
☐ Hardy, herbaceous

Planted in groups in herbaceous and mixed borders, golden rod provides a magnificent display of frothy, vivid yellow plumes of flowers. This bushy, vigorous plant has lance-shaped, mid green or golden green leaves. It can be rampant but there is a range of less invasive hybrids.

Popular species

Solidago canadensis, 90cm-1.8m (3-6ft) high and up to 90cm (3ft) across, is a vigorous, upright species with sharply serrated, mid green leaves and broad yellow flower plumes. It is suited to semi-wild gardens. The best known variety is 'Golden Wings'.

Solidago × *hybrida*, syn. *S.* × *arendsii*, covers a group of non-invasive hybrids with golden-green leaves and plumes or horizontally spreading sprays of flowers. They include: 'Cloth of Gold' (to 45cm/1½ft, deep yellow); 'Crown of Rays' (to 45cm/1½ft, yellow); 'Golden Dwarf' (to 30cm/1ft); 'Goldenmosa' (to 90cm/3ft, fluffy flower sprays); 'Golden Thumb' ('Queenie', to 30cm/1ft, golden yellow); 'Lemore' (to 60cm/2ft primrose yellow); and 'Peter Pan' (to 1.5m/5ft, bright yellow).

Cultivation

Plant from mid autumn to early spring in ordinary garden soil in sun or partial shade.

Propagation Golden rods quickly exhaust the soil and should be divided and replanted regularly, from mid autumn to early spring.

Pests and diseases Tortrix caterpillars may spin the leaves together and eat them. Powdery mildew shows as a white coating.

SOLOMON'S SEAL – see *Polygonatum*
SOUTHERNWOOD – see *Artemisia*
SPEEDWELL – see *Veronica*
SPIDERWORT – see *Tradescantia*
SPLEENWORT – see *Asplenium*
SPURGE – see *Euphorbia*

Stachys

betony

Stachys lanata 'Silver Carpet'

- ☐ Height 30-75cm (1-2½ft)
- ☐ Planting distance 30-45cm (1-1½ft)
- ☐ Flowers late spring to late summer
- ☐ Ordinary, well-drained garden soil
- ☐ Sun or partial shade
- ☐ Hardy, herbaceous or evergreen

Betony is an outstanding ground cover plant. Its flower spikes are in shades of purple and pink over a dense, leafy, silver or mid to bright green carpet. The species described below are herbaceous unless otherwise stated.

Popular species
Stachys (*Betonica*) *grandiflora* (woundwort), syn. *S. macrantha*, is up to 75cm (2½ft) high and 30cm (1ft) across. Mat-forming, it has rosettes of broad, corrugated, mid to dark green leaves and whorls of purple flowers. Varieties include:

Stachys lanata in flower

'Rosea' (rose); 'Superba' (rich rose-purple) and 'Violacea' (violet-purple).
Stachys lanata (lamb's tongue, lamb's ear, woolly betony), syn. *S. olympica* is an evergrey species grown primarily for its foliage. It is up to 45cm (1½ft) high and 30cm (1ft) across. It forms a mat of tongue-shaped, pale silvery green, woolly leaves. Spikes of purple flowers appear in mid summer. Varieties include: 'Olympica' (silver-white leaves, pinkish flowers); 'Sheila McQueen' (larger leaves and flowers than the species); and 'Silver Carpet' (non-flowering).
Stachys spicata, up to 45cm (1½ft) high and across, has bright green puckered leaves and bright pink flowers throughout summer.

Cultivation
Plant from early autumn to mid spring in ordinary, well-drained garden soil in sun or partial shade. Remove flower stems in late autumn.
Propagation All species and varieties spread rapidly by underground runners and many also self-seed. If necessary, divide and replant the roots from mid autumn to mid spring.
Pests and diseases Trouble free.

STAR-FLOWERED LILY-OF-THE-VALLEY – see *Smilacina*
STINKING HELLEBORE – see *Helleborus*

Stipa

feather or needle grass

Stipa calamagrostis

- ☐ Height 75cm-1.2m (2½-4ft)
- ☐ Planting distance 45-60cm (1½-2ft)
- ☐ Flowers early summer to early autumn
- ☐ Fertile, well-drained soil
- ☐ Full sun
- ☐ Moderately hardy, herbaceous or evergreen

Feather grass is a light airy plant, making a good feature for lawns and borders. It forms a clump of narrow mid to grey-green leaves and has handsome feathery flower plumes which can be dried for winter arrangements.

Popular species
Stipa calamagrostis, up to 1.2m (4ft) high, has compact tufts of grey-green leaves, and silvery to brown flower plumes.
Stipa gigantea, a near-evergreen up to 1.2m (4ft) high, forms a dense clump of grey-green leaves with silvery buff-violet flower plumes.
Stipa pennata, up to 75cm (2½ft) high, is an herbaceous grass with mid green leaves and silvery-buff flower plumes ideal for drying.

Cultivation
Plant in early to mid spring in fertile, light soil in full sun.
Propagation Divide and replant in early to mid spring.
Sow seeds outdoors in mid spring. Transplant the seedlings to their permanent positions in late spring to early summer.
Pests and diseases Trouble free.

STOKE'S ASTER – see *Stokesia*

Stachys grandiflora

Stokesia
Stokes' aster, cornflower aster

Stokesia laevis

- ☐ Height 30-45cm (1-1½ft)
- ☐ Planting distance 45cm (1½ft)
- ☐ Flowers late summer to mid autumn
- ☐ Well-drained soil
- ☐ Sun or light shade
- ☐ Very hardy, herbaceous

Despite the showy flowers composed of notched florets in shades of blue, lilac and pink or white, Stokes' aster (*Stokesia laevis*, syn. *S. cyanea*) is not a well-known plant.

The individual blooms are up to 7.5cm (3in) across and appear in succession over several months; the lance-shaped leaves are mid green.

Stokes' aster is easy to care for and provides a long-lasting show.

Varieties include: 'Alba' (to 30cm/1ft, white); 'Blue Danube' (light blue); 'Blue Star' (to 30cm/1ft, light blue); 'Wyoming' (to 40cm/16in, deep blue).

Cultivation
Plant in mid spring in any well-drained soil in sun or light shade. Support with twiggy sticks.
Propagation Divide and replant in mid spring.

Sow seeds in early spring. When the seedlings are large enough to handle, prick out into boxes. Grow on in nursery rows and plant out the following mid spring. Hybrid plants raised from seed seldom come true, but may give good colour forms which should be propagated by division.
Pests and diseases Trouble free.

Stylophorum
celandine poppy, wood poppy

Stylophorum diphyllum

- ☐ Height 30-40cm (12-16in)
- ☐ Planting distance 30cm (1ft)
- ☐ Flowers late spring to early summer
- ☐ Rich soil
- ☐ Partial shade
- ☐ Very hardy, herbaceous

The delightful celandine poppy (*Stylophorum diphyllum*) is a charming sight in partial shade with its clusters of gleaming yellow poppy-like blooms and downy lobed leaves.

The flowers, which measure up to 5cm (2in) across and appear from late spring to early summer, are followed by silvery seed pods.

Cultivation
Plant from autumn to spring in rich, moist soil in partial shade.
Propagation Divide and replant the roots in autumn or spring.

Alternatively, sow seeds in a cold frame in early spring. Prick the seedlings out into nursery rows and grow on until autumn or spring, then plant them out.
Pests and diseases Trouble free.

STONECROP – see *Sedum*
STRAWFLOWER – see *Helichrysum*
SUNDROPS – see *Oenothera*
SUNFLOWER – see *Helianthus*
SWEET BERGAMOT – see *Monarda*
SWEET ROCKET – see *Hesperis*
SWEET WOODRUFF – see *Galium*

Symphytum
comfrey

Symphytum grandiflorum 'Hidcote Pink'

- ☐ Height 20cm-1.2m (8in-4ft)
- ☐ Planting distance 38-60cm (15-24in)
- ☐ Flowers mid spring to late summer
- ☐ Ordinary or rich, moist soil
- ☐ Sun or shade
- ☐ Hardy, herbaceous

Comfrey's rough, coarse-textured leaves and pretty tubular flowers in shades of purple-blue and pink or white, provide excellent ground cover for moist borders or as specimen plants by water.

The hairy mid green leaves are usually broadly lance-shaped, and the flowers are held in sprays on branching stems.

Popular species
Symphytum caucasicum (blue comfrey), up to 60cm (2ft) high and 45cm (1½ft) across, is suitable for wild gardens where it will flourish in shady conditions. The drooping, bell-shaped flowers are pink when they open, changing later to blue. They appear from mid spring to early summer.

Symphytum grandiflorum, up to 20cm (8in) high and 38cm (15in) across, spreads rapidly to form good ground cover. The drooping sprays of white flowers, from mid spring to early summer, are short lived. The variety 'Hidcote Pink' has pale pink flowers opening from maroon-red buds.

Symphytum rubrum

Tellima grandiflora

Tellima
fringecup

Thalictrum
meadow rue

Thalictrum aquilegifolium

□ Height 75cm-1.8m (2½-6ft)
□ Planting distance 60cm (2ft)
□ Flowers mid spring to late summer
□ Any ordinary or rich moist soil
□ Sun or light shade
□ Hardy, herbaceous

Symphytum officinale (common comfrey, boneset), up to 1.2m (4ft) high and 60cm (2ft) across, is particularly suitable for wild or very informal gardens. It has yellowish white, pink or purple flowers in early summer.

Symphytum orientale, up to 60cm (2ft) high, has white flowers from late spring to early summer. This species is short-lived but self-seeds readily.

Symphytum rubrum, up to 38cm (15in) high, has finer leaves than the other species and sprays of deep red flowers from late spring to late summer.

Symphytum × uplandicum 'Variegatum', up to 1.2m (4ft) high and across, has hairy, white-edged, grey-green leaves and purplish pink flowers in summer.

Cultivation
Plant in mid to late autumn or early to mid spring in ordinary garden soil in sun or shade. *S. rubrum* prefers rich moist soil in partial shade. *S. caucasicum* occasionally requires staking. After flowering, cut back all flowering stems to basal growth.
Propagation Divide and replant the fleshy roots in mid autumn or early spring.
Pests and diseases Trouble free.

□ Height 45-60cm (1½-2ft)
□ Planting distance 45cm (1½ft)
□ Flowers mid spring to early summer
□ Ordinary garden soil
□ Partial shade
□ Hardy, semi-evergreen

An effective ground cover plant, fringecup (*Tellima grandiflora*) is grown mainly for its broad maple-like foliage, which forms a thick mat close to the ground, topped from mid spring with spikes of numerous bell-shaped flowers.

The hairy, lobed leaves are bright green and measure up to 10cm (4in) across. The flowers are greenish white to green-yellow, turning reddish as they age.

The leaves of the variety 'Purpurea' turn purplish in winter.

Fringecup does well in a shaded border or in a wild garden.

Cultivation
Plant from early autumn to early spring in ordinary garden soil. Fringecup prefers partial shade, but it is an adaptable plant and tolerates sun or quite dry shade beneath trees. Cut off the flower spikes after flowering unless seeds are required.
Propagation Divide and replant from early autumn to early spring.
Sow seeds when ripe or in early spring in a cold frame. The purple-leaved form does not come true from seed.
Pests and diseases Generally trouble free.

The deeply divided leaves and fluffy flower sprays of meadow rue make it a lovely soft-textured plant for borders and much sought after by flower arrangers.

The leaves vary from mid green to blue or grey-green and are often divided into numerous small leaflets like maidenhair fern. The sprays of tiny flowers, which have no true petals, come in shades of pink, purple and yellow.

Popular species
Thalictrum aquilegifolium, up to 90cm (3ft) high and 45cm (1½ft) across, has finely divided, grey-blue, glossy leaves. Sprays of fluffy mauve or purple flowers appear from late spring to mid summer. Varieties include: 'Album' (up to 90cm/3ft, white); 'Dwarf Purple' (up to 75cm/2½ft, purple-mauve); 'Purpureum' (1.2m/4ft, pale purple); and 'Thundercloud' (deep purple).

Thalictrum delavayi, (often sold as *T. dipterocarpum*), up to 1.8m (6ft) high and 60cm (2ft) across, has dainty, mid green and slightly glossy leaves and large loose panicles of lilac-mauve flowers with yellow stamens. It flowers from early to late summer. Varieties include: 'Album' (to 90cm/3ft, white); and 'Hewitt's Double' (to 90cm/3ft, mauve double flowers, likes shade and rich soil).

Thalictrum delavayi

Thalictrum minus (often sold as *T. adiantifolium*) is an ultra-hardy species up to 90cm (3ft) high and 30cm (1ft) across. It has grey-green leaves divided into numerous small leaflets and rather insignificant and loose sprays of purple-green flowers in mid summer.

Thalictrum rochebrunianum (often spelt *rocquebrunianum*) is an erect species reaching a height of 1.2m (4ft) and 60cm (2ft) across. It has fern-like leaves on purple-blue stems and loose sprays of rose-lavender flowers with yellow stamens from mid to late summer.

Thalictrum speciosissimum (often listed as *T. glaucum* or *T. flavum glaucum*) is up to 1.5m (5ft) high and 60cm (2ft) across. It has deeply divided blue-grey foliage and sprays of fluffy yellow flowers from mid to late summer.

Cultivation
Plant in early to mid spring in sun or light shade. Any ordinary garden soil is suitable, but meadow rue particularly thrives in rich, moist soil.

Propagation Divide and replant the roots in early to mid spring. Divided plants are slow to become established; apart from the double forms, which are infertile, it is best propagated from seed.

Sow seeds in early spring in a cold frame. When they are large enough to handle, prick out the seedlings. Grow on in a nursery bed until the following early to mid spring.

Pests and diseases Trouble free.

Thalictrum aquilegifolium 'Album'

Thelypteris
thelypteris

Thelypteris phegopteris

☐ Height 30-60cm (1-2ft)
☐ Planting distance 45-60cm (1½-2ft)
☐ Foliage plant
☐ Moist, acid or neutral soil
☐ Partial shade
☐ Hardy, herbaceous fern

Thelypteris is an ideal fern for the smaller garden with acid soil, and looks lovely by the waterside. It forms a clump of light, mid green or yellow-green fronds, often deeply cut and graceful.

Popular species
Thelypteris (*Phegopteris*) *hexagonoptera* (broad beech fern), up to 45cm (1½ft) high and across, has mid green fronds and tolerates some sun and dryness.

Thelypteris (*Dryopteris*) *noveboracensis* (New York fern), up to 60cm (2ft) high and across, has yellow-green fronds and tolerates sun in moist situations.

Thelypteris palustris (marsh fern), syn. *Dryopteris thelypteris*, is up to 60cm (2ft) tall with yellow-green fronds. This species likes a moist soil, not too acid, near a pool.

Thelypteris phegopteris (beech fern), up to 45cm (1½ft) high and across, has light green, flimsy fronds, and can be invasive.

Cultivation
Plant from mid autumn to early spring in moist acid soil in partial shade, though *T. palustris* likes neutral, boggy soil.

Propagation Sow the dust-like spores in early spring. Or lift and divide the rhizomes in mid autumn to early spring.

Pests and diseases Trouble free.

Tiarella

foam flower, tiarella

Tiarella cordifolia

☐ Height 30-45cm (1-1½ft)
☐ Planting distance 30cm (1ft)
☐ Flowers late spring to late summer
☐ Acid or ordinary soil, moist or well-drained
☐ Cool shady site
☐ Hardy, semi-evergreen

With its mat of lobed, light to mid green leaves, topped with spikes of foamy cream to white flowers, tiarella is a beautiful plant which makes excellent ground cover in cool, moist soil.

Popular species

Tiarella cordifolia, up to 30cm (1ft) high, has maple-like, pale to mid green leaves which turn bronze in winter. Spikes, about 15cm (6in) high, of cream-white flowers appear from late spring to early summer. This species spreads by surface runners.

Tiarella trifoliata, up to 45cm (1½ft) high has ivy-shaped, mid green leaves and narrow white flower plumes up to 25cm (10in) high throughout summer.

Cultivation

Plant in mid autumn or early to mid spring in a shady, cool site and in acid to neutral soil that is moisture-retentive; *T. cordifolia* in particular needs moist soil and is apt to die back if the ground dries out. Young outside growths may be replanted in early to mid autumn to fill in gaps.

Propagation Divide and replant the roots of tiarella in mid autumn or mid spring.

Sow seeds in a cold frame in early spring. When the seedlings are large enough to handle, prick out into boxes and then into a nursery bed. Plant out in a permanent site the following early spring.

Pests and diseases Generally trouble free.

TICKSEED – see *Coreopsis*
TOADFLAX – see *Linaria*
TOAD LILY – see *Tricyrtis*

Tolmiea

piggy-back plant

Tolmiea menziesii 'Aurea'

☐ Height 15-60cm (6in-2ft)
☐ Planting distance 38cm (15in)
☐ Flowers early summer
☐ Well-drained, humus-rich soil
☐ Partial shade or sun
☐ Moderately hardy, evergreen

Piggy-back plant (*Tolmiea menziesii*) makes an attractive ground cover plant for rich soils. Its common name refers to the plantlets that are produced on the backs of the leaves.

It spreads by rhizomes, forming tufts of hairy, mid green, maple-like leaves. In early summer slender branching stems with spires of rather insignificant green-white, red-flushed tubular flowers rise up to 60cm (2ft) over the foliage.

The variety 'Aurea' has yellow marbling on the leaves.

Cultivation

Plant in mid autumn or early spring in well-drained, humus-rich soil. Partial shade is ideal but the plant tolerates sun.

Propagation Detach leaves bearing well-developed plantlets and root in seed trays or pots.

Alternatively, peg down leaves bearing immature plantlets on to the soil, where they will root readily. Then lift and replant.

Pests and diseases Generally trouble free.

TORCH LILY – see *Kniphofia*

Tradescantia
spiderwort

Tradescantia × andersoniana 'Isis'

☐ Height 45-60cm (1½-2ft)
☐ Planting distance 45cm, (1½ft)
☐ Flowers early summer to early autumn
☐ Ordinary, well-drained soil
☐ Sun or partial shade
☐ Hardy, herbaceous

The garden varieties of spiderwort are hardy relatives of the well-known house plants.

Their main parent is *Tradescantia virginiana*, a border plant with dull green, pointed, strap-shaped leaves. Unusual three-petalled flowers in shades of blue, purple, red and pink or white appear throughout summer, and are up to 4cm (1½in) across.

Hybrids, correctly listed under the name *T. × andersoniana* but sometimes sold as *T. virginiana*, include: 'Caerulea Plena' (light blue); 'Blue Stone' (deep blue); 'Isis' (rich royal purple); 'Osprey' (white with fluffy blue centres) and 'Purple Dome' (purple).

Cultivation
Plant from mid autumn to early spring in sun or partial shade and in any well-drained but moisture-retentive soil. Provide twiggy sticks on exposed sites.

Tradescantia 'Osprey'

Propagation Divide the roots every three or four years in early to mid spring.

Seeds may be sown in a cold frame in early spring but named varieties do not come true. When the seedlings are large enough to handle, prick out into boxes. Grow on in a nursery bed and plant out in mid autumn.

Pests and diseases Slugs may eat shoots. A physiological disorder may cause browning of the leaves which shrivel and fall.

TREE POPPY – see *Romneya*

Tricyrtis
toad lily

Tricyrtis formosana

☐ Height 60-90cm (2-3ft)
☐ Planting distance 45-60cm (1½-2ft)
☐ Flowers early autumn
☐ Rich moist soil
☐ Partial shade
☐ Moderately hardy, herbaceous

Toad lily is a striking upright plant with white funnel-shaped flowers heavily spotted with mauve or purple. They appear in early autumn in loose, branched clusters at the top of the leafy stems and have prominent stamens. They are excellent for cutting. The oval, pointed leaves are up to 15cm (6in) long.

Popular species
Tricyrtis formosana, up to 60cm (2ft) high, has mauve-spotted flowers and deep green leaves. The variety *T. f. stolonifera* has a spreading growth habit.
Tricyrtis hirta, up to 90cm (3ft) high, has hairy leaves and lilac-spotted flowers.

Cultivation
Plant in mid spring in rich, moist soil in partial shade with shelter.
Propagation Divide and replant the rhizomatous roots in spring.

Alternatively, germinate seeds in mid spring in a cold frame. Prick out and grow on under glass until the following mid spring then plant out in permanent site.
Pests and diseases Slugs and snails may eat the leaves.

Trollius
globe flower

Trollius chinensis

Trollius europaeus

- ☐ Height 45-75cm (1½-2½ft)
- ☐ Planting distance 38-45cm (15-18in)
- ☐ Flowers late spring to early summer
- ☐ Ordinary, preferably moist garden soil
- ☐ Sun or partial shade
- ☐ Hardy, herbaceous

The gleaming yellow to orange blooms of globe flower rise like mini suns against a mass of lobed leaves – a delightful sight by the waterside, its favourite habitat.

Globe flower has mid to deep green leaves which are round to oval and deeply cleft into toothed lobes. The blooms resemble large, incurved buttercups up to 6cm (2½in) across and are carried on stems 75cm (2½ft) high.

This plant, which is poisonous, likes partial shade or sun, provided its roots are kept moist.

Popular species

Trollius asiaticus, up to 45cm (1½ft) high and 30cm (1ft) across, has orange-yellow flowers up to 5cm (2in) wide in late spring to early summer.

Trollius chinensis (often sold as *T. ledebourii*), up to 75cm (2½ft) high and 38cm (15in) across, has open-petalled golden-orange flowers up to 6cm (2½in) across. The centres are filled with long prominent stamens. The varieties 'Golden Queen' and 'Imperial Orange' have deep orange flowers.

Trollius europaeus (common globe flower), up to 60cm (2ft) high and 45cm (1½ft) across, has lemon-yellow flowers.

Trollius × *hybridus*, up to 75cm (2½ft) high, has flowers up to 6cm (2½in) across. Hybrids include:

'Alabaster' (ivory-yellow); 'Canary Bird' (pale yellow); 'Earliest of All' (medium yellow); 'Fireglobe' (deep orange-yellow); 'Goldquelle' (very large mid yellow flowers); 'Lemon Queen' (pale yellow); 'Prichard's Giant' (tall, medium yellow); and 'Salamander' (fiery orange).

Cultivation

Plant in mid autumn or mid spring in ordinary, preferably moist soil in sun or partial shade. Water freely during dry weather. Cut the flower stems back to the base after flowering to encourage a second flush of blooms.

Propagation Divide and replant the fibrous roots in early to mid autumn or mid spring.

Sow seeds in a cold frame as soon as ripe or from early autumn to mid spring. Old seeds may take over a year to germinate. When the seedlings are large enough to handle, prick out into nursery rows. Plant out in mid autumn to mid spring of the following year.

Pests and diseases Smut shows on leaves and stems as blister-like swellings which burst open to release a mass of black spores.

Valeriana

valerian

Valeriana phu 'Aurea'

☐ Height 90cm-1.5m (3-5ft)
☐ Planting distance 60cm-1.5m (2-5ft)
☐ Flowers late spring to late summer
☐ Ordinary garden soil
☐ Full sun
☐ Hardy, herbaceous

The hardy perennial valerians include many species that are either short-lived or weeds, but the following are easy-grown and long-lived plants suitable for sunny herbaceous borders. They are erect plants, the tall flower stems rising above dense leaf clumps to terminate in loosely branched clusters.

Popular species

Valeriana officinalis (common or cat's valerian), up to 1.2m (4ft) high and 90cm (3ft) across, forms a basal clump of leaves divided into lance-shaped leaflets and bears loose, flattened clusters of white, pink or mauve flowers with an unpleasant scent if bruised.

Valeriana phu 'Aurea', up to 90cm (3ft) high and 60cm (2ft) across, has deeply cut, bright yellow leaves, turning greener as they age. It bears dense 15cm (6in) long sprays of white tubular flowers in late summer.

Valeriana sambucifolia, an upright, vigorous species up to 1.5m (5ft) high and 60cm (2ft) across, has dark green divided leaves and branched flattish heads of pale pink flowers in early to mid summer. It is suitable for the back of a border.

Cultivation

Plant from mid autumn to early

Valeriana officinalis

spring in ordinary garden soil in full sun. Stake the taller species in early spring, especially on exposed sites and in moist soil. Remove the faded flower stems in mid autumn.

Propagation Divide and replant the roots from mid autumn to early spring.

V. sambucifolia is easily raised from seed. Sow the seeds outside in mid spring. When the seedlings are large enough to handle, prick out into a nursery bed. Set the young plants out in mid autumn in the permanent site.

Pests and diseases Generally trouble free.

Veratrum

false hellebore, helleborine

Veratrum album

☐ Height 90cm-2.1m (3-7ft)
☐ Planting distance 45-75cm (1½-2½ft)
☐ Flowers mid to late summer
☐ Moist, light soil
☐ Partial shade
☐ Ultra-hardy, herbaceous

False hellebore's stiff, narrow spikes or sprays of densely packed, minute flowers and large, fan-like, pleated leaves make a stately feature for borders. The roots of all species are poisonous.

Popular species

Veratrum album up to 1.2m (4ft) high and 45cm (1½ft) across, has light green leaves and green-white flowers.

Veratrum nigrum, up to 1.2m (4ft) high, has mid to dark green leaves and dense, maroon-black flower spikes up to 90cm (3ft) long, in late summer, followed by attractive seed heads.

Veratrum viride, up to 2.1m (7ft) high, has mid green leaves and branching sprays of yellow-green flowers in mid summer.

Cultivation

Plant in mid autumn or early spring in moist, light soil in partial shade.

Propagation Divide and replant in mid autumn or early to mid spring.

Sow seeds when ripe or in mid autumn in a cold frame. When the seedlings are large enough to handle, prick them out and grow on in a nursery bed. The plants take three or four years to reach flowering size.

Pests and diseases Trouble free.

Verbascum

mullein

Verbascum 'Cotswold Queen'

Verbascum longifolia

Verbascum 'Pink Domino'

- ☐ Height 60cm-1.8m (2-6ft)
- ☐ Planting distance 30-60cm (1-2ft)
- ☐ Flowers early summer to late autumn
- ☐ Any ordinary, well-drained garden soil
- ☐ Sunny site
- ☐ Hardy, herbaceous

Mullein, with its strong, branching flower spikes, is a majestic feature for borders and for planting in semi-wild settings. The plant, which has several bushy dwarf forms, has saucer-shaped flowers in shades of yellow, pink, purple or white. The leaves, lance-shaped or oblong, are mid to dark green or grey-green, and they and the stems are sometimes felted with white or yellow hairs.

Popular species

Verbascum chaixii, up to 1.5m (5ft) high, has tongue-shaped, grey-green woolly leaves and yellow flowers with purple stamens, borne in branched spikes in mid to late summer. 'Album' has white flowers.

Verbascum × hybridum is a group of summer-flowering hybrids with 30-60cm (1-2ft) flower spikes. Varieties include: 'C. L. Adams' (to 1.8m/6ft, deep yellow, magenta eye); 'Cotswold Beauty' (biscuit-yellow and lilac); 'Cotswold Gem' (terracotta and yellow); 'Cotswold Queen' (amber, buff centre); 'Gainsborough' (primrose-yellow, grey leaves); 'Golden Bush' (to 60cm/2ft, bushy, small clear-yellow long-lasting flowers, pink eye); 'Mont Blanc' (white, grey leaves); and 'Pink Domino' (deep rose, dark leaves).

Verbascum longifolia is up to 1.2m (4ft) high and 60cm (2ft) across. It has hairy lance-shaped basal leaves, up to 60cm (2ft) long and bears golden yellow flowers in dense spikes throughout summer.

Verbascum olympicum is an imposing plant, 1.8m (6ft) or more tall. Long-lived and suitable for wild gardens, the tall stems rise from rosettes of hairy, lance-shaped grey leaves and carry bright golden yellow flowers in widely branched spikes from early summer into autumn.

Verbascum thapsiforme, syn. *V. densiflorum*, is up to 1.5m (5ft) high and 60cm (2ft) across. Rosette-forming, with felted, crinkly, mid-green, oblong leaves densely covered with yellow hairs. Tapering spikes of yellow flowers appear throughout summer.

Cultivation

Plant in early autumn or from early to mid spring in any well-drained soil in full sun. Stake tall varieties in exposed sites. Remove the flower spikes as they fade to encourage later blooms and to prevent self-seeding.

Propagation Increase the true species, which often seed themselves, from seed sown in mid spring in a cold frame. When large enough to handle, prick the seedlings out into a nursery bed and grow on until early autumn, then move them to their flowering sites.

Increased named varieties, which do not come true from seed, from 7.5cm (3in) long root cuttings taken in late winter or early spring. Root in a cold frame, then transfer them to an outdoor nursery bed and grow on until early autumn when they can be moved to permanent sites.

Pests and diseases Trouble free.

Verbena

verbena

Verbena × hybrida 'Sissinghurst'

Verbena × hybrida

☐ Height 20cm-1.5m (8in-5ft)
☐ Planting distance 30-60cm (1-2ft)
☐ Flowers early summer to mid autumn
☐ Any fertile, well-drained soil
☐ Sun
☐ Half-hardy and hardy, herbaceous

Originally from South America, verbenas are hardy only in sheltered gardens in southern Britain. Although perennial in growth habit, they will flower in their first year from seed and are popular plants for summer bedding, valued for their long flowering period. Given greenhouse care during the winter, they will flower year after year or prized specimens can be perpetuated from cuttings or division.

The mid to dark green leaves are generally ovate and prominently toothed. The fragrant flowers resemble primroses but are borne in showy clusters.

Popular species

Verbena bonariensis grows 1.2-1.5m (4-5ft) tall, with strong, hairy and branching stems set with rough-textured dark green leaves and topped from early summer onwards with purple-lilac flower clusters. Hardy in sheltered gardens.

Verbena canadensis (rose verbena) is a sprawling plant, reaching a height of 20cm (8in) and spreading to 40cm (16in), rooting as it goes. Valuable for edging and ground cover of borders and beds. The flowers are in shades of rose-pink and lilac, sometimes white.

Verbena × hybrida is a large group of colourful verbenas, popular for summer bedding. They are bushy plants, 15-30cm (6-12in) tall, with dark green, toothed and often finely divided leaves. Ideal for planting in large groups in borders and beds, with their tight flower clusters that begin to open in early summer and continue until the first frosts. Colour selections include the compact 'Blaze' (23cm/9in, bright scarlet); 'Sissinghurst' (to 30cm/12in, rose-pink); and 'Sparkle Mixed' (15cm/6in, scarlet, pink and purple with white centres).

Verbena peruviana is a trailing plant suitable for bedding in baskets, in rock gardens and raised beds. Growing only 10cm (4in) tall, the sprawling stems bear grey-green, oblong and toothed leaves, studded with a profusion of bright scarlet flower clusters for many months. Near hardy.

Verbena rigida, syn. *V. venosa*, is hardy in most years and situations. It grows up to 60cm (2ft) tall from tuberous roots and bears erect stems with dark green, narrowly ovate, stiff and finely toothed leaves. The compact, claret-purple flower clusters are about 5cm (2in) wide. 'Alba' is pure white.

Cultivation

Plant verbenas in late spring, in any good, humus-rich and well-drained soil and in full sun. They are resistant to drought; pinch out the growing points to induce side-branching and dead-head regularly to prolong the flowering season. Except in very sheltered gardens it is advisable to lift the plants before the first autumn frost and place them in boxes of compost. Store the boxes in a frost-free greenhouse for the winter, starting them into new growth in early spring.

Propagation Take 5-8cm (2-3in) cuttings from overwintered plants in mid spring and root them, preferably in a propagator at a temperature of 10-13°C (50-55°F). Pot up the rooted cuttings singly and plant out when danger of frost is past.

Stored plants of *V. bonariensis* and *V. rigida* can be increased by division of the roots when new growth is evident.

All verbenas can be raised from seed sown under glass from mid winter to early spring at a temperature of 18-21°C (64-70°F). Germination is erratic and may take several weeks. Prick out the seedlings into boxes and harden them off before planting out in late spring or early summer.

Pests and diseases Aphids may infest young plants and check growth.

Veronica

speedwell

Veronica gentianoides

☐ Height 20cm-1.5m (8in-5ft)
☐ Planting distance 23-60cm (9-24in)
☐ Flowers late spring to early autumn
☐ Well-drained, humus-rich, moisture-retentive garden soil
☐ Sun or partial shade
☐ Hardy, herbaceous

Grown for its profuse spikes or sprays of flowers in a range of outstanding blues, speedwell is a beautiful soft-textured plant. It is an ideal plant for borders and for edging.

The following species are of upright habit and bear oval to lance-shaped leaves that are generally mid to dark green, and sometimes silvery or grey-green. The long-lasting, saucer-shaped flowers composed of a short tube opening out into four irregularly shaped petals also come in shades of purple and pink or white. They are borne on terminal spikes.

Popular species

Veronica exaltata grows 1.5m (5ft) tall and is suitable for the back of a border. It bears lance-shaped mid green leaves and carries densely packed spikes, up to 23cm (9in) long, of soft pale blue flowers in mid to late summer.

Veronica gentianoides, up to 38cm (15in) high and 23cm (9in) across, forms a mat of glossy dark green leaves and bears very pale blue loose flower spikes in early summer. It is suitable for edging. The variety 'Variegata' has leaves marbled with cream white.

Veronica incana (woolly speedwell, sometimes sold as *V. candida*), up to 38cm (15in) high and 23cm (9in) across, has silvery, toothed and lance-shaped leaves and 15cm (6in) long loose spikes of mid blue flowers produced in succession throughout the summer.

Veronica longifolia 'Icicle'

171

Veronica spicata 'Pavanne'

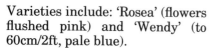

Veronica incana

Veronica teucrium 'Shirley Blue'

Varieties include: 'Rosea' (flowers flushed pink) and 'Wendy' (to 60cm/2ft, pale blue).

Veronica longifolia, up to 1.2m (4ft) high and 45cm (1½ft) across, has toothed oblong to lance-shaped, mid or dark green leaves and 15cm (6in) long spikes of deep purple-blue flowers from early to late summer. Varieties and hybrids include: 'Foerster's Blue' (to 75cm/2½ft, deep blue); 'Icicle' (to 60cm/2ft, white); and *V. subsessilis* (syn. *V. longifolia subsessilis* or *V. hendersonii*, to 90cm/3ft, branched spikes, royal blue).

Veronica spicata, up to 45cm (1½ft) high and 30cm (1ft) across, forms a neat clump of toothed mid green leaves and bears dense spikes up to 15cm (6in) long of blue flowers from early to late summer. Varieties include: 'Alba' (white); 'Barcarolle' (rose-pink); 'Blue Fox' (bright lavender blue); 'Pavanne' (tall, greyish foliage, pink flowers); 'Red Fox' (reddish pink); and 'Saraband' (deep lavender-blue).

Veronica teucrium, syn. *V. latifolia*, up to 60cm (2ft) high and 45cm (1½ft) across, has short sprays of blue to reddish flowers. Varieties include 'Crater Lake Blue' (to 38cm/15in, ultra-marine blue); 'Shirley Blue' (deep blue) and 'Trehane' (to 20cm/8in, golden green leaves, deep blue flowers).

Veronica virginica, up to 1.5m (5ft) high and 60cm (2ft) across, has whorls of pointed mid green leaves and branched sprays up to 25cm (10in) long of pale blue flowers from mid summer to early autumn. Varieties include: 'Alba' (white) and 'Rosea' (pink).

Cultivation

Plant speedwell from mid autumn to mid spring in well-drained garden soil, enriched with well-rotted manure. The soil should be moisture-retentive and the site in full sun or partial shade. Stake with twiggy sticks in exposed positions and cut all stems down to just above ground level after flowering or in late autumn.

Propagation Lift and divide perennial species every three years in early to mid spring.
Pests and diseases Powdery mildew may turn the foliage grey-white and disfigure it.

Viola

viola, violetta, violet

Viola 'Ardross Gem'

☐ Height 5-30cm (2-12in)
☐ Planting distance 10-38cm (4-15in)
☐ Flowers late winter to mid summer and autumn
☐ Any fertile, moist, well-drained soil
☐ Sun or partial shade
☐ Hardy, herbaceous or evergreen

Violas, violettas and violets are delightful perennial plants for edging beds and borders, for ground cover beneath trees and for planting in raised beds and rock gardens.

Their profuse five-petalled flowers, which appear throughout spring to mid summer and sometimes again in autumn, are renowned for their intense violets and deep blues, but also come in shades of mauve, paler blues, yellow and pink or white. They are close relations of the annual summer and winter-flowering pansies. Violas and violettas have flat flowers with overlapping petals, but violettas are smaller than violas. Violets have narrower petals with spurs at the back.

The leaves range from pale to dark green and may be oval or heart-shaped and are often lobed. The species described are herbaceous unless otherwise stated.

Viola biflora

Viola 'Jackanapes'

Viola cornuta 'Lilacina' and 'Alba'

Popular species

Viola biflora, 5-7.5cm (2-3in) high and spreading to 30cm (1ft) across, has bright green, kidney-shaped leaves and vivid yellow violet-shaped flowers up to 2cm (¾in) wide in late spring.

Viola cornuta (horned violet), 10-30cm (4-12in) high and up to 38cm (15in) across, has mid green leaves with rounded teeth, and in early and mid summer bears deep lavender, 2.5cm (1in) wide narrow-petalled flowers with a slender spur. Varieties include: 'Alba' (white); 'Belmont Blue' or 'Boughton Blue' (pale sky blue); 'Lilacina' (soft lilac); and 'Minor' (to 5cm/2in, small pale lilac flowers).

Viola cucullata, syn. *V. obliqua* (marsh violet) forms a mat 7.5-15cm (3-6in) high and 30cm (1ft) across. It has pale green, heart-shaped leaves and fragrant violet-like flowers up to 2.5cm (1in) across, ranging from white to violet with darker veining on the lower petals. It blooms in late spring and early summer.

Viola gracilis, 10cm (4in) high and

30cm (1ft) across, has mid green, toothed leaves and deep purple viola-shaped flowers with long spurs in late spring and early summer. Varieties are more usually cultivated than the species and include: 'Moonlight' (clear primrose-yellow); and 'Major' (large, deep purple blue flowers).

Viola hederacea, up to 7.5cm (3in)

high and 25cm (10in) across, is only moderately hardy. It has white-edged, violet-blue, almost spurless, violet-shaped flowers from late spring into early autumn.

Viola labradorica 'Purpurea', 10-12cm (4-5in) high and 30cm (1ft) across, is an evergreen species with purplish green leaves and violet-like mauve flowers in late spring.

Viola lutea (mountain pansy), up to 20cm (8in) high and 38cm (15in) across, has evergreen foliage and yellow flowers with brown or purple veins in late spring and early summer.

Viola odorata (sweet violet), 10-15cm (4-6in) high and 30cm (1ft) or more across, spread by runners. It forms evergreen mats of heart-shaped, mid to dark green leaves and, from late winter to mid

Viola labradorica 'Purpurea'

Woodsia
woodsia

Viola 'Molly Sanderson'

Viola odorata 'Christmas'

Woodsia obtusa

□ Height 10-40cm (4-16in)
□ Planting distance 20-40cm (8-16in)
□ Foliage plant
□ Gritty, moist soil
□ Partial shade
□ Ultra-hardy, herbaceous

spring, produces violet-shaped flowers in shades of purple to white, and sometimes pink. Single-flowered hybrids include: 'Christmas' (white); 'Coeur d'Alsace' (fragrant, pink); 'Czar' (fragrant, violet-purple); Governor Herrick' (purple); 'John Raddenbury' (fragrant, blue); 'Lianne' (red-purple); 'Mrs. R. Barton' (fragrant, white); 'Princess of Wales' (very fragrant, blue-violet); and 'White Czar' (fragrant, white feathered violet and yellow). Double-flowered hybrids (Parma violets) include 'Duchess de Parme' (very fragrant, mauve) and 'Marie Louise' (very fragrant, violet and white).

Viola hybrids are usually up to 15cm (6in) high and 38cm (15in) across with fragrant flowers up to 5cm (2in) wide in late spring and early summer. They include 'Ardross Gem' (blue and bronze-gold); 'Irish Molly' (khaki-yellow, bronzed centre); 'Jackanapes' (yellow and brown-red); 'Jersey Gem' (purple-blue); 'Maggie Mott' (silvery mauve, cream centre); and 'Molly Sanderson' (near black).

Violetta hybrids, up to 15cm (6in) high and 30cm (1ft) across, with 2.5cm (1in) wide fragrant flowers in late spring include: 'Buttercup' (yellow); 'Dawn' (primrose-yellow); 'Pippa' (mauve, yellow eye); 'Purity' (very fragrant, white); and 'Rebecca' (very fragrant, cream flecked violet).

Cultivation
Plant violas in early to mid autumn or early to mid spring in a sunny or partially shaded site. They thrive in any fertile, moist but well-drained soil

Propagation Sow seeds in early spring or mid summer, outdoors in a damp, shaded site. Transplant the seedlings to a nursery bed and grow on until early to mid autumn. Or germinate seeds in a cold frame. Prick off into pots, and plant out as before.

Named varieties are better propagated from 2.5-5cm (1-2in) basal shoots in mid summer and rooted in a cold frame. Pot up and plant out from early autumn to early spring.

Pests and diseases Slugs and caterpillars may devour the plants. Red spider mites may weaken and disfigure them. Rust distorts the stems which swell and bear pustules producing yellow-orange spores; brown spores appear in late summer and disfigure the plants.

Woodsia is a useful small fern, forming a tuft of dull green or greyish green fronds. It thrives in the poorest soil and makes good ground cover.

Popular species
Woodsia ilvensis, 10-20cm (4-8in) high and 20cm (8in) across, has dull green lacy fronds on reddish stalks.
Woodsia obtusa, up to 40cm (16in) high and across, has greyish green fronds covered with hairs.

Cultivation
Plant in mid spring in partial shade, in gritty, moist soil or in wall crevices. *W. obtusa* thrives in limestone soils.
Propagation Lift and divide in spring. Alternatively, sow the dust-like spores in early spring or mid to late summer.
Pests and diseases Trouble free.

ACKNOWLEDGEMENTS

Photographer's credits
Gillian Beckett 49(tl), 58(tl), 69(tr), 92(tr), 123(tl), 132(tr), 133(tr), 138 (tr); Biofotos/Heather Angel 29(tr), 34(tr), 92(tl), 125(tl), 142, 143(tl), 152(tr), 164(tr); Boys Syndication(Jacqui Hurst) 144(tr); Eric Crichton 9(t), 12(b), 20(tl), 21(b), 22(tl), 23(tl,b), 24(tr), 25(tr), 26(tl,b), 27(tr), 30, 31(tl,tr), 32(t,c), 33, 34(tl,b), 35(tr,c), 36(tl,tr), 37(tl), 38, 39(tc,c), 40(b), 41(tc,tr), 42(tl,tr,b), 43(tl,tr), 44(t,bl), 45(tr), 46(tl,tr), 48(tl), 52(tr), 53(tr), 54(tl,tr), 55, 56(tl,tr), 59(tl), 60(tl), 61(tl,c), 62, 66(tr), 67(tr,c), 68, 71(tl,tr,b), 73(tl,tc), 74(tr), 75(tr), 76(b), 77(bl), 78(t,c), 79(c), 80(tr), 81, 85(tr), 86(tl), 87(tl), 88(b), 89(tl,tr), 90(tl,b), 92(tc), 93(tl,tr), 94(tr,b), 95(tl,b), 96(tl,tr), 97(c), 98(tl,tr), 100(c), 101(tr), 102(tr), 103(tr), 104(tl,tr), 105(tl,tr), 106(tl), 107(tl,tc), 108(tl), 109(l), 110, 111(tl), 112(tl,tc), 113(tl,tr,c), 115(tr), 116(tl), 117(tl,tc,tr), 118(tr,c), 119(b), 120(tr,c), 122(tl,tr), 126(tl,tc,tr), 127(tc), 128(tl,tr), 129(tl), 131(tl,tr), 133(tl), 135(tl,tr,c), 136(tr), 137(tr), 138(tl), 138(b), 139(tl,c), 140(l,r), 141(tl,tc,tr,c), 143(tr,c), 144(tl), 145(b), 149(tl,tc), 150(tl), 153(tr), 154(tr), 156(b), 160(t), 161(b), 167(l,r), 170(tr), 171(t,b), 172(tr); Philippe Ferret 82(t), 84(tl,b); Garden Picture Library (Brian Carter) 36(c), 39(tr), 48(tr), 59(tr), 60(tr), 87(tc), 111(tr), 127(tl), 148(tl), 168(tr), (John Glover) 1, 157(t), (Carole Hellman) 151(tl), (Michelle LaMontagne) 121, (Clay Perry) 2-3, (David Russell) 19(tl), 36(tc), 50(tl), (Ron Sutherland)10(b), 11(t), 75(tc), 156(t), (Brigitte Thomas) 14, (Didier Willeby) 27(tl); John Glover front cover(bc,br), 40(tr), 46(b), 115(tl), 153(tl); Derek Gould 69(tl), 82(b), 89(b), 98(c), 124(b); Derek & Lyn Gould 131(tl), 169(tr); Insight Picture Library 130(b); Michelle LaMontagne 22(tr), 100(tr), 101(tl), 106(tc); Andrew Lawson 23(tr), 125(tr), 166(tr); S & O Mathews front cover(tc), 25(l), 37(tr), 63(tl), 67(tl), 70(tl), 72(t), 76(t), 85(tl), 106(tr), 119(tr,cr), 158, back cover; Tania Midgley 24(b), 39(tl,b), 41(tl), 54(b), 65(tr), 77(br), 86(tr), 94(tl), 95(tr), 100(tl), 102(tl), 108(tr,c), 116(tr), 118(b), 119(tl), 120(tl,tc), 122(c), 123(tr), 148(tr), 165(l); Natural Image (Bob Gibbons) 161(tc), 162(tr), 168(c), (Liz Gibbons) 161(tl); Philippe Perdereau 66(tl); Photos Horticultural/Michael Warren front cover(tl,tr,cl,cc,cr,bl), 4-5, 16(l,r), 17(tl,tr,b), 18(tl,b), 19(tr,b), 20(tr), 24(tl), 28(tl), 35(tl), 44(br), 47(tl,tr), 50(tr), 51(tr), 52(tl), 53(tl), 57(tl,tr), 58(tr), 61(tr), 63(tr), 64(c), 65(tl,c), 69(c), 70(tr), 72(b), 73(tr), 74(tl,tc), 77(t), 79(t), 80(tl), 83(t), 86(b), 87(tr), 88(t), 90(tr), 91, 97(tl,tr), 98(b), 99(tr), 101(b), 107(b), 112(tr), 114(tl,tr), 118(tl), 124(t), 127(tr), 129(tl), 130(tl,tr), 132(tc), 133(b), 134(tr), 136(tl,b), 137(tl,c), 144(bl,br), 145(tl,tr), 146(tl,tr), 150(tr,b), 151(tc,tr), 152(tl), 155, 157(b), 159(tl,tr), 160(b), 161(tr), 162(tl,tc), 163(tl,tc), 164(tl,b), 165(r), 166(tl), 168(tl), 170(tl), 172(c), (Andrew Lawson) 163(tr), Harry Smith Collection 16(c), 25(cr), 26(tr), 28(tr), 29(tl), 31(b), 37(tc), 40(tl), 45(tl), 49(tr), 51(tl), 58(b), 64(t), 75(tl), 99(tl,tc), 103(tl), 105(b), 107(tr), 109(r), 129(tr), 134(tl,c), 139(tr), 147, 149(tr), 154(tl), 166(c), 169(tl), 170(c), 172(tl); Harry Smith Collection/Polunin Collection 18(tr); David Squire 21(t); Brigitte Thomas 12(t); EWA 9(b), (Clare College) 8, (Jerry Harpur) 10(t), 12-13(t), 13(b); EWA/Jenkyn Place (Jerry Harpur) 6-7.

Illustrators
Readers Digest 11(b), (Shirley Felts) 83(b); Anne Winterbotham 84(tr).

Typesetting SX COMPOSING, ESSEX; Printing & Binding PRINTER INDUSTRIA, GRÁFICA S.A. BARCELONA
Separations COLOURSCAN OVERSEAS CO PTE LTD, SINGAPORE; Paper PERIGORD-CONDAT, FRANCE

53-005-1